# A SHORT INTRODUCTION TO CLASSICAL MYTH

## BARRY B. POWELL

UNIVERSITY OF WISCONSIN–MADISON

Prentice
Hall

Upper Saddle River, New Jersey 07458

**Library of Congress Cataloging-in-Publication Data**

Powell, Barry B.
    A short introduction to classical myth  /  Barry B. Powell
    p. cm.
    Includes bibliographical references and index.
    ISBN 0–13–025839–3
    1. Mythology, Classical.    I. Title.

  BL 723 .P69 2002
  292.1'3—dc21

                                             2001032998


President: J. Philip Miller
Editor-in-chief: Leah Jewell
Senior Managing Editor: Mary Rottino
Production Liaison: Fran Russello
Editorial/Production Supervision: Bruce Hobart (Pine Tree Composition)
Prepress and Manufacturing Buyer: Mary Ann Gloriarde
Marketing Manager: Rachel Falk
Art Director: Jayne Conte
Cover Design: Bruce Kenselaar
Cover Art: Andokides Painter. Hercules captures Cerberus with the aid of Athena.
Red figure attic amphora. Archaic, ca. 520–510 BC. Inv. F204 Louvre, Paris, France.
Giraudon/Art Resource, NY
Photo Researcher: Patricia Powell

For permission to use copyrighted material, grateful
acknowledgment is made to the copyright holders listed
throughout the text, which is considered an extension
of this copyright page.

This book was set in 10/12 Baskerville by Pine Tree Composition, Inc.,
and printed and bound by Courier Companies, Inc.
The cover was printed by Phoenix Color Corp.

    ©2002 by Pearson Education, Inc.
         Upper Saddle River, New Jersey 07458

Printed in the United States of America
10   9   8   7   6   5   4   3   2   1

0-13-025839-3

Pearson Education Ltd., London
Pearson Education Australia Pty. Limited, Sydney
Pearson Education Singapore, Pte. Ltd.
Pearson Education North Asia Ltd., Hong Kong
Pearson Education Canada, Ltd., Toronto
Person Educaión de Mexico, S.A. de C.V.
Pearson Education—Japan, Tokyo
Pearson Education Malaysia, Pte. Ltd.
Pearson Education, Upper Saddle River, New Jersey

*To Jeff Walter*
*animae dimidium meae (Horace* Odes *1.3.8)*

It's all new t' me,
Like some mystery,
It could even be like a myth.

# CONTENTS

# LIST OF FIGURES

# PREFACE

CLASSICAL MYTH IS A BIG TOPIC, made unruly by the richness of original sources in Greek and Latin, and sometimes in ancient Near Eastern languages. In this short book, I hope to guide the reader in understanding the origin of the concept *myth* in the ancient world and to describe the plethora of interpretive approaches applied to myth, which had begun already in the ancient world almost before the concept myth had taken a firm hold. I attempt to fill in the social and historical background essential to understanding classical myth, without which literary classics hang in a void. Finally, I attempt to provide in brief compass the historical and theoretical background necessary to understand classical myth as we find it in its primary sources in Homer, Hesiod, the tragedians, the historians, Ovid, Vergil, and in Greek art. While I am always deeply indebted to earlier commentators on myth, much material is original to this book, especially observations on myth and folktale and myth and art. In studying classical myth, we are studying the roots and history of Western civilization. For this reason there is no topic more compelling or rewarding, but the topic is complex and often bewildering. I hope that this book will assist the student or general reader to find a way through the forest of classical myth.

I wish to extend my thanks to the following reviewers who made invaluable sugestions for the improvement of this book: Susan Prince, University of Colorado; Rachel Kitzinger, Vassar College; Peter Struck, University of Pennsylvania; William C. West III, University of North Carolina–Chapel Hill; and David Engel, Penn State University. I have cited by name various translators who have provided the English translations (usually modified) of excerpts from ancient works. Either I or my colleague Herbert M. Howe translated all other passages. I would like to thank above all J. Philip Miller of Prentice-Hall, who saw the need for a book of this kind and who has stood behind me every step of the way. My wife Patricia has endured the arduous labor of assembling permissions and finding the best illustrations. Every effort has been made to contact the copyright holders, but should there be errors or omissions, the publisher will be happy to insert appropriate acknowledgment in any subsequent edition.

I gratefully acknowledge these sources for permission to use figures in Chapter 15: Archaeolology Receipts Fund (TAP), Athens, Figures 3, 6, 11, 13; British Museum, Figures 1, 2, 5, 7, 10; Elvehjem Museum of Art, University of Wisconsin-Madison, Figure 12; J. Paul Getty Museum, Los Angeles, Figure 9; Oriental Institute, University of Chicago, Figures 8, 14; Superintendent of Archaeology of Basilicata, Policoro, Figure 15; Superintendent of Archaelolgy for Etruria Meridionale, Rome, Figure 4; University of Wisconsin Photo Archive, Figure 16.

—*B.B.P.*
Madison, 2001

# CHAPTER 1

# WHAT IS A MYTH?

WHAT IS A MYTH? Faced with difficult problems of definition, some scholars have denied that there is any coherent concept behind the word *myth*, either in the classical period or at any other time or in any other place. If true, we would have little to write about in this book. Undoubtedly, the word *myth* has had an intricate history, meaning different things to different people, and it continues to invoke a broad range of meanings. For us, it most readily means "an untrue story." But myth is like the sea-god Proteus in Greek myth, who could take on many shapes and yet remain the same god. In this chapter let us review the principal issues.

Because our intellectual world is made up of words, we would not have the concept myth without the word myth. No pre-Greek culture had any word approximating myth (or religion, for that matter, with which myth is easily confused). Ancient Babylonians or Egyptians, no matter how learned or inquisitive, could not have discussed the myths (or religion) of their peoples in just those terms. In order to understand myth, we will want to look at the history of this and related words. Did the Greek word *muthos* create the concept, or did myth exist in its own right, waiting to be discovered by the Greeks, even as today we have discovered quarks and quasars?

## MYTH IN HOMER AND HESIOD

The Greek word *muthos* has no known etymology. It appears already in Homer, who seems to have dictated his great epics the *Iliad* and the *Odyssey* sometime in the eighth century BC, perhaps to the man who invented the Greek alphabet.[1] To Homer *muthos* seems to refer to an emphatic utterance or command, usually when a person in power is speaking in public, at length, and with emotional force: Such is a *muthos*. Sometimes the speaker recounts things that happened in the past to underline the importance of the command or exhortation, so that from the beginning *muthos* refers to a kind of story, or at least a narration.

We find the very earliest example of *muthos* in the opening scene of the *Iliad*, when a local priest of Apollo named Chryses (**krī**-sēz comes to the Greek camp to demand the return of his daughter, whom Agamemnon, leader of the Greek armies, has taken captive:

> Then all the rest of the Achaeans° shouted agreement,
> to respect the priest and accept the wonderful ransom,
> yet that did not please the heart of Agamemnon, son of Atreus,
> but he sent him away harshly and laid upon him a stern *muthos*:
>     "Let me not find you, old man, by the hollow ships,
> either tarrying now or coming back later,
> or your staff and the wreath of the god will not protect you.
> Her I will not set free. Sooner shall old age come upon her
> in our house, in Argos, far from her native land,
> as she walks back and forth before the loom and serves my bed.
> So go, do not anger me, if you wish a safe return."
>
> HOMER, Iliad 1.22–32, trans. A. T. Murray, modified

*Achaeans:* Homer's word for the Greeks, which he uses interchangeably with Danaäns and Argives.

Agamemnon's *muthos* is a threat, then, a declaration of power by a man of power. The *muthos* is not just a statement, but a kind of action creating an effect. The sheer power of *muthos*, in ancient times and today, has always been part of its nature.

Another word in Homer also refers to speech, *epos* (plural *epea*), which unlike *muthos* has a clear etymology. *Epos* is related to Latin *vox*, our word

---

[1]The author's own theory about the origin of the Greek alphabet (*Homer and the Origin of the Greek Alphabet*, Cambridge, 1991). The theory is enlightening to the study of myth, but others have interpreted the evidence in other ways. BC stands for "before Christ"; AD stands for the Latin *anno Domini*, "in the year of the Lord." Sometimes today you see BCE, "before the common era," and CE, "common era," but both systems are based on the hypothetical year of the birth of Jesus of Nazareth. In fact the year of his birth is unknown, but may have been seven or eight BC.

*voice.* From *epos* comes *epic,* a literary genre that includes the *Iliad,* the *Odyssey,* and other long poems. Homer does not always clearly distinguish between *epos,* which later will designate the genre in which Homer was composing, and *muthos,* which gives our word myth. Note the use of *epea* in the following passage from Book 20 of the *Iliad.* Achilles, maddened with anger because Hector has killed his friend Patroclus, charges across the Trojan plain looking for Hector, killing everyone in sight. He meets Aeneas, a prince of the royal house of Troy (destined, in Roman myth, to found the race of the Romans in Italy). Achilles taunts Aeneas by reminding him of an earlier meeting when Aeneas fled:

> Then Aeneas answered him and said,
> "Son of Peleus, think not to frighten me with *epea,* as if I were a child,
> knowing that I too know well how to utter insults and abuse.
> We know each other's genealogy, and each other's parents,
> for we have heard the *epea* told in olden days by mortal men,
> though neither you, nor I, have ever seen each other's parents with our
>     own eyes.
> They say that you are the son of blameless Peleus,
> and that your mother was Thetis of the beautiful tresses, daughter of the
>     sea;
> as for myself, I declare that I am son of great-hearted Anchises, and my
>     mother is Aphrodite.
> Of these shall one pair or the other mourn a dear son on this day,
> for not with childish *epea,* I think, will we part and return from the battle.

HOMER, *Iliad* 20.246–50, trans. A. T. Murray, modified

Aeneas goes on to tell Achilles how Zeus begot Dardanus, who founded Dardania on Mount Ida; that Dardanus had a son Erichthonius, who owned three thousand mares, some loved by the North Wind; Erichthonius begot Tros, first king of the Trojans, who had three sons, Ilus, Assaracus, and beautiful Ganymede, whom Zeus took to heaven; Ilus begot Laomedon, who fathered Tithonus, Priam (who begot Hector), Clytius, and Hicetaon, whereas the son of Assaracus was Capys, who fathered Anchises, father of Aeneas—back to where the list began! In this elaborate passage, *epea* at first refers to such insults, authoritative utterances that might well have been called *muthoi,* then refers to such oral stories about heroic ancestors that we today might well call myths. In a college course on myth, one spends a good deal of time learning just such "mythical" genealogies as those Aeneas describes.

Achilles' reply to Aeneas nicely illustrates Homer's ambiguous use of the terms *muthoi* and *epea:*

> Both of us know insults *to pronounce as muthoi (muthesthai),*
> very many of them; a ship with a hundred benches could not bear the
>     load!

> Loose is the tongue of mortals, and there are many *muthoi* in it,
> of all kinds, and of *epea* the range is wide on this side and on that.
> Whatever *epos* you speak, such shall you also hear!
>
> HOMER, *Iliad,* 20.246–50, trans. A. T. Murray, modified

In Homer, the oldest poet of Western civilization, *epos* seems to be the gener-alized term, referring to speech of any kind (and eventually to *epic,* the po-etic genre that the *Iliad* and the *Odyssey* exemplify). *Muthos,* on the other hand, may refer to a forceful, authoritative, extended speech, although Homer makes no rigorous distinction and simple metrical requirements may in some cases determine his use of one word rather than another. In Homer *muthos* never implies a lack of *truth.* Whether or not myth exists in Homer's poems, Homer's own word *muthos* does not refer to it.

The usual Greek word for truth is *alêtheia,* which really means "a not-forgetting" (as in the mythical river Lêthê [lē-thē], "forgetfulness," + *a-* = "no"). Another word for true is *etumon,* as in our word *etymology* ("a true ac-count"). Hesiod, Homer's near-contemporary, does explicitly contrast truth with falsehood in the telling of tales, although he does not use the word *muthos.* For him the opposite of true is something that is *pseudos,* "false." At the beginning of his poem the *Theogony* (c. 700 BC ?), which tells of the origin of the gods and the cosmos, Hesiod describes how he received his power to tell stories from the Muses, spirits who inhabit the mountains near Hesiod's home. The Muses bathe in cool springs, then by night dance through the woods veiled in mist, singing of gods. Once, they came to Hesiod as he watched his flocks, and said:

> "Shepherds of the wilderness, wretched things of shame, mere bellies,
> we know how to speak many *pseudea* ["false things"] as though they were
> *etumea* ["true things"];
> we know too, when we wish, to utter *alêtheia.*
> So said the ready-voiced daughters of great Zeus,
> and they plucked and gave me a rod, a shoot of blooming laurel,
> a marvelous thing, and breathed into me a godlike voice
> to celebrate things that will be and things that happened before.
> They urged me to sing of the race of the blessed gods that are eternal,
> but always to sing of themselves both first and last.
>
> HESIOD, *Theogony,* 26–35, trans. H. G. Evelyn White, modified

Near the beginning of the Greek tradition, therefore, already stands the assertion that song can be true or false. Being animal-like in their hunger and greed, singers and their audiences are "mere bellies," the Muses suggest, and so could never know the truth without their own divine assistance, which they are prepared to give. Yet there is nothing in the word *muthos* that con-notes falsehood.

## *MUTHOS* IN PINDAR

The earliest sign of a new meaning to *muthos,* one approaching our own, appears in the poet Pindar, who lived two hundred years after Homer and Hesiod in the late sixth century BC (522–438 BC) at the beginning of the Classical Period. Whereas we know nothing at all about Homer, and almost nothing about Hesiod, Pindar belonged to the highest Theban nobility. Pindar was one of Greece's greatest poets, but also one of the most difficult, writing songs in an artificial, allusive language performed to the accompaniment of complex melodies and dance rhythms, now completely lost. He wrote his poems under contract for pay and sold them to clients from Greek states as far distant from Greece as Sicily and North Africa. He is one of the earliest known professional writers.

The purpose of Greek poetry was to delight and entertain, as Homer tells us several times, but Pindar also had a moral, or religious, purpose. He wished to improve on the immoral and unedifying tales reported in the *epea* of Homer and other poets, which violated Pindar's sense of propriety. For example, an old story told the following about the hero Pelops (pē-lops), after whom the Peloponnesus was named ("Island of Pelops," the southern peninsula of Greece). Pelops was so lovely that Poseidon fell in love with him. Pelops' father Tantalus, so blessed that he dined with the gods, one day invited the gods to his house to dine. There he chopped Pelops into pieces and cooked him in a stew, to see if the gods were as wise as supposed. The foolish Tantalus wished to test them. Of course the gods immediately recognized Tantalus' impious deed, except for Demeter. Being absentminded from sorrow over her daughter Persephonê's disappearance into the underworld, she ate Pelops' shoulder. The indignant gods reassembled the pieces and replaced the devoured shoulder with one of ivory.

Pindar does not like this old story, thinks it false, and intends to reform its immoral content in his poem *Olympian 1,* a song he wrote for Hiero, a tyrant of Syracuse in Sicily, when Hiero's charioteer won the four-horse chariot race in 478 BC at Olympia. The general myth of Pelops is suitable for Pindar's poem because Pelops was supposed to have settled in Pisa, site of the Olympic games, after migrating from Lydia in Asia Minor and defeating a local king in a chariot race. Here for the first time *muthos* is presented as a story that can be false. The "grace of words," poetry, has made false *muthos* seem true, Pindar says (even as the Muses told Hesiod they could sing songs that were true or false). Pindar is himself a poet, but with the grace of his own words he now wishes to tell the true *muthos* about Pelops. Poseidon fell in love with Pelops and carried him to heaven to be his sexual consort. When neighbors saw that he was gone, they concocted the false *muthos* about the cannibal feast. Divine pederasty is noble, divine cannibalism definitely not:

Come, take the Dorian lyre down from its peg,
if the splendor of Pisa and of Pherenicus placed your mind under the influence of sweetest thoughts,
when that horse ran swiftly beside the Alpheus,° not needing
to be spurred on in the race, and brought victory to his master Hiero.

Hiero's glory shines in the settlement of
fine men founded by Lydian Pelops,
with whom the mighty holder of the earth
Poseidon fell in love, when Clotho° took him out of the pure cauldron,
furnished
with a gleaming ivory shoulder. Yes, there are many marvels, and yet I
suppose the
*muthoi* of mortals beyond the *alathê* ["true"[2]] account can be deceptive,
stories adorned
with embroidered *pseudea* ["lies"]
and Grace, who fashions all gentle things for men,°
confers esteem and often
contrives to make believable the unbelievable. But the days to come are
the wisest witnesses.
A man should speak well of the gods, for the blame is
less that way. Son of Tantalus,
I will speak of you, contrary to what was said before.
When your father invited the gods to a very well-ordered banquet at his
own dear Sipylus,
in return for the meals he had enjoyed,
then it was that the god of the splendid
trident seized you,
his mind overcome with desire, and carried you away on his team of
golden horses
to the highest home of widely honored Zeus, to which at a later time
Ganymede
came also, to perform the same service for Zeus.
But when you disappeared,
and people did not bring you back to your mother,
for all their searching, right away
some envious neighbor whispered that they cut you limb from limb with
a knife into the water's rolling boil over the fire,
and among the tables at the last course
they divided and ate your flesh.

For me it is impossible to call one of the blessed gods a glutton. I stand
back from it.

PINDAR, *Olympian 1,* 17–53, trans. Diane Arnson. Svarlien, modified

---

*Alpheus:* a river near Pisa.    *Clotho:* goddess of fate.    *all gentle things for men:* i.e., the loveliness of song.

---

[2]The word is spelled differently in Pindars dialect.

The old story about Pelops is a "myth," an untrue account. His own story is the truth.

Pindar lived at a critical moment in the history of Western culture, and the turbulence of his intellectual world is again reflected in a poem called *Nemean* 7, in honor of a victor in the boy's Pancration (a combination of boxing and wrestling). In this poem, Pindar expressly describes the power of song to falsify the truth. Such is not Pindar's purpose—his song will celebrate *alêtheia*, "not-forgetting," of the great deeds of the athlete he is paid to praise. Homer, by contrast, Pindar says, through the power of his song made Odysseus' deeds seem greater than they were. According to the story, Odysseus spoke so well that he received the arms of the dead Achilles, not the more-deserving Ajax, who then killed himself for shame:

> And I expect that the *logos* ["account"] of Odysseus
> exceeded his experiences, through the sweet *epea* of Homer,
> for there is a certain solemnity in his *pseudea* ["lies"] and winged artfulness,
> and poetic skill deceives, leading us astray with *muthoi*. The mass of men
> has a blind heart. For if they had been able to see *alêtheia* ["truth"], then
>     mighty Ajax, in anger over the arms,
> would never have planted in his chest the smooth sword—Ajax, who was
>     the most powerful in battle, except for Achilles ...

> Pindar, Nemean 7, 20–27, trans. Diane Arnson. Svarlien, modified

Pindar's word for "account," *logos*, extremely rare in Homer and Hesiod, will become the historian Herodotus' preferred word for a story of any kind (we will discuss the historians' contribution more fully in Chapter 9); Herodotus lived one generation after Pindar. The word *logos* is of clear etymology and comes from a root meaning "to pick out," as when one assembles the elements in an account. From the same root comes the verb "to read," because the reader picks out the sounds from the letters. Pindar's use of *muthos* as a persuasive but potentially untrue tale is directly antecedent to the modern popular usage, "No, that's just a myth."

## *MUTHOS* IN PLATO

In the fourth century BC, Plato (428?–347 BC), whose writings provide the foundation for Western philosophy, draws the distinction between *muthos*, a "story," and *logos*, an "account" that accords with reason and truth, in a far more self-conscious way. In several cases, however, he deliberately blurs the distinction between the two. For example, he refers to the *logoi* of Aesop (*Phaedo* 60d), although later he calls them *muthoi* (61b). In the dialogue called *Protagoras*, Protagoras is speaking to Socrates and wonders how to present his argument:

> "... shall I, as an old man speaking to his juniors, put my demonstration in the form of a *muthos*, or of a *logos*?"

Many of the company sitting by him urged him to treat his subject however he pleased.

"Well then," he said, "I fancy the more agreeable way is for me to tell you a *muthos*. There was once a time when there were gods, but no mortal creatures. And when it came time to create these, the gods molded their forms in the earth of a mixture made of earth and fire and all substances that are mixed with fire and earth . . ."

PLATO, *Protagoras* 320c–d, trans. W. R. M. Lamb, modified

and so on, describing how Prometheus and Epimetheus meted out different faculties to the creatures of the world, making some strong in one thing, weak in another, but always providing a strategy for survival. Soon Epimetheus had handed out all the qualities. Only humans were left. How would they survive? Prometheus gave them fire, stolen from Hephaestus, and Athena gave them practical skills:

And now that humans were partakers of a divine portion, they, in the first place, by their nearness of kin to deity, were the only creature that worshiped gods, and set themselves to establish altars and holy images; and secondly, they soon were enabled by their skill to articulate speech and words, and to invent dwellings, clothes, sandals, beds, and the foods that are of the earth. Thus far provided, humans dwelt separately in the beginning. There were no cities, so that they were being destroyed by the wild beasts, since these were in all ways stronger than they; and although their skill in handiwork was a sufficient aid in respect of food, in their warfare with the beasts it was defective; for as yet they had no civic art, which includes the art of war. So they sought to band themselves together and secure their lives by founding cities. Now as often as they were banded together they did wrong to one another through the lack of civic art and thus they began to be scattered again and to perish. So Zeus, fearing that our race was in danger of utter destruction, sent Hermes to bring respect and justice among men, to the end that there should be regulation of cities and friendly ties to draw them together. Then Hermes asked Zeus in what manner then was he to give men right and respect . . . : "To all," replied Zeus, "let all have their share, for cities cannot be formed if only a few have a share of these as of other arts. And make thereto a law of my ordaining, that he who cannot partake of respect and justice shall die the death as a public pest." Hence it comes about, Socrates, that people in cities, and especially in Athens, consider it the concern of a few to advise on cases of artistic excellence or good craftsmanship, and if anyone outside the few gives advice they disallow it, as you say, and not without reason, as I think: but when they meet for a consultation on political skill, where they should be guided throughout by justice and good sense, they naturally allow advice from everybody, since it is held that everyone should partake of this skill, or else that states cannot be. This, Socrates, is how this came to pass."

PLATO, *Protagoras* 322a–323, trans. W. R. M. Lamb, modified

Protagoras begins his account of origins as did the ancient Mesopotamians, by explaining how humans were made of mud. Hesiod's Pandora, too, was made of mud, then decorated by gifts from the gods; in reading Plato, we are meant to think of Hesiod's account. As in Hesiod's account, Protagoras' *muthos* is set in a primeval time, concerns the doings of gods, and describes how things came to be the way that they are, qualities still sought today in definitions of myth. His story quickly becomes a description, however, of how the uniquely close relation between humans and the gods led to the invention of religion and language, which in turn led to the establishment of cities, which required justice and a sense of mutual respect for good governance. It is easy to see how what began as *muthos,* a story with a traditional primordial setting and gods as agents, has changed to a different kind of explanation for how present practice came to be. Plato's Protagoras himself recognizes how he has changed the terms of his discourse, from *muthos* to *logos,* when he comes to the topic of whether *aretê,* "virtue," can be taught:

> I have yet to deal with your remaining problem about good men, why it is that these good men have their sons taught the subjects in the regular teachers' courses, and so far make them wise, but do not make them excel in that *aretê* ["virtue"] wherein consists their own goodness. On this point, Socrates, I shall give you a *logos* instead of *muthos.*
>
> PLATO, *Protagoras* 324d, trans. W. R. M. Lamb, modified

And he goes on to explain his thinking on this matter.

Another example appears in the *Phaedrus* (274c–275b), where Socrates tells what he calls a *muthos,* the story of the Egyptian god Theuth's (= Thoth) discovery of writing. The story preserves expected features of myth, telling how in a primordial era a god established for all time a feature of human life. But no sooner has Socrates finished his *muthos* than Phaedrus protests about Socrates' *logos!* In these examples we can see how Plato seems to play with the distinction between *muthos,* a traditional tale whose veracity is suspect, and *logos,* anything said, but with a greater claim to credibility than a *muthos.*

The distinction continues earlier speculation going back to Hesiod about truth and falsity in traditional tales and is explicit in a passage in Plato's *Gorgias,* where Socrates invokes gods and stories about the other world in order to present a philosophical basis for ethical behavior. Socrates recognizes that the traditional elements belong to *muthoi,* tales, but that the meaning of the story is a *logos,* a truthful, reasoned account:

> Socrates: Listen now to a fine *logos,* which you will regard as a *muthos,* I imagine, but I as an actual *logos.* What I am about to tell you I mean to offer as the truth [*alêthê*]. According to Homer [*Il.* 15.187ff.], Zeus, Poseidon, and Pluto divided the sovereignty among themselves when they took it over from their father. In the time of Cronus there was a law concerning mankind, which holds to this day among the gods, that every man who has passed a just and holy life departs after death to the Isles of the Blest, where

he dwells in happiness apart from pain. But whoever has lived unjustly and impiously goes to the dungeon of punishment and sorrow that, as you know, they call Tartarus. In the time of Cronus there were judges of these men, and still in the reign of Zeus—living men to judge the living on the last day of life. In this way cases were being poorly adjudged. Pluto and the overseers from the Isles of the Blest came before Zeus and reported that men were being assigned to either dwelling place undeservedly.

Zeus said, "I will put a stop to these proceedings. Present cases are ill judged because those who are on trial are tried in their clothing, for they are tried alive. Now many," said he, "who have wicked souls are clad in fair bodies and ancestry and wealth, and at their judgment appear many witnesses to testify that their lives have been just. Now, the judges are confounded not only by their evidence but at the same time by being clothed themselves while they sit in judgment, having their own soul muffled in the veil of eyes and ears and the whole body. Thus all these are a hindrance to them, their own clothing no less than those of the judged. Well, first of all," he said, "we must put a stop to their foreknowledge of their death; for this they at present foreknow. However, Prometheus has already been given the word to stop this in them. Next they must be stripped bare of all those things before they are tried, for they must stand their trial dead. Their judge also must be naked, dead, beholding with very soul the very soul of each immediately upon death, bereft of all kin and having left behind on earth all that fine array, so the judgment may be just. Now I, knowing all this before you, have appointed my own sons to be judges; two from Asia, Minos and Rhadamanthys, and one from Europe, Aeacus. These, when their life is ended, shall give judgment in the meadow at the dividing of the road, whence are the two ways leading, one to the Isles of the Blest, and the other to Tartarus. And those who come from Asia Rhadamanthys shall try, and those from Europe, Aeacus, and to Minos I will give the privilege of the final decision, if the other two are in any doubt. In this way the judgment upon this journey of mankind may be supremely just.

"This, Callicles, is what I have heard and believe to be true [*alêthê*]; and from these *logoi* we must draw some such moral as this: death, as it seems to me, is actually nothing but the disconnection of two things, the soul and the body, from each other. And so when they are disconnected from one another, each of them keeps its own condition very much as it was when the man was alive, the body having its own nature, with its treatments and experiences all manifest upon it."

PLATO, Gorgias 523a–524b, trans. W. R. M. Lamb, modified

Plato's system of reward and punishment in the other world was to influence profoundly medieval Christian notions of the afterworld.

Plato returns to the same *logos* about a moral system of reward and punishment in his dialogue the *Republic,* again making use of terms and concepts from traditional myths. In this *muthos* he allows for a purification of the soul before it returns to another human life—for the presence, in more modern terms, of a Purgatory ("place of purification") as well as an Inferno and a Paradise. Plato describes the experience of a man named Er (perhaps "spring," hence rebirth) who came from the land of Pamphylia (a real place in southern Anatolia, but = "land of all races" or "everyman's land"). Er was killed in battle. Ten days afterward, when the bodies were being placed on a funeral pyre to be burned, he was found to be still alive and able to tell his story. He and all the other dead found themselves, he said, in a place where openings on either side led up or down. The souls were judged and were punished or rewarded tenfold for the evil or good they had done in life. For as much as a thousand years they suffered torment or enjoyed bliss. After this they returned to the place of judgment and were offered a choice of the lives they would live when they returned to earth. A herald took a number of lots (already prepared by Clotho, one of the Fates), from the knees of Lachesis (another of the Fates) and proclaimed, "Souls of a day, here you begin a new period of life. Nobody will choose for you. You must make your own decision. Do not blame the god for it, the responsibility will be your own." The souls then picked what they wanted. The famous singer Orpheus chose to be a swan; Thersites, an ugly Greek warrior at Troy, chose to be a monkey; Agamemnon, king of the Greek forces at Troy, chose to be an eagle; Odysseus, whose former life had taught him the folly of ambition, hunted for a long time before he found what he wanted: a quiet and obscure life, one that everyone before him had rejected.

The third of the Fates, Atropos, confirmed the destiny that each soul chose and the souls were led to the Spring of Forgetfulness, Lêthê, whose waters made them forget their past life (truth, we remember is *alêtheia*, "not forgetting").

> And after they had fallen asleep and it was the middle of the night, there was a sound of thunder and a quaking of the earth, and they were suddenly wafted thence, one this way, one that, upward to their birth like shooting stars. Er himself, he said, was not allowed to drink of the water, yet how and in what way he returned to the body he said he did not know, but suddenly recovering his sight he saw himself at dawn lying on the funeral pyre. And so, Glaucon, the *muthos* was saved, as the saying is, and was not lost.
>
> PLATO, *Republic* 621b, trans. P. Shorey, modified

Plato, perhaps following an innovation in diction first introduced by Herodotus (see Chapter 9), distinguished *muthos* from *logos,* the one having a greater claim to the truth than the other. From this distinction emerges our own meaning of myth as an untrue tale. Plato was famous for his *muthoi,* which he seems to have viewed as vehicles complementary to *logos* in the expression of truth. *Muthos* as an approach to the comprehension of reality has the power to entertain and to impress by image and narrative, which *logos* can never do. Plato never says explicitly that *muthoi* contain special or hidden truths, which the clever can ferret out, but he implies something like that in the passage of the *Gorgias* discussed previously, where the same account is first called *muthos,* then *logos.* Later followers of Plato, the neoplatonists, aggressively viewed myth in this way, and to some extent so do we.

## *MUTHOS* IN ARISTOTLE

Not until Aristotle does the word *logos* seem to take on a fairly consistent meaning of reason or "a reasoned account," as opposed explicitly to *muthos,* "a false account," or as we would say, a "myth." In the earliest work of literary criticism, and the most influential, Aristotle first spoke of *muthos* as "plot," a narrative structure consisting of a beginning, middle, and an end. The *muthos* of tragedy, Aristotle wrote, is "the imitation [*mimesis*] of an action. By *muthos* I mean the arrangement of the incidents" (Aristotle, *Poetics* 1450a). He continues:

> . . . we must next discuss the proper arrangement of the incidents since this is the first and most important thing in tragedy. We have laid it down that tragedy is the imitation of an action that is whole and complete and of a certain importance, since a thing may be a whole and yet have no importance. A whole is that which has a beginning and middle and end. A beginning is that which is not a necessary consequent of anything else but after which something else exists or happens as a natural result. An end on the contrary is that which is inevitably or, as a rule, the natural result of something else but from which nothing else follows; a middle follows something else and something follows from it. Well-constructed *muthoi* must not therefore begin and end at random, but must embody the principles we have stated.
>
> ARISTOTLE, *Poetics* 1450b, trans. W. H. Fyfe, modified

In a good *muthos,* or plot, first a situation is established; then the main character faces conflict; then the conflict is resolved. Aristotle's description of the construction of plot, *muthos,* remains true today, repeated endlessly in novels and feature films: Boy meets girl (the beginning), boy loses girl (the middle), boy finds girl (the end). If, following Aristotle, we think of myths as having plots, in addition to other qualities, we need a beginning, a middle, and an end of a story to have a myth. In casual speech we may say that the Greek god Zeus, for example, is a myth, but strictly speaking, Zeus is not a myth: He is a character in myth, in the plotted stories that tell of his exploits. Belief in the existence of this or that god, the observance of this or that ritual in a god's honor, and religious symbols are not myths.

There is no plot without characters. In the beginning of a typical *muthos,* in the setup, we are introduced to characters in a certain situation. *Character* comes from a Greek word meaning "a certain mental imprint." Helen is the lovely seductress, self-pitying but charming to every male. Odysseus is the clever man who can persuade anyone to do anything. Agamemnon is the blustering braggart, using political authority to swell his self-importance against the best interests of his people. Hector is the family man with much to protect, but doomed to a frightful end, like his family, whom he cannot save. Achilles is the warrior-intellectual, questioning the very foundations of his traditional culture by rejecting Agamemnon's offer of rich gifts to return to battle. Character is the sum of the choices one makes. In myths, the characters may be gods, goddesses, or other supernatural beings, but they may also be human beings or even animals who speak and act in the manner of human beings.

In the complex development of the concept of myth, the Greek word *myth* came to mean not simply an untrue story (as it can in Pindar), but an untrue story that may nonetheless contain some truth or have something important to say to us. Plato rejects the lies of the poets and contrasts *muthos* (story) with *logos* (account), but still creates his own "myths." Aristotle also champions *logos* but nonetheless thinks that tragedy (whose core component is myth or story) is "truer than history":

> The writings of Herodotus could be put into verse and yet would still be a kind of history, whether written in meter or not. The real difference is this, that one tells what happened and the other what might happen. For this reason poetry is something more philosophical and serious than history, because poetry tends to give general truths while history gives particular facts.
>
> ARISTOTLE, *Poetics* 1451b, trans. W. H. Fyfe, modified

The notion that myth contains a special truth was fully elaborated by the Stoic philosophers and led to allegorical interpretations of classical myth, dominant until the nineteenth century and still commonly found (see chapters 2 and 3).

## MODERN DEFINITIONS

Already in the late eighth or early seventh century BC, Hesiod articulated the problem of truthfulness in a story, and by the fifth century BC Pindar has demarcated the difference between a tale that can be false, *muthos*, and one based on reason, *logos*. Later, Plato and Aristotle refine such distinctions. Strikingly, modern discussions of myth neglect the problem of truth in story to emphasize the social origins of myth, calling it simply a *traditional tale* (from Latin *trado*, "hand over"). Partly, this emphasis grows from impatience with the problem of truth, especially in literature. More importantly, Homeric studies have revealed how Homer's poems are the product of a long development during which one generation of singers passed on to a younger generation techniques for telling stories in verse and the stories themselves. Because Homer's poems obviously contain myths, or their plots are myths, myths are therefore traditional tales, which maintain contact with the past and hand on inherited wisdom to the future. Traditional tales explain a society to itself, promulgating its concerns and values. They describe patterns of behavior as models for members of a society, especially in times of crisis.

For example, in Homer's *Iliad,* Achilles tries to persuade King Priam of Troy to eat at a time when Priam is heartbroken for his son Hector, whom Achilles himself has killed. Without classifying his speech as *muthos* or anything else, Achilles tells the story of Niobê (**nī**-ō-bē), a Theban princess. Although Artemis and Apollo had killed her seven sons and seven daughters, still she ate, and so should Priam, Achilles advises. Four hundred years later, when the philosopher Socrates was on trial for his life, he defended his insistence on telling the truth in spite of threats against him by recalling the example of Achilles, ashamed to live as a coward and preferring to die bravely before the walls of Troy (*Apology* 28b–c).

When stories are traditional, they are also anonymous. In contrast to such modern forms of storytelling as Leo Tolstoy's *War and Peace* or J. D. Salinger's *Catcher in the Rye* or George Lucas's *Star Wars* films, myths do not have identifiable authors. Literary works based on myths may have authors, but the myths themselves do not. So the Greek dramatist Sophocles wrote a play about Oedipus the king, but the *myth* of Oedipus existed long before, and no one can say who created it.

The anonymity of traditional tales helps us to understand why the Greeks, following the lead of the philosopher Plato, eventually came to contrast *muthos,* "story, plot, myth," with *logos,* "account." The teller of a *logos* takes responsibility for the truth of what is said. A *logos* is a reasoned explanation of something that emphasizes a continuing causal sequence, as in the proofs of plane geometry. We still use the suffix *-logy* to indicate a reasoned inquiry into a topic, as anthropo*logy,* "study of human beings," bio*logy,* "study of life forms," or even mytho*logy,* "study of myth." By contrast, the teller of a *muthos* does not claim personal responsibility for what is said. After all, the teller did not invent the story, but only passed it on.

Myth as "traditional tale," therefore, is a way of defining myth by describing how it was transmitted, avoiding the problem of its essence. The definition appeals to those who deny that myth has an essence, but does require that we have an oral tradition, if we want a myth. Unfortunately, we find ourselves in an awkward position when applying this criterion to the nontraditional stories told by such celebrated ancient authors as Aeschylus, Euripides, Sophocles, Apollonius of Rhodes, and Vergil. Perhaps many knew the story of the man who married his mother—surely a traditional tale—but Sophocles seems to have invented his self-blinding. Is the famous self-blinding of Oedipus not part of the myth, then, not *mythi*cal? Just because Sophocles composed in writing, are his utterances, his *muthoi*, different in kind from those of the ancient *singers*, who composed without the aid of writing? Oral poets constantly altered their tradition too (although they claim not to), and many believe that such events as Odysseus' meeting with the beautiful nymph Calypso in the *Odyssey*, or with the princess Nausicaä on the shore, were invented by Homer whole-cloth.

During the process of oral transmission, a traditional tale is subject to constant change because different narrators of a story have different motives and emphasize or embroider on different aspects. The story of Niobê could easily illustrate the dangers of self-assertion (Niobê bragged that she had more children than the mother of Apollo and Artemis), but Achilles uses the story to prove that grief can be lessened by food. Homer describes Achilles' anguished choice between a short glorious life and a long inglorious one, but never presents the choice as between courage and cowardice, the meaning that Socrates gives to the story. Both Homer and Sophocles report that Oedipus, king of Thebes, killed his father and married his mother, but in Homer's account Oedipus continues to rule after the truth comes out, whereas in Sophocles' play he pokes pins in his eyes and leaves the city, a wretched wanderer. Neither is the "true" version of which the other is a variant, although we might argue that a version originating before writing is more traditional. Still, the myth of Oedipus is the complex of all the variants, however many there may be. The *Iliad* and the *Odyssey*, just as we have them, are Homer's invention, then, although made up of very much that is traditional. How can we be sure that Homer's poems are myths, whereas stories created in writing are not, just because they have authors?

Perceiving the difficulty emerging from a definition of myth based on the study of modern singers of tales, some critics have wished to ask that myth also be *serious*, not just traditional. By serious is meant the presence and activity of gods in the story, on the presumption that gods are "serious." Unfortunately, this refinement presumably excludes the rollicking and unserious story of the adultery of Ares and Aphrodite told in the *Odyssey*, one of the most famous myths. The story of Sophocles' *Antigonê*, too, will drop from the category *myth*: not only does the story appear to be Sophocles' invention, but gods play no direct part in it. Seriousness, whatever that means, may surely sometimes be an ingredient in myth, and myths may be handed down in oral tradition, but such definitions will not encompass the rich body of stories that come to us from the ancient world.

Such is a brief history of the word and concept *myth*. As many questions are raised as answered. We are left in the uncomfortable position of agreeing only that myths are those stories always called myths, without always being sure why. We have no choice but to live with such ambiguities. We face a similar dilemma when trying to define other concepts of broad cultural and historical importance—religion or philosophy, for example. In later chapters we will return to the problems of definition.

## FURTHER READING

Buxton, R. G. A., ed., *From Myth to Reason?* (Oxford, 1999). Includes the argument that myths are organically connected with Platonic argument.

Detienne, M., *The Creation of Mythology,* trans. M. Cook (Chicago, 1986). Doubts the category "myth" is valid.

Kirk, G. S., *Myth: Its Meaning and Function in Ancient and Other Cultures* (Berkeley, 1970). Good on problems of definition.

Martin, R. P., *The Language of Heroes. Speech and Performance in the Iliad* (Ithaca, 1989). Good on the meaning of *muthos* in Homer.

# CHAPTER 2

# THE MEANING OF MYTH I: ANCIENT AND PREMODERN THEORIES

WHAT DO THESE mythical stories handed down from the unknown past, often bizarre or mysterious, signify? Disturbed by the irrational and often immoral content of their traditional tales, Greek intellectuals had already posed these questions in ancient times, initiating a long tradition of theoretical inquiry into the nature and meaning of myth. Some ancient Greeks rejected the traditional stories completely, but others developed elaborate theories to show that the myths contain profound truths, despite their initial implausibility. This tradition was developed further in the Middle Ages and the Renaissance. In the modern era, with the development of new fields of inquiry, the factual or philosophic truth of myth has ceased to be the only question considered. Anthropologists, for example, are concerned with the social function of myth, and psychologists develop theories about the emotional needs that myth reflects and satisfies. In this chapter we trace some of the major phases in the history of the *interpretation of myth* from ancient times up to the premodern age.

## GREEK THEORIES

Through their rationalism the Greeks were the first people to become fully self-conscious and critical of their own traditions. The inquiry was closely bound up with Greek philosophy, which began partly in speculation about the nature of myth, then developed into a system of reasoning about causes and effects and about the nature of things that was independent of traditional—that is, mythical—explanations. The Greek philosophers wanted to reduce dependence on explanations that used the anthropomorphic categories of Greek religion so prominent in Greek traditional tales. They criticized the traditional stories for their implausible and irrational details or immoral content. Already in the sixth century BC, Xenophanes (ksen-o-fan-ēz) of Colophon (in Asia Minor) complained of the ethical weakness of the Olympians, insisting that popular notions about the gods must be wrong:

> In my opinion mortals have created their gods with the dress and voice and appearance of mortals. If cattle and horses had hands and wanted to draw or carve as men do, the cattle would show their gods in the form of cattle and horses would show them as horses, with the same form and appearance as their own. The Ethiopians say that their gods have snub noses and black skins, while the Thracians say that theirs have blue eyes and red hair.
>
> XENOPHANES, fragment 21 B 14–16 (Diels–Kranz)

And:

> One god is greatest among gods and men, but his appearance and thought are nothing like ours.
>
> XENOPHANES, fragment 21 B 23 (Diels–Kranz)

Xenophanes, who lived about two hundred years after Homer, questions the very existence of the gods that populate Greek myth and, by implication, attacks the truth of the traditional tales cherished by the Greeks as their cultural heritage. Plato, a friend of Socrates and founder of the immensely influential Academy during the fourth century BC in Athens, criticized such tales even more severely, as we have seen. He thought that the irrational stories of Homer and other poets had a corrupting influence because they presented to the untutored mind a false image of reality. In his ideal state, described in the *Republic,* Plato banned the poets and their lying tales (*Republic* 606e). On the other hand, Plato was aware that some important truths lie beyond the grasp of human reason. Indeed, the burden of his philosophy was to demonstrate the existence of timeless eternal realities behind the transient and changing surface of the everyday world, realities Plato called "Ideas" or "Forms" (= Greek *eidoa*).[1] As we saw in Chapter 1, although Plato opposed traditional myth, he considered mythlike stories to be an appropriate vehicle for giving expression to these truths. So he wrote his own "myths,"

---

[1] Whence our word *idealism*—belief in values not apparent in the material world.

dealing especially with the soul's fate after death, but also with the nature of being and of the perfect political order. The "myth of Atlantis," a philosophical utopia far out at sea, was Plato's invention.

Other Greek thinkers went beyond Plato, asserting that even the traditional myths Plato had vigorously criticized could be seen to contain a kernel of philosophical or historical truth. The task, they thought, was to interpret the myths so that this kernel would come to light. Despite their bizarre or immoral content, the traditional stories meant something other than what they appeared at first glance to mean. In this way there was no need to dismiss the myths as mere errors, containing nothing that need be taken seriously. They must be *allegories,* the Greeks argued, stories that look like one thing on the surface, but are really something else inside.

Allegory is a Greek word that means "saying something in a different way" or "saying something different from what appears to be said." In allegorizing myth, the story is translated from its initial frame of reference into another that is more acceptable. For example, Daphnê's transformation into a laurel tree to escape the clutches of Apollo can be explained as an allegory about chastity. The story does not mean that a girl, pursued by Apollo, literally was changed into a tree, but promulgates the view that abstinence from sexual intercourse can, at least for a woman, be desirable. Allegory is closely related to *symbolism,* which means "something put together with something else," because in both allegory and symbolism one thing points to and brings another thing to mind. Thus Daphnê can be interpreted as a symbol of virginity.

The allegorical or symbolic meaning found in any given story depended entirely on the frame of reference that the ancient interpreter believed to be "true." Because Greek philosophers were concerned primarily with "the truth" in such fields as cosmology, history, and—as in the case of Daphnê—morality, the meanings they found in myth generally originated in these spheres.

## PHYSICAL ALLEGORY

Theagenes (thē-**a**-jen-ēz), who lived in southern Italy during the later sixth century BC, is said to have been the first to use the allegorical method. None of his writing survives, but later commentators say that he explained mythical accounts of battle among the gods as representing conflicts among natural forces. In Theagenes' cosmology, dry is opposite to wet, hot to cold; water extinguishes fire, fire evaporates water. Such natural oppositions, Theagenes thought, must be embodied in Homer's story in the *Iliad* (20.54ff.) of Apollo who, armed with his arrows, faces Poseidon: Apollo stands for fire, Poseidon for water. The mythical conflict of the two gods is the allegorical expression of a basic cosmological principle concerning the opposition of fire and water. Other allegorists did not hesitate to apply allegory in psychological interpretations as well, making Athena personify rational thought; Ares, irrational violence; Aphrodite, desire; and Hermes, reason.

During the Hellenistic Period, the Stoic philosophers refined physical allegory into a powerful tool that could be applied to any myth. For example, they argued that the Greek creation myths contained profound truths about the origin of the universe. The story of Uranus' castration was explained as meaning that the original creative element of the universe, "fiery air" (= Uranus), begot its offspring spontaneously without the assistance of sexual union. Likewise, the Stoics identified Cronus with *chronos* (= "time"), and his role in creation was interpreted to mean that all things were begotten by time. The children of Cronus are the ages, and the story that Cronus devoured them means that "time consumes the ages." The story that Zeus overthrew Cronus and bound him in the underworld means that time, although great in extent, is nonetheless limited.

The interpretation of Cronus as *chronos* illustrates how the Stoics used etymology, speculation about "the true meaning of a word," to reinforce allegory; the meaning of a word or name can reveal the meaning of a myth. The famous biographer Plutarch (c. AD 50–125) offers another example. He interprets the story of Demeter (de-**mē**-ter) and Persephonê (per-**sef**-o-nē) as an allegory conveying an important insight about life after death. According to Plutarch, Demeter is the earth, Hades the shadow cast by the earth, and Persephonê herself the moon, which reflects the light of the sun. He proves this by reminding us that Persephonê's other name, Korê, means in Greek not only "girl," but also "pupil of the eye." As the eye (*korê* = "pupil") acts like a mirror reflecting little images of objects, so does the moon reflect the light of the sun. Korê, or pupil/Persephonê, is the moon, and the story of Persephonê's descent into the underworld and subsequent return refers to the waxing and waning of the moon, when the moon slips in and out of the shadow of the earth, Hades' realm. By extension, the story of Persephonê's descent and return means that after losing their bodies at death, human beings exist as souls and minds in Hades. If they are blameless, however, they may subsequently escape to the sun as pure minds. By adding a philosophical meaning, Plutarch's physical allegory turns the myth into a vehicle for what he considers a deeper truth.

The etymologies offered by the Stoics, which depended on similarity in sound, must have seemed reasonable in a society where myth was still part of the living, aural language. In reality, their etymologies were often quite fantastic; the science of linguistics was poorly developed in the ancient world. We now know that the name Cronus is etymologically unrelated to the word *chronos*. But through this false etymology arose the common picture of Father Time as the Grim Reaper, an old man carrying a sickle, because C(h)ronus/Time castrated his father with a sickle.

Roman writers who followed the Stoic philosophy also used Latin etymologies to interpret myths. For example, they argued that Juno (corresponding to Hera in Greek myth) was really air because the Greek (and Latin) word for air (*aêr, aura*) sounded like *Hera*. This etymology was supported by the belief that air lay just beneath the aether, or upper atmosphere, symbolized in myth by Jupiter. The position of air (= Juno) just beneath aether (= Jupiter, Juno's mate) was the true meaning of the story that Jupiter united with Juno in sexual embrace!

These physical allegorical interpretations attempted to explain a cultural inheritance from a distant, preliterate past in the light of sophisticated philosophical thought about forces in nature. The allegorists had no notion that myths arose at different times and in different cultural conditions and for different reasons (a mistake easy to make). Through their explanations, the allegorists were able to maintain the respectability of the traditional tales, which were otherwise liable to rejection because of their patent factual errors or offensive moral content. In addition to protecting the respectability and social utility of traditional stories, physical allegory was a philosophically respectable way of bringing to light hidden, even mysterious truths about the world (for example, that time devours all things).

## HISTORICAL ALLEGORY: EUHEMERISM

Allegorical interpretation of myth goes back to the sixth century BC, but about 300 BC the Greek mythographer Euhemerus (yū-**hē**-mer-us) offered a new approach, according to which myth was thought to reveal historical rather than cosmological truth. Euhemerus wrote a book describing a journey to three fabulously wealthy islands in the Indian Ocean. On the main island, Panchaea (modeled after Plato's Atlantis), Euhemerus said that he had found a golden column on which was inscribed the history of the reigns of early human kings. This alleged history suggested a very different interpretation of Greek myth.

First to rule, according to Euhemerus' story, was Uranus, so called because he was learned in the study of the heavens. From union with his human wife, Hestia, Uranus begot the Titans and Cronus. The column gave further information about Uranus' successors, Cronus, Zeus, and their families. The war in heaven and Cronus' swallowing his children were explained as recollections of palace intrigues. During his reign, according to the column, Zeus was said to have traveled the earth teaching the arts of civilized life, banning such reprehensible religious practices as cannibalism and founding temples. According to the story, he actually lived for a while on Mount Olympus, then, at the end of a long life, Zeus retired to Crete, died, and was buried near Cnossus. That is why the Cretans spoke of "the tomb of Zeus."

Although Euhemerus' story of the inscribed column is a fiction, his underlying theory is quite plausible and enters many modern interpretations of myth. By asserting that gods were in origin great men, so respected that they were worshiped after death, he attempted to explain myth as a form of early history. From his book comes the modern term *euhemerism,* the thesis that gods once were human. Many features of the Greek mythical tradition lent themselves to explanation along these lines. The gods, after all, were organized in a family on Olympus, and they looked and acted like Greek aristocrats. The god Asclepius shows many signs of having once been a real man, a famous doctor.[2] As for such deified heroes as Heracles, everyone always thought them to be real men anyway, who had actually lived, founded cities, and done great deeds. Euhemerus' thesis derived convenient support from the politics of Hellenistic monarchs, especially in Egypt, who presented themselves to their peoples as gods incarnate and who included the native gods in their dynastic genealogies. The deification of dead Hellenistic rulers made more plausible the notion that great humans of the past had, with the passage of time, become more than human. Behind myth lay history; certainly Heinrich Schliemann, excavator of Troy and Mycenae, believed this.

An approach closely related to that of Euhemerus is found in a handbook on myth called *On Incredible Things,* of which an excerpt survives, written by Palaephatus (pal-ē-fat-us), a contemporary of Euhemerus. Palaephatus' special contribution was to explain myths as originating from a misunderstanding of language. According to Palaephatus, Actaeon, for example, was not really transformed into a stag and torn apart by his dogs; rather, he was ruined by spending too much money on his hunting dogs. The myth arose when neighborhood gossip began to tell of how "poor Actaeon is being devoured by his dogs." Similarly, the Lernaean Hydra against which Heracles fought was not really, as many said, a water snake (assisted by a dangerous crab) from whose many necks two heads would grow every time he cut one off; only by cauterizing the severed necks did Heracles overcome the beast. Lernus, he claimed, was a king in the Peloponnesus who went to war with the Mycenaeans. Near Lernus' border was a town called Hydra, garrisoned by fifty archers in a tower. According to Palaephatus, Heracles was sent with some troops to attack the town, but when he used fire against the archers, two new ones would take the place of every one who fell. Lernus called in additional help from a mercenary army led by a certain Carcinus (= "crab"). Carcinus was so effective that Iphicles, Heracles' nephew, had to come to his uncle's aid with another contingent from Thebes. At last they succeeded in burning Hydra. In origin, then, the myth told of a "General Heracles who destroyed Watertown ("Hydra"), defended by General Crabb, by using fire as an assault weapon against persistent defenders." The interpretation of myth

---

[2]Recent research suggests, however, that he was a healing god from the northern Levant.

as a "disease of language" was to undergo a surprisingly successful renaissance in the theories of Max Müller in the nineteenth century AD (see next chapter).

## MORAL ALLEGORY

The interpretation of myth as a system of advice on good and bad behavior, or moral allegory, was more highly developed than physical or historical allegory. We have already seen a crude example of it in the explanation of the story of Apollo and Daphnê as exhorting young women to remain chaste. So the Harpies who rob Phineus of his food are really prostitutes who ruin young men through their high fees. The goddesses in the Judgment of Paris represent three kinds of life: the active (Hera), the contemplative (Athena), and the amorous (Aphrodite), among which every man (Paris) must choose. The coupling of Leda and the Swan is an allegory for the joining of Power (Zeus) and Injustice (Leda, who is raped), whose fruit is inevitably scandal and discord (Helen).

Such interpretations, like those of the physical and historical allegorists, fail to preserve myth, whatever the intentions of their practitioners, for they remove the charm of the original story and replace it with a trite truism or historical or physical incident. An intellectual movement linked loosely to Platonism dealt with myth more positively and gently. Although Plato himself rejected traditional myths, later writers influenced by Plato were able to find in these same myths allegorical expressions of profound metaphysical truths. In the final centuries of the pagan era (AD 200–500), the *neoplatonists* revived and developed many of Plato's theories and became the major philosophic movement of the day. Neoplatonists, like their founder Plato, believed in a higher dimension of reality beyond the limits of time and space, where perfection and absolute truth—that which is always and everywhere the same— could be found. This higher world is accessible to us through our minds, if they are freed from our bodies and senses. The material universe, by contrast, yields only an inferior knowledge based on sense perception, at best imperfect and ultimately false because everything in the material world is always changing. The material world in which we live, reported to us by our senses, is nonetheless to some extent modeled after the perfect rational world. By virtue of that connection, the changing, imperfect material world has many features that point to, or symbolize, the unchanging perfect blueprint that lies behind the corrupt world of the senses. Thus transient physical beauty, such as a sunset, symbolizes eternal beauty. In the same way, say the neoplatonists, myths give us hints about the moral world beyond. Neoplatonism lends itself to allegory, although of a kind that does not reduce myth to literal fact, but expands it into a vehicle for discovering profound truths, usually moral, about a higher domain hidden behind appearance.

Plotinus, for example, the founder of neoplatonism in the third century AD, held that myth describes timeless realities in the form of temporal events. He saw a correspondence between the generational sequence

- Uranus

- Cronus

- Zeus

and the three great principles of reality:

- Unity (unchanging, the same in all parts = Uranus)

- Intellect (unchanging, but plural = Cronus)

- Soul (plural and subject to change and motion = Zeus)

Plotinus' student Porphyry produced an extremely complex interpretation of Homer's description of the cave of the nymphs on Ithaca, where Odysseus hides his treasure after returning from his wanderings (*Odyssey* 13.102–112). The cave, he argues, represents the universe because it is generated from matter and is natural; the nymphs, as spirits of water, represent the ceaseless flow of events within time; the looms of stone on which they weave represent souls descending to incarnation, as the flesh is woven on the bones (the stones of the body). The moral truths are obvious: The material world, including our bodies, is an illusion and unworthy of our aspiration. The increasing interest of neoplatonists in such allegories reflects an effort to rehabilitate myth and to establish its value for revealing higher truths in face of the growing threat from Christianity. In the end Christianity swallowed neoplatonism: St. Augustine (AD 354–430) began as a dualist (believer in two opposed principles), became a neoplatonist, and ended as one of the greatest of Christian theologians.

## MEDIEVAL AND RENAISSANCE THEORIES

Platonic modes of thinking exerted powerful influence on early Christian theology. Both myth itself and the various methods devised for interpreting it were part and parcel of the cultural heritage taken over by the church. Although some church fathers rejected allegory on the ground that it was a way of holding onto pagan myth, most found allegorical interpretation a legitimate way to interpret pagan myth, especially when a moral encouragement of righteous conduct could be found lurking within the tale. The allegorical method whereby moral meanings were drawn from old stories was also applied extensively to the Bible. For example, the frankly erotic content of the Song of Solomon, which tells of sexual love between a man and a woman, was explained as an allegory of God's love for the church (in fact the poem descends from secular Egyptian love poetry). Euhemerism was a useful method of analysis for the Christians because it served to justify the authority of the church by proving that pagan religion was idolatry, just as Christians and Jews had always maintained.

The ancient methods of interpretation lived on, but direct acquaintance with classical culture and its literature declined drastically, especially in the Latin-speaking West. The myths were now known principally through handbooks, which became increasingly important and elaborate. One of the most influential was the *Mythologies* of Fulgentius (ful-**jen**-shus), a North African Christian of the sixth century AD. On reading his account of some god, the reader would find a succinct entry that included both the facts of the story and a moral based on an allegorical interpretation.[3] For example, the story of Liber (the Latin equivalent of the Greek wine-god Dionysus) was understood to be an allegory in which Semelê, the mother of Dionysus, and her three sisters represent four stages of intoxication: (1) too much wine, (2) the forgetfulness it causes, (3) lust, and (4) sheer madness. The interpretation is supported with typical etymological explanations: the first sister (and first stage of drunkenness) is Ino, linked to *vinum* and *oinos*, the Latin and Greek words for "wine"; Autonoë is fancifully said to mean in Greek "ignorant of herself"; Semelê is explained as a combination of *sôma* = "body" and *luein* = "release"—a "release from bodily inhibitions, hence lust"; Agavê is insanity because she cut off her son's head, which only an insane person would do. Drunkenness, obviously, is to be avoided at all costs.

Such material reappeared in other handbooks over the next centuries and for a long time made up the basic source of myths available in the West. Interpretation had become more complex and important than the myths themselves, whose telling might consist of little more than a few key details. Allegory continued to focus on acceptable moral meanings. *Ovide moralizé* ("Ovid Moralized"), a text originally in French that went through many versions from AD 1300 on, listed interpretations of the often racy myths retold in Ovid's poetry. The story of Daphnê transformed into a laurel tree to escape the lustful Apollo is explained as an allegory for the moral that chastity, like the laurel, remains as cool as a river and always blooms, but never bears fruit. The story may also be understood as a botanical allegory (the warmth of the sun, Apollo, when combined with water, Daphnê, makes the laurel flourish) or even a medical allegory (chased by a rapist, she dies from exhaustion under a laurel tree). Such interpretations reached a wider public through Christian sermons, which could use Odysseus' encounter with the Sirens, for example, as an object lesson of the temptations posed by pleasure during a Christian's voyage through life.

---

[3]Fulgentius gives the allegorical interpretation of the Judgment of Paris mentioned previously.

Part of the renewed emphasis given to classical culture at the time of the Renaissance came from interest in Platonism. The Platonic conviction that myth contains profound symbolic truth concerning higher spiritual realms was attractive to Christian culture and led to a vogue for even more elaborate allegory that combined pagan and Christian elements. Repeating arguments made earlier by the neoplatonists, whom they deeply admired, students of classical myth during the Renaissance maintained that bizarre, shocking features were actually the surest sign of truth in a myth. Only those who earnestly sought the truth would not be put off by repulsive surface appearances, but would penetrate to the deeper riches hidden beneath.

The medieval and Renaissance alchemists, who believed that a knowledge of nature's secrets would allow them to transform common metals into gold or silver, found a different kind of truth in classical myth, reviving in new form Greek physical allegory. Accepting neoplatonic ideas about the relationship between matter and spirit, they put allegorical interpretation of myth to use in their description of secret physical processes. The figure of Hermes (= Mercury), for example, was taken to be a ready-made allegory of chemical facts about the element Mercury. The alchemical work *Atalanta Fugiens* ("Atalanta Running Away"), published in 1617 by Michael Maier, is an excellent case in point. Building on a long tradition, he provided his text with pictures and a musical score, "so that your eyes and ears may take in the emblems, but your reason searches out the hidden signs." Both text and pictures treat the mythical tradition as a treasure trove of alchemical allegory. Atalanta was identified with "volatile" mercury, which "flees," and Hippomenes, the suitor whom she allowed to outrun her, is the sulfur that overcomes her, that is, effects a chemical reaction. The golden apples that Hippomenes cast to slow Atalanta's flight are another ingredient retarding the process.

Together with such specialized esoteric texts, handbooks continued to provide basic information along with interpretations for artists or writers. Myth had virtually become a language for talking about timeless truths, and in the seventeenth century the theory that pagan myth was a distorted version of biblical history reemerged with vigor. Scholars gathered evidence intended to show that many details in Homer were muddled versions of events in the Old Testament. The siege of Troy was explained as a recasting of Joshua's attack on Jericho. Odysseus' wanderings reflected those of the patriarchs. Nysa, the mountain where Dionysus was raised, becomes an anagram for *Syna* (= Sinai).

## THEORIES OF THE ENLIGHTENMENT

Such interpretations fell under serious attack in the eighteenth century as part of the profound cultural revolution called the Enlightenment. As the institutional power of the church waned in response to political and social changes in Europe, everything traditional was subject to reexamination, usually with a notable lack of sympathy. Because few things were so traditional as myth, the authority of mythical accounts (including the Bible) and the value of allegory for preserving their worth were increasingly questioned.

Bernard Fontenelle's book *De l'origine des fables,* "The Origin of Fables" (1724), is a landmark monument of the radical change in attitude taking place, initially in France. This seminal book paved the way for many of the central ideas of the Enlightenment. Fontenelle took a detached, wholly disenchanted stance and laid down a whole range of new principles for dealing with myth. Instead of seeking deep, esoteric truths, he saw in myth the product of error, beyond saving by allegory. Myth was rooted in the ignorance of humans living at earlier stages of cultural development. Fontenelle shifted the emphasis of theory from interpreting myth to explaining the origin of myth, which, he asserts, originates and develops in savagery and ignorance. Some scholars date the modern meaning of myth as a fanciful tale, or the notion that it exists as a discrete category at all, to Fontenelle's writings. We may also view the modern definition of myth as a "traditional tale" as a refinement of Fontenelle's approach.

Information about the cultures of the American Indians and other preliterate peoples coming in from missionaries or colonial administrators was a source for Fontenelle's ideas. Such information justified his distinguishing the "primitive" mind from the enlightened and his finding of parallels between the "primitive" cultures of his day and that of the early Greeks. Greek myth, too, he assumed, was the product of a "primitive" mode of thought. This radical, new, and dramatic approach, taking as its premise the notion of progressive evolutionary development away from an earlier condition of savagery to present conditions of civilization, was destined to shape Western thought for the coming centuries and continues to do so today.

The Italian Giambattista Vico (jom-ba-**tēs**-ta **vē**-kō), sometimes regarded as the first modern historian (*Scienza Nuova,* "New Science," 1725), accepted this evolutionary approach to the understanding of the past. History, he thought, was the study of the origin and unfolding of human society and institutions. This view was unlike that of his contemporaries, who regarded history as the biographies of great men or as the record of the unfolding of God's will. Vico argued that history moves in great cycles, each of which has three phases, the same in every cycle, but modified by new circumstances and developments.

The first phase in each cycle is the Age of Gods. In our own cycle this was the period immediately after the flood. In the Age of Gods human activity is limited to a struggle for physical survival. People live close to nature, whose power they understand only as a display of anger by a mighty god. From this phase comes the image of God and of gods as terrible and wrathful beings and what we in this book call "divine myth" (for the categories of myth, see Chapter 6). In the next phase, the Age of Heroes, nature becomes separated from humankind. Emerging social institutions are connected with personified gods and heroes about whom stories are told; from the Age of Heroes descend "legends." The third and last stage (we live in one now) is the Age of Man, in which reason replaces instinctive imagination and passion. Philosophy arises in this phase.

Vico's theory is one of the earliest of many efforts to understand myth as part of an all-embracing history of ideas. Allegory, in his view, deals only with particular myths. What was really needed, Vico thought, was to discover a principle of myth itself in human consciousness. Myth originated in the earlier phases of culture, when humankind's thinking was highly concrete. At that time language, originally monosyllabic and versified, expressed a poetry and ritual more powerful than any we know today, a direct representation of reality. This is why myth is so personal and dramatic, so disconcerting to us who live in the "rational" Age of Man. By recognizing that ways of thinking change fundamentally, Vico avoided two common pitfalls associated with evolutionary schemes: He did not simply idealize preliterate culture, and he recognized that earlier forms of understanding, which cannot be fully grasped by the standards of rational thought, are valid in their own terms

## FURTHER READING

### ANCIENT THEORIES

Guthrie, W. K. C., *The Greek Philosophers, from Thales to Aristotle* (New York, 1960). Lucid condensation of how philosophy emerged from myth in the Archaic and Classical Periods, with bibliography for further exploration.

Kirk, G. S., and J. E. Raven, *The Presocratic Philosophers: A Critical History with a Selection of Texts* (Cambridge, England, 1962). The earliest critics of traditional explanations of the world, including Xenophanes.

Lamberton, R., *Homer the Theologian: Neoplatonist Allegorical Reading and the Growth of the Epic Tradition* (Berkeley, 1986). Excellent on allegorical interpretations in the ancient world and their transmission to the medieval world.

### MEDIEVAL AND RENAISSANCE THEORIES

Allen, D. C., *Mysteriously Meant: The Rediscovery of Pagan Symbolism and Allegorical Interpretation in the Renaissance* (Ann Arbor, 1970). Surveys the use of allegory in the Renaissance.

Allen, S. H., et al., ed., *Survival of the Gods: Classical Mythology in Medieval Art* (Providence, 1987). Based on an exhibition, contains excellent essay on facets of the survival of classical myth, with excellent illustrations.

Bush, D., *Mythology and the Renaissance Tradition in English Poetry* (Minneapolis, 1932; New York, 1963). Good on the postclassical uses of mythology, with a list, chronologically arranged, of poems on mythological subjects.

Seznec, J., *The Survival of the Pagan Gods: The Mythological Tradition and Its Place in Renaissance Humanism* (New York, 1953; reprinted Princeton, 1994). Scholarly description of how the Greek gods were recast and reinterpreted in European literature and art after the triumph of Christianity—the most useful book on this topic.

### THEORIES OF THE ENLIGHTENMENT

Marsak, L. M., trans. and ed., *The Achievement of Bernard le Bovier de Fontenelle* (New York, 1970). Introduction to Fontenelle, with selections from his works.

# CHAPTER 3

# THE MEANING OF MYTH II: MODERN THEORIES

ALTHOUGH THERE HAVE BEEN many disagreements in emphasis, approaches to myth since the Enlightenment either have used an evolutionary perspective, which assumes that myths are the relics of savagery, or have studied myth with the methods of the social sciences, which assume that myth reflects ways of thinking different from our own. Both approaches are closely related, and in either case the effect is to reduce myth to a cultural relic. The counterview of myth as valid and understandable in its own terms, however, did not entirely disappear at the time of the Enlightenment, and it surfaced again in the Romantic movement during the late eighteenth and early nineteenth centuries.

## ROMANTIC THEORIES

Romanticism was a reaction against what many saw as the arrogance, superficiality, and outright blindness of the Enlightenment. Opposing the Enlightenment's confident rationalism, the Romantics saw the emotional side of experience as most distinctively human: intense feeling, awareness of powerful but obscure forces, abnormal states, and a direct intuitive relationship to nature. Whereas thinkers of the Enlightenment attacked myth as a product of primitive mental and emotional states, the Romantics returned to myth as a vehicle for regaining lost truths. Such ideals were expressed mostly in poetry, painting, and music, but ambitious philosophical theories, especially in Germany, argued for the timeless truth of myth and for its continuing vital role in the modern world.

An explanation of how this could be, that myth embodies timeless truths, was given by Friedrich Creuzer in his long book *Symbolism and Mythology of the Ancient Peoples, Especially the Greeks* (1810). Creuzer's explanation was one of several to emerge from the great intellectual discovery of the Indo-Europeans in the late eighteenth century.[1] Their original homeland was apparently in central Asia, perhaps east of the Caspian Sea. Beginning in the fourth millennium BC, the Indo-Europeans seem to have migrated in all directions into Europe and Asia, bringing with them their linguistic and cultural traditions. Most of what is known about them is inferred from a reconstruction of the language they spoke, called proto-Indo-European. Although we have no written record or other direct evidence for this long-extinct hypothetical language, much of its vocabulary, and even some of its grammatical structure, can be reconstructed from the many ancient and modern languages descended from it. Most European languages (except Basque, Finnish, Hungarian, and Estonian) and many others spoken as far east as central India (including Armenian, Iranian, and Sanskrit, but not the Semitic languages) are descended from the hypothetical parent proto–Indo-European.[2]

Creuzer thought that the Indo-Europeans must have possessed primordial revealed truths. He interpreted all myth, in neoplatonic fashion, as a set of symbols for such universal truths, intimations of which could be found in Indian religious texts, first studied in Europe at this time. As the Aryans—that is, the Indo-Europeans—spread from their homeland, the once pristine truth became obscure, preserved only in symbolic forms by a priestly elite, refracted like pure light broken into various colors by a lens. The different mythologies of the Indo-European peoples are those colors, each expressing in its own idiom a truth that was originally, Creuzer thought, symbolized visually by means of hieroglyphs, like those of Egypt.

According to Creuzer, then, myth is a way of dealing with absolute, infinite truth in finite narrative form. But whereas truth is ultimately rational and abstract, myth is dramatic and concrete. For example, the golden rope by which

---

[1]The discovery is usually credited to Sir William Jones, chief justice of India, founder of the Royal Asiatic Society, presented in a lecture in 1796.

[2]Today more than 1.6 billion people, on every continent, speak or understand Indo-European languages. Europe's colonies in the Americas, Africa, Asia, and Australia carried English, Spanish, Portuguese, Russian, and French into new lands, where today they continue to absorb and replace native languages. The spread of the Indo-European language family is one of the most remarkable events in the history of the human race.

Zeus could suspend sea and earth if he chose (*Iliad* 8.18–19) symbolizes the divine energy that supports the world. This is the same cosmic energy described as a thread of pearls in the Sanskrit classic, "Song of the Blessed One." Each mythic image—the golden rope and the string of pearls—descends ultimately from a single primordial revelation to humankind of truth about the nature of reality.

Another imaginative, partly Romantic theory was advanced by Johann Bachofen (*Das Mutterrecht,* "Mother Right," 1861), a student of Roman law who noticed that women enjoyed considerable status in some ancient legal and social systems. All modern theories of a matriarchal phase in early human social development go back to Bachofen, who concluded that the patriarchal authority, which has long dominated all present-day societies, was preceded by a stage during which women exercised great influence in their capacity as mothers. Much of his evidence for this claim came from classical myth, which he considered to contain hidden truths about early human social structure. According to Bachofen's explanation, the earliest nomadic hunting phase, represented in myth by Aphrodite, was lawless, when women were victims of violence. In a later phase, represented by Demeter, the institutions of agriculture and marriage were introduced, and values clustering around the mother encouraged peace and feelings of communal affection. On the other hand, the aggressive potential in woman's nature was reflected in myths about the Amazons.

Although Bachofen described favorably the early "mother right," he recognized a third, and higher, Apollonian phase, represented by Rome. Here the older, more primitive communal mother right was overthrown, and authority was invested in law that embodied the higher values of patriarchy, individuality, and rationality. His scheme, which influenced later Marxist theory, combined speculation about a happier, maternal past with a typically evolutionary pattern that moved through earthly and lunar phases to the present solar triumph of the patriarchal principle.

Friedrich Engels, one of the founders of modern communism, took Bachofen's position in his book *The Origin of the Family, Private Property, and the State* (1883).[3] Before the evolution of the state and the family, women ruled society and were free to have intercourse with whomever they pleased, so that no son ever knew his father. The eminent Russian folklorist Vladimir Propp (1895–1970), writing under the Soviet regime, pointed out that such was the situation of Oedipus, who had intercourse with his own mother: The myth must, therefore, be a historical reminiscence of the shift from a matriarchal to a patriarchal organization of society. According to Propp, in the Greek legend the shepherds who transported Oedipus to the wild and then

---

[3]In Communist China, such teaching about the history of social organization is still official doctrine.

to Corinth stand for the foster parents who in a primitive matriarchy cared for the children. Oedipus' age-mates reflect some early collective, before the evolution of the family.

## ANTHROPOLOGICAL THEORIES

The flood of information about newly discovered cultures pouring into Europe from colonial outposts and journeys of exploration did seem to support the view that myth is a symptom of intellectual backwardness, and students of myth formulated many variations on the concept of "primitive" societies and "primitive" ways of thinking by which classical myth could be understood. During the second half of the nineteenth century, the process of integrating diverse data into general theories of development was further encouraged by Charles Darwin's theory of biological evolution advanced in his *The Origin of Species* (1859). From such studies emerged what is now called anthropology.

One of the most influential of these formulations was advanced by the British Edward Tylor, who presented his theory of universal cultural evolution proceeding through several stages in *Primitive Culture* (1871). Tylor explained the "quaint fancies and wild legends of the lower tribes" in terms of an original stage that he called *animistic.* Animism is the belief that everything has a soul. Myth and religion, which are natural consequences of such a belief, do not ultimately come from inherently poetic language, as Vico thought. Instead, myth is a mistaken science or philosophy, rooted in fear or ignorance, but designed to explain natural phenomena.

A number of other theories were advanced about the primitive state through which all human societies must pass. The model for the evolution of human societies was drawn from the biological evolution of a species. Thus societies that represent earlier stages can exist, although only in isolated backwaters, at the same time as more evolved societies. Technologically primitive communities still intact in Australia and the practices and beliefs of European peasants were sources of information.

This general approach was especially popularized by the British Andrew Lang (*Myth, Literature, and Religion,* 1887). Trained as a classicist, he was a prolific essayist, historian, poet, sports writer, and critic, one of the leading intellectuals of his day.[4] Deeply affected by the interest in evolution, he at first accepted Tylor's laws of cultural development, but as he examined the evidence more critically, he came to believe that there must have been more than a single pattern of development. Myth was indeed, as Tylor maintained, a protoscientific effort at explanation, but the primitive stage of culture was

---

[4]His retelling of traditional stories in the *Blue Fairy Book* and others, which he published with his wife, are still popular among children.

not always a time of confused ideas about natural forces. Faced with examples of what seemed to be ethical monotheism among "savages," Lang argued that monotheism must in some cases have actually preceded animism and polytheistic myth, into which it subsequently degenerated.

To most scholars, then, myth was explicable essentially as reflecting an early, clumsy effort to do what science later did better—explain why things are the way they are. Sir James Frazer, a classical scholar and one of the founders of modern anthropology, accepted the validity of social evolution as an explanation with universal application. With immense industry Frazer gathered evidence from all over the world, from American Indians, from Africans, from Melanesians, as scientific evidence from which decisive conclusions about the meaning of myth could be drawn.

Frazer's celebrated book, *The Golden Bough,* is often ranked as one of the most influential works of modern times. It began as two volumes published in 1890 and reached twelve volumes in the 1911–1915 edition. Frazer started by inquiring into the ancient tradition that a "King of the Wood" ruled at Aricia, a village near Rome. The King of the Wood, so the story went, was never secure in his power because at any time another man might challenge him to hand-to-hand combat, kill him, and take over the realm. Before the duel could take place, however, the challenger had to break off a golden bough from a sacred tree in the grove—hence the title of Frazer's book.

Frazer searched the world over for evidence of his thesis that the story of the golden bough is a late survival of a primordial human social and religious institution in which the King of the Wood embodied and ensured the fertility of the realm. When his waning power threatened the well-being of the people, the king had to be killed and a young, vital successor placed on the throne. The king must die that the people might live. As embodiment of a fertility or "corn"[5] god, his life and death represent the fundamental vitality of nature. The stories of Phrygian Attis, Greek Adonis, Egyptian Osiris, and Greek Dionysus are mythical projections of this pattern.

On the basis of this hypothetical primordial rite, Frazer attempted to account for much that we find in myths and religions worldwide. The king's life was hemmed in by an elaborate system of taboos. If he broke a taboo, his ability to help his people would be lessened, much as a grounded battery loses its charge. Here, Frazer argued, is the origin of the do's and do not's in every religion and of the many violated taboos in myth. Because the old king must die, many myths tell of the death of kings and gods. These stories, he thought, arose as explanations for real rituals in which a king actually was killed. The origin of myth is thus closely tied to religious ritual. This is *the ritual theory of myth,* and in modified forms, it still has supporters today.

---

[5]Corn, in British usage, means any sort of grain; in American usage corn is usually limited to maize.

Frazer's understanding of myth as a secondary elaboration of ritual exerted immediate influence. Like others influenced by evolutionary thought, Frazer wanted to formulate a comprehensive theory of cultural development. To that end he replaced Tylor's animism with "magic," understood as a mechanical operation used by primitive peoples as part of a ritual to coerce impersonal natural or supernatural forces to obey human wishes. When humans realized that magic was often ineffective, religion was born. The propitiation of quasi human gods replaced coercion through magic. Science, in turn, was destined to replace religion. Myth is associated especially with the religious phase of development because myth is characterized by a belief in personal forces that act in stories, whereas science and magic are concerned with impersonal forces.

Europeans of the late nineteenth century were preoccupied by the concept of progress. Especially in England, progress was thought of as change for the better and, in fact, implicit in the principle of evolution. Like writers on myth during the Enlightenment, Frazer ignored the possibility that change may not always bring improvement. Frazer himself did no field work. He integrated into his master scheme a vast body of data, often carelessly gathered, and manipulated it to fit his theory.

In the twentieth century, anthropological method was much improved by Bronislaw Malinowski (*Magic, Science, and Religion,* 1948), who was born in Poland but pursued his career chiefly in England. Influenced by French sociological thought, his own theory was based directly on field work carried out between 1914 and 1918 among the Trobrianders, the people of a remote island complex southeast of New Guinea. Objecting to the evolutionary understanding of myth as protoscience, Malinowski held that its purpose was to serve as a "charter," a justification for the way things are. This is the *charter theory of myth.*

For example, a story might be told to justify so-and-so's ownership of a certain part of the island—because that is where so-and-so's ancestors sprang from the ground. According to Malinowski, myths justify and validate economic, political, social, and religious realities. Myth is not to be explained according to hypothetical patterns of cultural evolution at all, but from its social function, from how myth helps to deal with the practical problems of living. Malinowski is usually considered the founder of *functionalism,* the notion that the function of a practice determines the form it takes.

## LINGUISTIC THEORIES

The science of Indo-European linguistics, which made great advances in the nineteenth century, was the basis for another allegorical approach to myth in theories advanced by Max Müller (1823–1900), the leading Sanskrit scholar of his day, a vigorous rival of Andrew Lang. Müller, a German-born Oxford don, saw in nearly every myth, whether about heroes or gods, an allegory of the struggle between sunlight and darkness. Hence this method of interpretation is called *solar mythology*. Müller's theory, like others inspired by evolutionary thought and the rapid growth of science, sought to understand myth as the effort of early peoples to explain prominent natural phenomena, such as storms or celestial bodies, but Müller's theory was unusually influential because of the linguistic support he provided for the central role assigned to the sun.

Take, for example, the fairly obscure story of Endymion and Selenê. Endymion was a handsome youth whom Selenê ("moon") saw as he lay sleeping in a cave. She fell deeply in love with him and bore him many children. The two were separated when Zeus allowed Endymion to choose anything he wanted: He chose to sleep forever, never growing old. Because the Greek *enduein* originally meant "to dive," the name Endymion at first simply described the sun's setting ("diving") in the sea. The original meaning of *enduein* faded and was misunderstood to refer to a person, Endymion ("Diver"). The mythical story of the love of Selenê and Endymion, then, began with the words "Selenê embraces Endymion," that is, "Moon embraces Diver," which in the metaphorical "primitive" expression of early peoples was a way of saying "the sun is setting and the moon is rising."

In effect, Max Müller combined ancient physical allegory with the theories of Palaephatus about the distortion of language. Myth, he thought, begins through a "disease of language" whereby the original meaning of language, especially in observations about solar phenomena, was gradually misunderstood and reinterpreted. Müller and his followers were able in this way to argue that bloody death in myth was really the red-streaked sunset, that Odysseus' imprisonment in a cave was the waxing and waning year, and that Achilles' destruction of his enemies was really the splendid sun breaking through the clouds. Midas was the sun gilding everything it touches, and the story of Phaëthon describes how excessive heat (Phaëthon's ride) causes drought that is finally broken by a thunderstorm (the bolt hurled by Zeus to kill Phaëthon).

It is easy to ridicule Müller's theories, but he did attempt to furnish a theoretical explanation for shifts in the meaning of the names of mythical figures. In this he differed from his many predecessors in the long history of allegory, who simply proclaimed, without justification, the truth of whatever came to their minds. Still, it was all too easy for Müller and his followers to find the sun everywhere. Like many ambitious theories of myth, this one began to refute itself. The theory was wittily parodied in a learned article by Andrew Lang that proved, by Müller's own methods, that Müller had never existed, but was himself a solar myth!

Solar mythology, like Creuzer's theories, arose under the influence of the discovery of proto-Indo-European. If it is possible to elucidate the origin and inner structure of modern European languages by comparing them with Greek, Latin, and Sanskrit, it should also be possible, according to the supporters of *Indo-European comparative mythology*, to elucidate European mythology in the same way and to discover essential patterns and original meanings of myth. For example, the Romans told a story about Mucius Scaevola ("Lefty") who deliberately burned off his right hand to demonstrate Roman bravery to an enemy king. The Norsemen, Indo-European speakers like the Romans, told a story about the war god Tiu (whence "Tuesday"), whose right hand was bitten off by the wolf Fenris, an enemy of the present order of creation: While biting off Tiu's hand, the distracted wolf was bound by an unbreakable chain. We could thus infer the existence of an original Indo-European story about a man who sacrificed his hand for the good of all. This story becomes a patriotic tale among the Romans, who emphasized civic duty, but among the Norsemen, who were concerned with the opposition between the cosmic forces of order and chaos, it became a tale of temporary world redemption (one day the Fenris wolf will escape its bonds and the world will end).

Indo-European comparative mythologists maintain that myths accompany language as it is passed on. (Creuzer had argued something similar, but believed in a period of primordial revelation.) They seek a common "grammar," or inner structure, in the stories. Such a grammar ought also to reveal something characteristic of Indo-European social traditions. This sort of interpretation was refined in the mid-twentieth century by French scholar Georges Dumézil (1898–1986), who correlated three hypothetical original classes in Indo-European society with the roles played by certain deities in Indo-European myth. These classes are rulers and priests, warriors, and food producers. Consider, for example, the story of the Judgment of Paris. Why does Hera attempt to bribe Paris with an offer of royal power, while Athena offers him military glory and Aphrodite offers him Helen? Because the three choices represent the three fundamental activities in Indo-European society: Hera stands for royal authority, the ruling class; Athena stands for the warrior class; and Aphrodite, who sponsors reproduction and sustenance, represents the food producers (you might expect Demeter). The division of the first function into rulers and priests is also reflected in myths about early Roman history. The first four kings, in order, are the political founder Romulus, a religious leader (Numa), a warrior (Tullus Hostilius,) and a provider (Ancus Marcius). Dumézil thus combines features of Malinowski's functional approach (myth justifies social patterns) with features of the structural approaches that we will consider shortly. However, so much is left to hypothesis in these reconstructions, and so contradictory or explicable in other ways is the evidence, that few scholars have accepted such explanations with confidence. It is striking how few traces of Indo-European culture we find among the Greeks.

## PSYCHOLOGICAL THEORIES

New fields of study of the past century inspired corresponding new theories of myth. Sociology and anthropology led to functionalism, linguistics led to Indo-European comparative mythology. Psychology, too, has brought with it both a key myth—the story of Oedipus—and a variety of new psychological theories.

At the time when anthropological approaches were developing, Sigmund Freud (1856–1939) advanced a view of myth based in the individual rather than in society. Myth, he thought, was a byproduct of personal psychological forces. Freud's theories of myth began with his thinking about the dreams of individuals. The mind of a sleeper works by different rules from the mind of the wakeful, although dream symbols can be correlated with things in the waking world. Freud formulated rules by which translation from symbolism in dreams to everyday reality takes place. For example, condensation occurs when several things from the waking world are fused together in a dream, perhaps with disturbing effect. Displacement occurs when something in a dream stands for something quite different in the waking world, even its opposite, as when an enemy represents a lover whom the sleeper does not entirely trust. Condensation and displacement are necessary to the dreamer because the true thought is morally or emotionally repugnant to the waking consciousness. Because the thought is still there, however, it must be dealt with, and the mind releases tension by dealing with the problem indirectly. Dreams are symptoms of psychological tensions that can affect the waking world of those suffering from mental disease, from neuroses.

How do the dreams of individuals result in myths, which belong to a whole people? They do, Freud thought, because myths are the collective and recurrent dreams of the race. An example in myth of dream condensation would be the mythical Centaurs, or Sirens, made up of two separate beings fused together; an example in myth of dream displacement would be the upward anatomical shift of a woman's pubic region to create the face of Medusa.

Freud also held that neuroses and their symbolic expression in dreams go back to the infant's experience of his or her personal sexuality. He emphasized the *Oedipus complex,* first set forth in *The Interpretation of Dreams* (1900). From this story, Sigmund Freud developed his notion that adult male psychology arises from the infant boy's sexual attraction to his mother and his hostility and jealousy toward his father, even as Oedipus married his mother and killed his father. Freud did not seek the origins of the legend in social history, as had the Soviet folklorist Vladimir Propp, but in the incest dreams of his patients, which he took to represent suppressed desires of childhood. The son wishes sexual contact with his mother, from whose breasts he feeds and in whose warm body he is daily encompassed. He resents the father's sexual demands on the mother, which displace him from her embrace. He wishes to kill the father, that he might have the mother to himself. Only by overcoming such hidden, taboo, and obviously unspoken desires might one become an adult, Freud thought.

The myth of Oedipus, then, emerges from primeval dreams. To make his point Freud ignored inconvenient parts of the legend, above all the story that at the end of his life Oedipus may have been taken up by the gods. Freud also ignores Oedipus' exposure as an infant and his great intelligence. Critics of Freud starkly complain that Freud's true intentions in his fantasies about human psychology were to denigrate human nature, to reduce it to raw and amoral animal impulse, a vision much in favor at the end of the nineteenth century. Like Oedipus, Freud says, we live in ignorance of our inner wishes that are so repugnant to morality, which Nature has forced upon us, but when we see them clearly, we seek to close our eyes. Critics have also asked whether Oedipus himself had an Oedipus complex; he does not seem to, but Freud was little interested in explaining the story itself.

In Freudian interpretation, stories that describe heroes slaying dragons and marrying maidens are really forms of the Oedipus complex, because they echo the son's repressed desire to kill his father (= the dragon) and have sexual intercourse with his mother (= the maiden). Cronus castrated Uranus because sons wish to deprive their fathers of sexual power, and they fear the same treatment from their own sons in turn. Mythical kings and queens represent parents, sharp weapons are the male sexual organ, and caves, rooms, and houses symbolize the mother's containing womb. The imagery of myths can therefore be translated into that of sex, often in specifically anatomical ways.

Freud saw myths as arising among a race in the way that dreams arise in the individual, but he also argued that individual psychological development repeats the psychological history of the whole race.[6] This is an adaptation of evolutionary thinking. The individual's dreams reflect the same primitive mode of consciousness that we find in myth, which are collective dreams preserved from the primitive childhood of the race. His theory is yet another that connects the mythical with the primitive and the irrational, an approach common since the Enlightenment. A Freudian reading of myth is allegory in yet another guise, translating mythical patterns and events into psychological patterns and events. But like Max Müller, and unlike earlier interpreters, Freud explained not merely how, but also why, shifts occur from one meaning to another.

---

[6]The notion that "ontogeny recapitulates phylogeny" (the development of the individual goes through the same stages as that of the race) was developed by embryologist August Weissman (1834–1914) some time before Freud.

Freud's associate Carl Jung (yung) (1875–1961) continued to explore the notion of an unconscious part of human nature. Like Freud, Jung discerned a complex symbolism that both conceals the unconscious and, to the psychiatrist, furnishes access to it. Jung did not believe, however, that the symbolism of the unconscious mind was predominantly sexual in nature, nor even that dream symbolism ultimately belonged to the individual.

Jung's theory resembles Eastern religious teachings in some respects. For him the consciousness of the individual is like a bay or an inlet on a great ocean of psychic activity, which he called the *collective unconscious* (Freud had implied as much with his notion of racial dreaming). Into the bay swim, from time to time, great beings that inhabit the deep. These are the *archetypes* (a Greek term also used by neoplatonists), timeless recurrent images on which our emotional world and our myths are built. Certain groups of archetypes may dominate the consciousness of entire cultures for periods of time. Jung spoke of such different archetypes as the Wise Old Man, the Earth Mother, and the Divine Child. The *mandala,* a perfectly symmetrical, geometric visual figure used for focusing the consciousness in Buddhist meditation, was considered by Jung to be an emblem of the total psychological integration that each person seeks and that myth reflects. In this sense myth can never be discarded from human life. Whether we know it or not, we live out myths in our own lives.[7]

A follower of Jung, Erich Neumann (1905–1960) used Jung's method to explain the common myth of the dragon-combat. The myth, he argued, symbolizes the breaking away of an individual's consciousness from the great collective unconscious of the world. The dragon represents the collective unconscious, always trying to swallow the hero, who symbolizes individual consciousness. The collective unconscious is also represented by the Great Mother goddess, the mother of all things, a recurrent type in myth and in the history of religion. Although the source of individual consciousness and of life itself, she threatens to swallow her own progeny. For this reason, the male hero, who typically undergoes great dangers, is often threatened by evil female forces—witches like the Greek Circê or monsters like the Mesopotamian Tiamat. At some point the monster may actually swallow the hero (as the whale swallowed Jonah), but defeat is always temporary. The psychological truth represented by the hero's ultimate victory over the dragon is the emergence of personal identity, the victory of the individ-

---

[7]Deeply influenced by Jung is Joseph Campbell, whose many books and even a TV series have popularized the notion of *Myths to Live By* (the title of one of Campbell's books: New York, 1981). Although interesting, Campbell's works have limited value to scholars because of his failure to distinguish between myth and religion and because of his eagerness to find a central hidden meaning (like so many before him) in all myths from all cultures. Most widely read is *The Hero with a Thousand Faces,* 2nd ed. (New York, 1968); see also *The Masks of God,* 4 vols. (New York, 1959–1968), and *The Power of Myth,* with Bill Moyers (New York, 1988).

ual consciousness over the threatening collective unconscious. The hero's reward—princess or treasure—represents the devouring collective unconscious in a tamed-down form, defeated, and now made fecund. The combat myth is really a description of an individual's psychological destiny.

## STRUCTURALIST THEORIES

A highly influential theory of myth interpretation is *structuralism,* especially as propounded by French anthropologist Claude Lévi-Strauss (1908–1994). Meaning in a traditional story is not conveyed by the content, he maintains, but by the structural relationships that one can discover behind the content. In this most rationalistic and abstract of theories, the meaning of myth is its pure form. Structural relationships are often so subtle that they can be made clear only by means of diagrams, charts, and formulas, which resemble mathematical formulas. The meaning of a story, then, is independent of any particular telling of it, residing ultimately in all possible variants of the story taken together. Far from confining himself to "traditional tales," Lévi-Strauss declared that even the interpretation of a myth is to be considered part of the myth, including Lévi-Strauss's own analyses, which are simply additional variants!

Lévi-Strauss finds the origin of myth in the principle that "mythical thought always works from the awareness of opposition toward their progressive mediation." Humans perceive the world in terms of sharp, intolerable dualities—hot and cold, bitter and sweet, raw and cooked, life and death. Because by nature we cannot tolerate opposition for which intermediaries do not exist, we bridge perceived contradictions by telling stories. For example, the story of Cronus fathering his children but refusing to allow them to be born, and of Uranus' son Cronus swallowing his children after they were born, could be said to mediate between the opposites of birth and death. The irreconcilable opposites are brought together by telling a story in which the same creature both generates and consumes his progeny. Homer's *Odyssey,* the story of a man who went to the land of the dead and returned, brings together the irreconcilable opposites of life and death: Although life and death are opposites, in myth we can tell how a man journeyed to the land of the dead and returned. Our binary perception of the world derives, Lévi-Strauss thinks, from the binary physical structure of our brains, which is supposed to make consciousness possible. Because of this binary structure, perceived oppositions can never be fully and finally reconciled—hence the dynamic quality of myth.

In 1955 Lévi-Strauss offered a celebrated new interpretation of the myth of Oedipus (see Further Reading at the end of this chapter). Despite its obscurity, his reading of the myth has attracted widespread comment. According to Lévi-Strauss, the myth has no message, but is the expression of the perception of irreconcilable claims about human origins. The Thebans claimed to be autochthonous, "sprung from the earth" (from the teeth of a dragon, according to the story). Thus Oedipus, "swollen-footed," is so called because creatures who spring from the earth, such as the snaky-footed Giants, have something wrong with their feet. On the other hand, the Thebans obviously sprang from their mothers' wombs, and Oedipus is certainly born from Queen Jocasta. Therefore the myth of Oedipus is said to bridge, through story, what cannot be bridged through logic.

Lévi-Strauss's interpretations are difficult to assess, in part because of the obscurity of his style. For example, in his essay on Oedipus he summarizes his argument in this way: The "overvaluation of blood relations is to their undervaluation as the attempt to escape autochthony is to the impossibility of succeeding in it." It is also hard to know when a true structure has been found because different possibilities for analysis so often exist. As an anthropologist, Lévi-Strauss worked principally among South American Indians, through whose myths he wished not only to discover the deep concerns, fears, and ambitions of these peoples, but to lay open the inner workings of the whole human mind. In this he follows the ancient tradition of commentators wishing to prove that secrets about human nature and human destiny are hidden in traditional tales. More specifically, Lévi-Strauss echoes the neoplatonists' program of discovering behind the stuff of myth an abstract pattern or code that explains the very nature of things.

In spite of its limitations, Lévi-Strauss's structural method of interpretation has had considerable exploratory power because it tries to bring out hitherto unnoticed facets of myth by bringing together whole systems of myth and, beyond that, by relating myth to broader aspects of culture. The method has been followed up for Greek myth by a group of Lévi-Strauss's followers, especially J.-P. Vernant, P. Vidal-Naquet, and M. Detienne. These authors, together with Claude Lévi-Strauss himself, are often called the *Paris school of myth criticism.*

We can take as an example of their method their treatment of the Greek pantheon. The usual way of studying the pantheon is to examine each god in isolation, speculating on his or her origin, and saying something about associated myths and rituals. According to Vernant, however, no one god can ever be understood in isolation, any more than can a single word; one must seek the "syntax," the complicated interrelationships that bind together all the gods in myth. Only then can one understand the conceptual universe of the Greeks.

For example, the traveler Pausanias noted that on the base of Phidias' statue of Zeus in Olympia were linked the names of Hestia and Hermes. Why? Because, according to Vernant, Hestia and Hermes embody the contrary but complementary aspects of the Greeks' apprehension of space. Hestia is the fixed point, the hearth at the center of the household and of the city; Hermes represents transition, movement, change, the connecting link between oppositions. The same polarity is echoed in Greek social life. As Hestia is to Hermes, so is woman to man: The woman stays at home, while the man travels abroad, conducts business, and wages war. Neither Hestia nor Hermes, then, can be understood in isolation because they constitute opposite poles of a single concept. To us this single concept is represented by the word *space,* but the Greeks, who are supposed to have lacked this abstract expression, represented the same notion by the different but complementary activities of Hestia and Hermes.[8]

By selecting and linking apparently disparate items taken from all aspects of culture, structuralist interpretations attempt to detect the rules shaping myth. The complexity of the enterprise points to both its possibilities and its hazards. Interplay between details and larger patterns yields fascinating insights, but the objectivity and significance of what emerges are a persistent difficulty. The universal claims of structuralist theory, professing as it does to be based on the very laws of human thought, permit it to be applied practically everywhere, but open it to criticism on the familiar ground of attempting too much.

## CONTEXTUAL APPROACHES

Such weaknesses are well described by the German scholar Walter Burkert in his book *Structure and History in Greek Mythology and Ritual* (1979), which has exercised strong influence on classical scholars. Burkert accepts the importance of structure in the study of myth, agreeing that the very identity of a tale is maintained by a structure of sense within it. The existence of this constant, partly invisible, internal structure makes it possible for us to say that Homer's story of Oedipus and Sophocles' story are both, despite their differences, "the myth of Oedipus." However, Burkert opposes Lévi-Strauss's indifference to changing cultural and historical conditions, which constantly impart different collective meanings to a myth. Cultural and historical context must always, Burkert insists, be taken into account.

Reviving in part the ritual theory of myth, Burkert argues that the structures that inform myth reflect biological or cultural *programs of actions.* An example of a cultural program of action can be found in the hunting practices of Paleolithic man. Forced to kill his prey in order to survive, but feeling a close relationship with and affection for animals, the hunter assuages his feelings of guilt through various ceremonies. After killing an animal, he makes a mock restoration by setting up its bones. This program of action can explain details in the myth of the hunter Actaeon, who was turned into a stag by Artemis, a goddess of hunting, and torn to pieces by his own dogs. The

[8]In fact several words in Greek do roughly correspond to our *space.*

story reflects a prehistoric ritual in which real animals were hunted by men in animal disguise—thus the dogs are personified in the mythical tradition to the extent of being given individual names. In one version of this myth, the dogs' grief-stricken howling at Actaeon's death is brought to an end when the Centaur Chiron makes an image of Actaeon, which the dogs mistake for their slain master. This making of the image of the slain man/animal, in Burkert's view, reflects the very old ritual reconstruction of the dead animal by the guilt-ridden hunter, actually practiced by tribal peoples.

Surely many ritual elements are reflected in Greek myth, including, no doubt, some drawn from Paleolithic hunting practice, and Burkert's remarks on religion and myth are always enlightening. However, his thesis that Greek sacrificial ritual, and the myths that reflect it, derive from ancient hunting practice leaves unexplained why Greek sacrificial ritual always used domestic animals, never wild animals captured for the purpose. His conviction that ancient hunters felt "guilty" about killing their prey is also open to criticism. Although hunters undoubtedly respect their prey, we usually think of guilt as an emotion arising from violating the social mores; killing animals did not violate the mores of Paleolithic hunters. No doubt one reason that ancient hunters reconstructed their slain prey was to ensure, through magic, that there might be still more animals to kill.

Feminist critics may also apply a contextual approach, using myth to cast light on underlying social realities related to gender or show how myths may actually construct reality; so the myth of Demeter explained to Greek women expected roles in marriage, childbearing, and religious cult, making such roles seem intrinsic and natural. We cannot be mechanical, however, in separating biologically determined patterns of behavior from culturally determined ones; such explanations sometimes assume that all gender differences, justified by myth, are conventional, which is not likely. Such criticism must also work with literary material generated by and for males, never by females for themselves.

The contextual approach to myth is complex, making use of insights from structural, historical, and comparative methods and appealing broadly to what we know about human biology, the history of religion, language, and anthropology.

## CONCLUSION

What are we to make of this long development, the history of the interpretation of Greek myths, of which we have given only brief highlights? One cannot help but be impressed by the abiding fascination that the Greek mythical tradition has exercised over the human mind. But what validity do these systems of interpreting myth have for our understanding of myth, if by "understanding" we mean placing something in a larger and more familiar context?

The ancient Greek theorists, puzzled by the strangeness of traditions taken from a preliterate and prephilosophic past, attempted to explain their own myths by assimilating them to "correct" models of reality as created by philosophy. They saw in myths allegories for philosophic descriptions of the physical world or, in Euhemerism, as a source for historical reconstruction of the human past, or as a set of examples for how one should behave. Later methods have worked much the same way, adapting myths to new models of reality as they emerged from Christian to modern times. We need to be aware that the scientific model of reality, which has increasingly dominated thought since the Enlightenment and especially since the nineteenth century, is only the latest in a long line of such models. Although the nineteenth-century theory of myth as a "disease of language" centering on natural phenomena was encouraged by scientific linguistics, it is remarkably similar to the interpretation proposed by Palaephatus in 300 BC. Modern psychological theories, especially those of Jung and Lévi-Strauss, offer explanations that in important ways repeat and refine an approach used by much earlier interpreters who sought in myth allegories of spiritual and psychological truths.

The strength of science lies in defining ideas precisely and treating them within strictly controlled guidelines. The power of humanistic studies, on the other hand, lies in their concern with the capacity of humans, as symbol-making beings, to create alternative worlds. Myth is one such alternative world, and the interpretation of myth is another; each is an expression of the same human capacity. Historically, the interpretation of myth is fully as important as myth itself and in fact occurs on a far grander scale. The interchangeable use of the words *myth* (the story itself) and *mythology* (reflection on myth) in English usage unintentionally points to this critical confusion, a fact recognized by structuralists when they suggest that interpretations of myths are only the addition of new myths to old. If myth embodies the tensions, values, and intellectual currents of the society that produces it, myth interpretation embodies those currents no less faithfully. A sketch of the history of myth interpretation turns out to be a sketch of the history of ideas. In the history of myth interpretation we can watch and study ever-changing intellectual fashions in relation to an unchanging body of material.

The grand theorizers about myth like to pick out this or that story, this or that figure, make impressive observations, and then speak as if their conclusions were applicable to all myths from all times and all places. But myths are so different from one another, and sometimes so ill-defined, that any universal definition is bound to be arbitrary and to serve theoretical interests of one's own; the history of the interpretation of myth richly demonstrates this fact. The scope of Greek myth both invites and refutes the fatal tendency to comprehensive claims, because Greek myth affords so rich a choice of test cases. With careful selection any theory will work well in particular instances, elucidating even minor points with astonishing clarity. Applied to the next myth, the theory may be unable to deal plausibly with even obvious features.

Classical myth taken together is too complex, too multifaceted to be explained by a single theory, as is fully recognized by the contextual approach, which I favor in this book (but not to the exclusion of other approaches, when appropriate). The complexity of myth is bound up with the complexity of human consciousness itself and with the special role that the Greeks, the inventors of the alphabet, played in the transition from an oral traditional culture to one that was alphabetic and self-critical. Greek myth, therefore, is a special case in the history of the human spirit. To understand it, we must make use of insights offered by different schools of interpretation. No one method of analysis will dissolve the endless mysteries of classical myth.

## FURTHER READING

### General Approaches

Bremmer, J., and F. Graf, eds., *Interpretations of Greek Mythology* (London, 1987). A collection of essays on various topics, by leading critics.

Cohen, P., "Theories of Myth," *Man,* new series 4 (1969): 337–353. Concise review of theories on the interpretation of myth.

Dundes, A., ed., *Sacred Narrative: Readings in the Theory of Myth* (Berkeley, 1984). Gathers important essays by major scholars on myth interpretation, edited by a leading folklorist.

Edmunds, L., ed., *Approaches to Greek Myth* (Baltimore, 1990). Essays on modern schools of myth interpretation, including myth and ritual, myth and history, Greek and Near Eastern mythology, Indo-European mythology, folklore, structuralism, psychoanalytic interpretation, and myth and Greek art.

Kirk, G. S., *The Nature of Greek Myths* (New York, 1974). Discusses "five monolithic theories"—nature myths, etiological myths, charter myths, myths that evoke a creative era, and myths that derive from rituals—and adds five additional theories that view myths as products of the psyche.

### Romantic Theories

Kamenetsky, C., *The Brothers Grimm and Their Critics, Folktales and the Quest for Meaning* (Athens, OH, 1992). The place of the Grimms' collection in the Romantic movement; extensive review of theories of folktale interpretation.

### Anthropological Theories

Fontenrose, J., *The Ritual Theory of Myth* (Berkeley, 1966; reprinted 1971). Argument against the theory that myth derives from ritual, by a leading scholar.

Frazer, J. G., *The New Golden Bough,* ed. T. Gaster (New York, 1959). A modern condensation of this seminal work.

Malinowski, B., *Magic, Science, and Religion, and Other Essays* (New York, 1948; reprinted Prospect Heights, IL, 1992). The anthropologist sets forth his charter theory of myth.

Vickery, J. B., *The Literary Impact of The Golden Bough* (Princeton, 1973). Résumé of Frazer's arguments and their influence.


### LINGUISTIC THEORIES

Dorson, R. M., "The Eclipse of Solar Mythology," in T. A. Sebeok, ed., *Myth: A Symposium* (Bloomington, IN, 1971), pp. 25–63. A witty account of the rise and fall of Max Müller's theory of nature mythology.

Müller, F. Max, *Comparative Mythology: An Essay*, ed. A. Smythe Palmer (London, 1909; reprinted Salem, NH, 1977, ed. R. M. Dorson). Müller's major statement on the principles of solar mythology.

Puhvel, J., *Comparative Mythology* (Baltimore, 1987; reprinted 1989). An up-to-date review of Indo-European elements in Greek myth, including the theories of Georges Dumézil (most of whose many publications are in French).


### PSYCHOLOGICAL THEORIES

Fordham, F., *An Introduction to Jung's Psychology*, with a foreword by Jung, 3rd ed. (Baltimore, 1966).

Jung, C. G., et al., *Man and His Symbols* (New York, 1968). Jung and his followers expound the theory of unconscious archetypes.

Mullahy, P., *Oedipus, Myth and Complex, A Review of Psychoanalytic Theory* (New York, 1948; reprinted 1955).

Neumann, E., *The Origins and History of Consciousness*, trans. R. F. C. Hull (Princeton, 1954; reprinted 1970). A student of Carl Jung, Neumann analyzes the story of the dragon-combat in terms of unconscious archetypes.

Wollheim, R., *Freud* (London, 1971). An introduction to Freud's thought for the beginner.


### STRUCTURALISM

Detienne, M., *The Creation of Mythology*, trans. Margaret Cook (Chicago, 1986). An important contribution to the "Paris School."

Gordon, R. L., ed., *Myth, Religion and Society*. Structuralist essays by M. Detienne, L. Gernet, J.-P. Vernant and P. Vidal-Naquet (Cambridge, England, 1981). Writings from the "Paris School."

Leach, E., *Claude Lévi-Strauss*, revised edition (New York, 1974; reprinted Chicago, 1989). Excellent presentation of the Straussian analysis of myth.

Lévi-Strauss, C., "The Structural Study of Myth," reprinted in T. A. Sebeok, ed., *Myth: A Symposium* (Bloomington, IN, 1971), pp. 81–106. A classic, much-criticized essay analyzing the myth of Oedipus.

Lévi-Strauss, C., *The Raw and the Cooked,* trans. J. and D. Weightman (Chicago, 1980). Volume 1 of his four-volume *Mythologiques* and a good introduction to his method and theories.

Vernant, J.-P., *Myth and Society in Ancient Greece,* trans. J. Lloyd (New York, 1990). Major statement by a leading member of the "Paris School."

### CONTEXTUAL APPROACHES

Burkert, W., *Structure and History in Greek Mythology and Ritual* (Berkeley, 1979). An influential modern contribution to theoretical approaches to Greek mythology. Contains a lucid explication and criticism of the school of Lévi-Strauss.

Powell, B. B., *Classical Myth,* 3rd ed. (New York, 2001). An expanded version of this book with many illustrations and selections from ancient literature.

# CHAPTER 4

# THE CULTURAL CONTEXT
# OF GREEK MYTH

MYTHS REFLECT the society that produces them. They cannot be separated from the physical, social, and spiritual worlds in which a people lives, or from a people's history. In this chapter we consider the background of the Greeks (and, briefly, the Romans), the nature of the land they lived in, their origins and history, how they lived as groups and individuals, and something about their values—what they hoped to achieve in life and how they hoped to do it.

## GREEK GEOGRAPHY

Greece was a poor country, barren and dry, in ancient times as today. Unlike the rich river valleys of Egypt and Mesopotamia, the rugged Balkan peninsula, the southeasternmost extension of Europe, does not seem to be a likely setting for the ancient civilization it produced (see map, inside front cover). Its rivers are too small to be navigable, and they dry up in the blazing heat of the mostly rainless summers. The Greek landscape is dominated by high mountains that occupy about three quarters of the land. A towering range, the Pindus, runs down the center of the peninsula, then continues into the sea, where its peaks appear as dry, rocky islands. Pindus is intersected by other ranges that cut across the peninsula. Between these ranges lies a series of small, isolated plains, the only places in Greece suitable for agriculture.

Here on these plains, nestled between the mountains and the sea, Greek civilization developed.

To the northeast on the Balkan peninsula are the plains of Thessaly and Macedonia. To their south lies the plain of Boeotia (bē-ō-sha, "cow-land"), whose principal settlement in ancient times was the city of Thebes, and the plain of Attica, whose capital was Athens. Farther south, on the smaller peninsula known as the Peloponnesus (pel-o-pon-**nē**-sus, = "island of Pelops") are other cultivable plains: Argolis, whose principal settlements were, in the Bronze Age, Tiryns (**ti**-rinz) and Mycenae (mī-**sē**-nē) and later, in the Classical Period, Argos and Corinth; Laconia, with the town of Sparta, also called Lacedaemon (las-e-**dē**-mon); Messenia (mes-**sē**-ni-a), whose most important settlement was Pylos; and Elis, site of the Olympic Games. All of these places figure importantly in Greek myth.

On these small plains the ancient Greeks grew wheat and barley, planted early in winter, when the rainy season began, and harvested in May. The olive, whose small, compact gray leaves resist the ferocious summer sun, grew abundantly in the lowlands and provided a delightful light oil for cooking, cleansing and anointing the body, and burning in lamps. Wine grapes grew on vines planted on the slopes that surrounded the plains. Goats, sheep, and pigs were kept for wool, milk, cheese, leather, and meat, but cattle were few because of the lack of forage. Horses were also scarce, and therefore highly valued; they were a source of great prestige, the pride of the ruling class.

As cultivable land was limited in Greece, so too were other resources. There was some gold in Thrace (far in the north), but none in Greece proper. There were a few deposits of silver (one at Laurium in Attica contributed to Athenian economic and military power). Most iron had to be imported, although important iron deposits in Laconia contributed to Spartan military supremacy. Greece imported copper from Cyprus. The source for tin, alloyed with copper to produce bronze, remains unknown.

The Greeks did have access to excellent deposits of limestone and clay. The best limestone was found on the island of Euboea (yū-**bē**-a) just east of the mainland (important for other reasons, discussed later in this chapter), on several smaller islands, and in Thessaly. Under high pressure, limestone crystallizes into marble, a lovely, workable stone used by the Greeks for sculpture and for the finest temples, like the Parthenon in Athens, which celebrated the goddess Athena.

Important deposits of marble were found on Mount Pentelicus near Athens and on the islands of Naxos and Paros. The finest clay, especially that found near Athens and Corinth, provided material for pottery, which the Greeks produced in great abundance and variety. Once fired, ceramic material is breakable, but its fragments are virtually indestructible. Exquisitely decorated Greek pots that imitated precious exemplars in silver and gold now lost, often expressly for use in burials, have been found all over the Mediterranean world. The pictures painted on these pots provide us with vivid illustrations of Greek myths and wonderfully illuminate many details of Greek social life.

But perhaps the greatest Greek natural resource was the sea. The Aegean (ē-**jē**-an) Sea, between the Balkan peninsula and Asia Minor, played a central role in the life of the ancient Greeks. Most of them lived near the sea and took from it the fish that was one of the staples of their diet, although Homeric heroes preferred to eat only flesh. The sea was also an avenue of communication with the world beyond the mountains that enclosed them.

Because of the islands scattered across the Aegean, a seafarer is almost never out of sight of land, and the Greeks learned early to travel long distances in small open boats. Several large islands dominate the others. Crete, the southernmost Aegean island, had an especially important role to play in the early history of Greece, but Euboea, Rhodes, Chios, and Lesbos also stand out. There are two principal groups of islands: the Cyclades (**sik**-la-dēz, "circle islands"), placed in a rough circle around the tiny central island of Delos, sacred to Apollo and Artemis; and the Sporades (**spor**-a-dēz), "scattered islands," which extend in two groups, one in the northwest Aegean near Thessaly, the other in the southeast Aegean. The southern Sporades include the twelve islands off the southwest coast of Asia Minor called Dodecanese (do-dek-a-**nēz**) ("twelve").

The paucity of cultivable land and natural resources led the Greeks to trade with other nations. A mastery of the sea allowed them to transport goods to and from foreign lands. They exported wine, olive oil, and pottery and brought back the metals and other goods they needed, especially grain and luxury items of exquisite workmanship. Later, they established colonies across the sea, on the coasts of Asia Minor to the east and in Italy to the west.

The geography of the Balkan peninsula influenced both the history and the myths of the Greeks. The extremely mountainous terrain discouraged communication by land and favored political independence; through most of ancient Greek history, the various cities remained autonomous political entities. Many Greek legends told of the great deeds of these cities' founders and early rulers. Myths also reflect the fact that the Greeks were the greatest seafaring people of the ancient world (together with the Semitic Phoenicians), as exemplified by the story of Odysseus' perilous sea journey home from the Trojan War.

## GREEK HISTORY

Greece was occupied even in the Paleolithic ("Old Stone") Age, before 7000 BC, but almost nothing is known of these early inhabitants. From the Neolithic ("New Stone") Age, 6000–3000 BC, survive foundation stones of houses, pottery, stone tools, and graves. These peoples lived in settled communities and practiced a rudimentary agriculture. Our evidence becomes richer with the advent of the Bronze Age around 3000 BC, after which we divide the archaeological and historical record into the following periods:

| | |
|---|---|
| Early and Middle Bronze Age | 3000–1600 BC |
| Mycenaean Age (Late Bronze Age) | 1600–1200 BC |
| Dark Age | 1200–800 BC |
| Archaic Period | 800–480 BC |
| Classical Period | 480–323 BC |
| Hellenistic Period | 323–31 BC |

The dates for these periods are to some extent arbitrary and conventional, but this scheme provides a useful framework for discussion.

## The Early and Middle Bronze Age (3000–1600 BC): The Origin of the Greeks

We do not regard the inhabitants of the mainland during the Early and Middle Bronze Age as Greeks because their cultural traditions were very different from those of the people who eventually became known by that name. We know nothing of their race or the language they spoke. They seem to have been modest farmers who worshiped goddesses of fertility believed able to increase the yield of their crops, a religion still vital among later Greeks and reflected prominently in some Greek myths.

We are far better informed about the inhabitants of the island of Crete, called Minoans after Minos, the legendary Cretan king, although again we know nothing of their ethnic affinities or language. From c. 2200 BC into the Mycenaean Age, c. 1450 BC, they built elaborate and costly palaces. The bull was important in their religious ritual, as was the double ax, or *labrys* (hence "labyrinth"), presumably the special tool by which bulls were sacrificed. They also worshiped a goddess of fertility. The Minoan palaces were not encircled by defensive walls, a fact that lends support to the remark by the Greek historian Thucydides (c. 460–401 BC) that the mythical "kingdom of Minos" dominated the seas.

The exact date of the arrival of the Indo-European Greeks in the southern Balkans cannot be established,[1] but the destruction of existing settlements in Greece around 2100 BC at the transition from Early to Middle Bronze Age suggests the arrival of a new people. From about the same time, we find the first evidence in Greece of the domestic horse, an animal elsewhere associated with the Indo-Europeans. As we have seen (Chapter 3), some think that basic patterns in Greek myth go back to the Indo-Europeans.

---

[1] For the Indo-Europeans, see Chapter 3.

The Greek language of later eras was probably not the tongue of the early Indo-European immigrants, but developed over the centuries after their arrival. The basic vocabulary of Greek is derived from the hypothetical proto-Indo-European parent language, but many words—particularly those for places, plants, and animals—seem to have been taken from the language of the earlier inhabitants, just as in America the names Manhattan, Chicago, and Wisconsin were taken from languages of pre-European inhabitants. There were also a considerable number of Semitic words in Greek, reflecting the Greeks' enormous debt to the earlier cultures of the variegated Semitic peoples (Akkadians, Babylonians, Phoenicians, Aramaeans, Hebrews) who lived in the Near East.

## The Mycenaean Age (1600–1200 BC)

We have little archaeological evidence from the Early and Middle Bronze Age in Greece, but spectacular ruins, as well as written documents, survive from the Late Bronze or Mycenaean Age, named for the impressive stone citadel of Mycenae in the Peloponnesus. Immensely rich tombs from about 1600 BC prove its wealth and importance and provide a convenient date for the beginning of the Mycenaean Age.

In the Mycenaean Age the Greeks were ruled by powerful kings. The kings and their retainers constituted a military and aristocratic elite; they were lovers of war who used bronze weapons, rode to battle in horse-drawn chariots, and concentrated great wealth in their hands. Independent kings built impressive strongholds from which they supervised highly controlled and centralized, although local, economies. Their greatest centers of power, in addition to Mycenae, were Thebes and Orchomenus in Boeotia, Athens in Attica, Pylos in Messenia, and Sparta in Laconia: All these centers (except Orchomenus) figure prominently in Greek myth, and we will encounter them repeatedly in the following chapters. Unlike the Minoan settlements, Mycenaean palaces were strongly fortified. The Mycenaean Greeks may have called themselves Achaeans (a-kē-anz), a word Homer uses to describe the men who attacked Troy.

About 1450 BC the Minoan civilization was destroyed and the palaces burned, perhaps by Mycenaeans from the mainland, when Mycenaeans occupied and rebuilt the principal palace at Cnossus. The palace was destroyed again around1375 BC by an unknown agency, never to be rebuilt. In the ruins we have found documents written in Greek in a nonalphabetic script called Linear B. Minoan art and religion made a deep impression on the Mycenaean Greeks and, through them, on subsequent European culture.

Linear B, the form of writing used by the Mycenaeans, was deciphered in 1952 by an English architect, Michael Ventris, one of the great intellectual accomplishments of the twentieth century. Without the advantage of such bilingual documents as the Rosetta Stone (which made it possible to decipher Egyptian hieroglyphics), Ventris proved that the writing consisted of about eighty nonalphabetic signs, each of which stood for a syllable. In addition to the tablets found at Cnossus in Crete, documents in Linear B have turned up at Pylos, Mycenae, and Thebes on the mainland, proving the cultural uniformity of the Mycenaeans. Linear B, preserved on clay tablets, may have originated as a modification of the earlier undeciphered Linear A writing, which may have preserved the Minoan language, presumably unrelated to Greek. Linear B was used only for keeping economic accounts. Although these records give us a great deal of information, Linear B was not used for recording literature.

The coincidence between centers of power in Mycenaean times and important locations in cycles of Greek legend—the Mycenae of Agamemnon, the Tiryns of Heracles, and the Thebes of Oedipus—makes probable that many Greek legends originated during the Mycenaean period. In the absence of some form of writing suitable for recording them, however, these tales could only be transmitted orally from one generation to the next. Sometimes non-Greek cities, Cnossus in Crete and Troy in Asia Minor, were provided with cycles of legend, but always as seen through Greek eyes. Of native traditions from such cities, we have no direct information.

## The Dark Age (1200–800 BC)

When Troy was destroyed by human hands about 1250 BC, perhaps assisted by an earthquake, the people then occupying the site were raising horses and using pottery similar to that found in Greece; because of the similarity in styles of pottery, some think that the Trojans of this period were in fact Greeks. Most scholars associate the destruction of 1250 BC with the legend of the Trojan War (although there is plenty of disagreement). Soon after 1200 BC, fire also destroyed most of the Mycenaean palaces on the mainland. Linear B writing disappeared forever. Greece sank into a Dark Age that lasted some 400 years.

Later Greeks attributed this destruction to an invasion by Greek-speaking peoples from northwest Greece, whom they called the Dorians, equated with the Sons of Heracles in Greek legend. Although modern scholars cannot confirm the Dorian invasion from archaeological evidence, it offers a plausible explanation for the widespread destruction of Mycenaean sites at about the same time. The Dorians, whether or not descendants of Heracles, seem to have replaced the Mycenaeans who earlier dominated Greece, except for remote and mountainous central Arcadia in the Peloponnesus. Dorians then pushed across the Aegean to Crete and other nearby islands and to the southern strip of Asia Minor, where they founded colonies.

Of the mainland settlements, Athens alone withstood the invaders. Many Greeks from other regions migrated eastward and resettled the Aegean islands. Refugees from the Peloponnesus, passing through Athens and now called Ionians, took possession of the central islands of the Aegean and founded colonies in the central sector of the western coast of Asia Minor. This central region, henceforth known as Ionia, had its greatest center at Miletus. Other refugees, the Aeolians, crossed from Thessaly to the island of Lesbos and to the northern portion of the coast of Asia Minor, henceforth called Aeolis. The famous poet Sappho (sixth century BC), whose poems are nearly the only documents to survive in the odd Aeolic dialect, lived on Lesbos, as did the great contemporary poet Alcaeus. By 900 BC, the map of Greece had been completely redrawn.

Very few archaeological remains survive from the Dark Age, a time of profound social disorganization, depopulation, and impoverishment. Petty kings with only local authority replaced the great monarchs of the Mycenaean Age. To judge from later traditions, Greek society was organized around the family and village. Many settlements were split by tribal and family feuds and, in the Dorian areas, by a great gulf between masters and subjects. What civilization remained seems to have centered on the long island of Euboea, just east of the mainland, where recent excavations have revealed rich burials, one a spectacular grave containing a warrior and his wife, with many rare and valuable objects, some of gold. We are now learning that Euboean settlements were the only Greek towns to carry on direct trade with the Near East throughout the Dark Age. These relationships were to play a central role in the subsequent revival of Greek culture: The alphabet first appears on Euboea, and the *Odyssey* tells of seafaring to the far West, where Euboeans at this time actually traveled.

## The Archaic Period (800–480 BC)

About 800 BC someone familiar with Phoenician writing, perhaps a bilingual Semite resident on Euboea,[2] seems to have invented the Greek alphabet by requiring that a rough indication of the vowel accompany each consonantal sign. Phoenician writing had only signs for consonants and could not be pronounced except by a native. The Greek alphabet was the first writing that encoded an approximation of the actual sound of the human voice, hence potentially a writing applicable to any human language. It is one of the most important inventions in the history of civilization, the basis for all Western

---

[2]According to the author's own researches.

culture and, except for minor changes, the same system of writing that appears on this page.

Within a generation, the revolutionary alphabetic technology had spread widely among the Greek people. At the same time, under Euboean leadership, the Greeks sent out colonies to the west, to southern Italy and Sicily, where they built cities and prospered greatly. The period of political and cultural revival that coincided with the invention of the alphabet marks the beginning of a new era in Greek history, the Archaic Period (800–480 BC).

The Archaic Period witnessed the emergence of the Greek *polis,* the politically independent city-state. Unlike the villagers of earlier eras, who defined their position by family relations, the members of a *polis* owed their allegiance to a social group defined by geography, economic interests, and military camaraderie. In the *polis* appeared for the first time the explicit concept of citizenship ("city-membership"), so important to the modern state. Only males were citizens and could participate in political affairs, that is, decide when to go to war and against whom; females lived in a separate world. Within the *polis,* the Greek citizen was in relentless competition with his neighbor. Greek cultural values depended on the spirit of male competition (unlike in Egypt, for example, where cooperation was the highest social value), and these values permeate the stories they told.

Another important development during the Archaic Period was the rebirth of commerce, sunk to a low ebb throughout the Dark Age. The Greeks' dependence on the sea for commerce, transportation, and food was essential to the formation of their character and had a direct influence on their social structure. Greece was never socially stratified in the elaborate fashion of the heavily populated and extravagantly wealthy river monarchies that grew up along the Nile and in Mesopotamia, between the Tigris and Euphrates rivers, and the Greeks' dependence on the sea served further to reduce distinctions of class. The sea is an equalizer: The sudden dangerous storms of the Aegean threatened captain and crew alike, when claims to good birth and upbringing had no survival value. Seafaring encouraged extreme individualism and offered rich rewards to the skilled adventurer willing to take risks. Seafaring was practiced almost entirely by free citizens, and in the *Odyssey* the Greeks invented the world's first tale of danger and wonder on the high sea.

In the sixth century BC commerce received an enormous stimulus from the introduction of coinage, universally accepted weights of portable, indestructible metal certified by civic authority. Before this time, money as we think of it did not exist. Coined money made possible capitalism and the enrichment of new social classes. The traditional aristocracy looked down on and bitterly opposed these upstarts, skillful only at accumulating wealth, and called them *kakoi,* the "bad men," while calling themselves *aristoi,* the "best men" (hence our "aristocrat"). Despite the scorn of the *aristoi,* economic and political power fell more and more into the hands of the *kakoi.*

Between 650 and 500 BC, many Greek city-states were ruled by strong men known as *tyrants,* who represented the interests of the commercial class against the traditional aristocracy. The word *tyrant* comes from a non-Greek language of Asia Minor and originally meant something like "ruler," but by the sixth century BC referred to a leader who had taken power by "unconstitutional" (that is, nontraditional) means. In the eyes of their aristocratic opponents, the tyrants were arbitrary despots, but tyrants often did much to enhance the wealth and power of the cities they ruled. Rarely did a tyrant give up power voluntarily. In cultural matters, however, the aristocracy clung to power. As the most literate class, its members were creators or sponsors of most Greek literature, art, and philosophy. They gave to "tyrant" the pejorative meaning it still has today. When speaking of Greek culture, we refer, with few exceptions, to the literary monuments produced by and for the *aristoi,* the free male citizens descended from old families. About the *kakoi,* the poor, slaves, women, and other noncitizens, most of whom were illiterate, we have little direct information.

## The Classical Period (480–323 BC)

During the latter part of the Archaic Period, Greece was threatened by a powerful rival from the east. The Persians, an Indo-European people living on the Iranian plateau east of Mesopotamia (= modern Iraq), had developed into a dynamic warrior state under the leadership of Cyrus the Great (600?–529 BC). Conquering and absorbing first the Semitic states of Mesopotamia, then Egypt, and finally advancing into Anatolia (modern Turkey) and southern Russia, Persia became the greatest empire the world had seen. Soon Persia absorbed the Greek colonies on the western coast of Asia minor.

In 508 BC, in Athens, a remarkable development took place: the emergence of the world's first *democracy* ("rule by the people"; *dêmos* = "people"), an outgrowth of the centuries-long dispute between *kakoi* and *aristoi.* Under the leadership of Cleisthenes (**klīs**-the-nēz), the social and political basis of the *polis* was completely reorganized so as to place the power of making decisions in the hands of all the adult male citizens, who may have numbered about 25,000. Citizens lived both in the countryside and in the city. Henceforth, authority in government came not from wealth and prominence of family, but from one's ability to persuade the large, unruly assembly of citizens.

From this unique political climate emerged many of the forms of civilization familiar to us today: written secular law, the rules of reason, the need for evidence in reaching the truth, history, popular entertainment, science, and philosophy. In Athens, ancient myths were recast as a new form of entertainment and instruction in the annual presentations of Athenian tragedy.

Democracy made the ordinary citizen feel he had responsibility for his own destiny, as in reality he did: Anyone could be heard and citizens made their own choice about when and whom to fight. The Persian army discovered to their sorrow the explosive power of this new form of government when they invaded mainland Greece in 490 BC. In a tremendous battle near the village of Marathon, about twenty-five miles from Athens, Athenian citizen soldiers smashed the professional Persian army and drove the invaders into the sea. "This proved," wrote the historian Herodotus, "if there were need of proof, how noble a thing is freedom" (*Histories* 5.78). An even greater Persian campaign launched ten years later, in 480 BC, also met with disaster, first in a naval battle off the island of Salamis near Athens and then on land near Plataea, in Boeotia (479 BC). This second stunning victory over the Persians, under Athenian leadership at sea and Spartan on land, fired the Greeks, and especially the Athenians, with an unprecedented self-confidence and eagerness to try out new forms of thought, social organization, and artistic expression. These amazing victories inspired the first study of *history* (Herodotus coined the word, which means "inquiry," in his great book) and mark the beginning of the brief Classical Period. In the popular marathon race, the Athenian victory of 490 BC is still celebrated around the world.[3] The enormous booty captured from the retreating Persian army greatly enriched the small city of Athens, as did its supremacy at sea, thanks to the new citizen navy.

During the Classical Period, the Golden Age of Greece, lived many of the most influential thinkers, artists, and politicians: the historians Herodotus and Thucydides; the tragedians Aeschylus, Sophocles, and Euripides and the comic dramatist Aristophanes; the statesman Pericles; the philosophers Socrates, Plato, and Aristotle; Ictinus, architect of the Parthenon; the sculptor Phidias; and the orator Demosthenes, to name only the most prominent. All these men were Athenians or residents of Athens, a testimony to the city's cultural supremacy, fostered by its radical democracy. From other cities during the Classical Period came the poet Pindar; Democritus, who fashioned the atomic theory of matter; and Hippocrates, "the father of medicine."

During the Classical Period the *polis* reached its greatest effectiveness, but also showed its worst faults. Some of the tragedies of this era illuminate the violent tensions many citizens no doubt felt between ancient loyalty to the family and current loyalty to the political state. Still, the *polis* triumphed as the ideal of social life. In the fourth century BC, Aristotle described the

---

[3]After the defeat of the Persians, a runner supposedly ran the twenty-five miles to Athens, announced the victory, and dropped dead (many scholars doubt this happened). In the Olympic Games at Athens in 1896, the marathon race was instituted to commemorate this event. In 1908 the distance was standardized at 26 miles, 385 yards.

*polis* as the perfect and natural fruit of a long social evolution. According to him, "man is by nature a political animal," that is, a being who reaches full potential only by living in a *polis.*

Although the proud and politically independent city-states struggled constantly and murderously against one another, the Greeks nonetheless maintained the sense of being a single people. They spoke a common language and used a common technology of writing and called themselves Hellenes (**hel**-ēnz), implying a common descent from the legendary Hellên (**hel**-lên).[4] They worshiped the same pantheon of gods and participated in Panhellenic religious and athletic festivals, especially at Olympia. Such regional events as the annual Panathenaic ("All-Athenian") festival in Athens gave the Greeks a sense of ethnic community. But political unity was beyond the reach of the freedom-loving Greeks. In the crisis of the Persian wars they combined briefly against the barbarian invader. Once the Persian threat receded, however, they settled into two loosely organized rival leagues, one led by Sparta, a military state ruled by an old-fashioned aristocracy, the other by democratic Athens. From 431 to 404 BC, these leagues fought each other in a ruinous conflict, known to history as the Peloponnesian War. Greece never recovered.

The Classical Period saw the development of Greek philosophy and history as powerful intellectual rivals to traditional myth. Such freethinkers as Xenophanes and such philosophers as Protagoras and Empedocles and later Plato and Aristotle challenged mythic accounts of the origin and nature of the universe, while the historian Thucydides rejected the conviction, heretofore universal, that gods determine the outcome of human events. The stories of gods and heroes were the common birthright of all Greece and were celebrated in painting, sculpture, song, and drama, but they were given new meanings in the intellectual ferment of this extraordinary age.

## The Hellenistic Period (323–31 BC)

The social and political system based on the *polis* was crippled in 338 BC when Philip II of Macedon, a region to the north of Greece, overran the Greek city-states and imposed his will on them. The Macedonian state was a feudal monarchy altogether unlike the Greek *polis;* although Philip admired Greek intellectual culture and Greek economic enterprise, he had no patience with the endless squabbles conducted in the name of "freedom." When he was killed in 336 BC in a palace intrigue, his twenty-year-old son

---

[4]Not to be confused with Helen of Troy. The term *Graioi,* "Greeks," comes from the Romans, who seem to have taken it from a northwestern Greek tribe living in Epirus, the backward territory across the Ionian Sea, which separates Italy from Greece.

Alexander inherited the throne. Moved by legends of the Trojan War and seeing himself as a latter-day Achilles, Alexander attacked the enormous Persian Empire, ostensibly to avenge the Persian invasions 150 years earlier. In a series of brilliant battles, he destroyed the Persian monarchy and occupied its vast territories. His conquests took him even beyond Persian domains into India. From 323 BC, when Alexander died of a fever (or was poisoned by rivals) at age thirty-two, we date what is known as the Hellenistic Period of Greek history.[5]

After his death Alexander's empire quickly broke up into separate and hostile kingdoms, but Greek culture now became world culture. Everywhere throughout the ancient East—in Syria, Mesopotamia, Palestine, and Egypt—cities were established on the Greek model, decorated in the Greek style, ruled by Greeks and speakers of Greek. The cultural capital shifted from Athens to Alexandria, a city Alexander himself had founded in the western delta of Egypt.

In 146 BC the Greek mainland was conquered by Rome, and other centers of Hellenistic culture met a similar fate in the years that followed. The end of the period can be dated to 31 BC, when Alexandria in Egypt fell into Roman hands after the suicide of Cleopatra VII, the last ruling descendant of the generals of Alexander.

## GREEK SOCIETY

Greek myths reflect the society in which they were transmitted, and to understand them we need to understand something about the social life of ancient Greece. Unfortunately, our knowledge of Greek society is rather limited. About conditions in the Bronze and Iron Ages we have archaeological evidence, but no written information except the accounting documents of Linear B. For the Archaic Period, we have the long poems of Homer and Hesiod, who lived in the eighth century BC, but almost nothing after them. We know more about Greek society in the Classical Period, largely because of the tragedies and other literary works that have survived from this era. But even here our knowledge is incomplete. Almost all the literary sources are of Athenian origin, and almost all were composed by aristocratic males. Most so-called descriptions of *Greek* social life are really descriptions of *Athenian* social life of the fifth and fourth centuries BC, although Athens was in many ways a unique community in ancient Greece. In this section we will nonetheless attempt to describe the general aspects of Greek society reflected in myth, especially those aspects that seem to us most foreign and distant.

---

[5] *Hellenic* refers to anything Greek (from the legendary Hellên, founder of the Greek race); *Hellenistic* refers to the historical period that began with the death of Alexander the Great.

## Slavery

Without slaves, ancient civilizations could not have existed. Tribal societies kill captives taken in war, or sometimes adopt the women and children, but the ancient Mediterranean civilizations of Greece and Rome were sufficiently wealthy to support vast numbers of slaves, upon which their economies depended. Slaves made up one-fourth to one-third of the workforce in classical Athens, and even men of modest means owned them. They made possible the leisure essential to Athenian democracy, allowing the citizens to argue in the law courts, debate public policy in the assembly, fight their enemies on land and sea, and practice the arts of rhetoric, philosophy, history, and science. The slaves in Greece were mostly captured in Thrace or further north in the Danube region, or they came from Asia Minor, sold into Greece by slave traders.

Slaves were chattel property and had no enforceable rights whatever. They could be killed or sexually used with impunity: Heracles, in one of his adventures, is sold as a slave to a foreign queen to serve as her sexual playmate. Slaves had no legal families of their own. They served in the household, but male slaves also performed work outside it, doing the same tasks as free men, with whom they often worked side by side on farms and in factories. Most unfortunate were those who worked in mines, under atrocious conditions, like the Athenian silver mines at Laurium (as many as 40,000 at one time). Slaves could receive salaries and often saved up enough money to purchase their freedom. In Roman civilization, freedmen—those born as slaves who had purchased or been given their freedom—developed into a powerful social caste and were highly influential in the governance of the Roman empire.

## Beliefs and Customs

Underlying many Greek myths is a way of thinking about the world that most people today would reject, at least in principle. For us to comprehend these myths, we must make an effort to understand their world view, one shared by many preliterate societies throughout the world.

One aspect of this view is the assignment of human qualities to natural forces. Although modern science rejects such notions, they were present in virtually all ancient societies and still have wide appeal; we still speak of Mother Nature and Father Time. The ancients also believed in magic. Modern science rejects the theory that we can manipulate the outside world by means of rituals and spells, but ancient peoples (and some modern ones) were certain that magic was effective. Myths talk endlessly about magical objects—amulets, a necklace that bears a curse, or such objects as a hat that makes the wearer invisible, sandals that enable one to fly, or a fruit that gives everlasting life.

Today we consider words to be unconnected to the objects or ideas that they represent (so that the same thought can be expressed in many languages), but magical theory assumes that words embody creative and effective power. If one commands emphatically that this or that take place, it will take place. Curses on the lips of the dying are extremely dangerous. The word or the name is the thing itself, its essence or soul.[6]

Closely related to the belief in magic is the conviction that the world is inhabited by spirits, especially the ghosts of the dead. From the fear of ghosts comes the belief in contamination (sometimes called "blood-guilt"), which the Greeks called *miasma*, "pollution," the same word used to describe the blood from childbirth. *Miasma* was thought to afflict a murderer because he was pursued by the spirit that lived in the blood he spilled. For this reason murderers were very dangerous company—their misfortune, destined to come, would afflict those around them. Fortunately, spirits and ghosts could be coerced by means of ritual or spells or persuaded by sacrifice or prayer.

Another common feature of the world view underlying myth is the taboo, a strict prohibition against some form of behavior. Many folktales turn on the plot of the "violated prohibition" and describe the terrible consequences that follow when one acts contrary to an authoritative command. An example appears in the folktale "Bluebeard." Bluebeard tells his new wife never to open a certain door, but she does so and discovers the corpses of Bluebeard's many earlier wives. Sometimes the violated prohibition has deep moral connotations, as in the biblical story of Adam and Eve. God commands, "You may freely eat of every tree of the garden, but of the tree of the knowledge of good and evil you must not eat." The penalty for violating this prohibition is that man must toil for his food, woman must suffer in childbirth, and both must die at last.

We divide the human world sharply from the natural, but in classical myth such distinctions were not necessary. Animals may have human qualities, including the power of speech. For example, in Homer's *Iliad* the horses of Achilles speak to him at a critical moment, warning him of impending death. A human may be born not of woman, but of something in the natural world: The handsome Adonis was born from a tree. Animals may raise humans, as in the story of the twins Romulus and Remus, the eventual founders of Rome; abandoned as infants, they were suckled by a she-wolf. Transformation of humans into animal or natural forms (rocks, trees, mountains, or stars) is common. A famous story was told about Narcissus (nar-**sis**-sus), a youth of tremendous good looks. His parents wished to know whether their son would have a long life. "Very long," a prophet replied, "if he does not

---

[6]Hence the biblical commandment, "You shall not take the name of Yahweh in vain."

look at his own face." When Narcissus was grown, he saw his face reflected in a spring. Reaching for the beautiful figure, he fell in and drowned (hence our term *narcissism* to mean "self love"). His body was changed into the flower that still bears his name.

Similarly, the supernatural world easily mixes with the human. A human being may be born of a god or spirit: Achilles' mother was Thetis, a sea nymph. Male gods commonly have intercourse with mortal women, who bear them mortal but superior human children; far less often, goddesses have intercourse with mortal men. The line between human and divine is not firmly drawn. Although Heracles was born a mortal, he became a god at death. Dionysus and Zeus were both gods, but both had tombs where their spirits were honored as those of dead mortals. We must remember, however, that such events reflect more the expectations and conventions of traditional tales than they tell us about the beliefs of the people who told those stories.

We think of the world as a complex machine, governed by natural law, through which we wander, dodging misfortune and doing the best we can. God may have made the world, but appears not to intervene directly in it (although in Christian doctrine God sent his son). The theory of natural law, however, is a Greek invention of the fifth century BC; it did not exist when Greek myth was forming and was probably never accepted by most Greeks. According to traditional Greek views, there are no chance events; every event in the world is connected with every other, if only we see how. At remote Dodona (do-**dō**-na) in northwestern Greece, servants of Zeus and his consort Dionê could interpret the rustling of the wind in an oak to answer questions written on lead tablets; some of these have survived. Especially important among the Etruscans and later the Romans was information drawn from examining the entrails of sacrificed animals and observing the flight of birds (called *augury,* hence our word inauguration, when auguries once were told). Professional prophets and seers play an important role in Greek myth.

Dreams were another way to discover hints of the future, for in sleep the spirit is loosely attached to the body and is in communication with the realms of Apollo, lord of prophecy. When Hecabê, queen of Troy, was pregnant, she dreamed that she gave birth to a bundle of sticks, from which emerged fiery serpents who set fire to Troy. A Trojan seer explained that the child would bring destruction to the city. He ordered the baby exposed on the mountain. Rescued by a shepherd, the child grew up to be Paris, who caused the war that destroyed Troy.

Greek myths often refer to social mores that, although common among preliterate societies, differ sharply from those of Greek society itself, at least in the historical period. Cannibalism, human sacrifice, cattle rustling, wife-theft, and blood vendetta as the ordinary response to homicide all figure prominently in Greek myth. For example, Thyestes, a prince of Mycenae, unknowingly ate his own sons cooked in a stew; his nephew Agamemnon killed his daughter Iphigenia to appease the goddess Artemis; one of Heracles' labors was to rustle the cattle of the monstrous Geryon; the Trojan War began when Paris abducted Helen, wife of Menelaüs; and Orestes, son of Agamemnon, killed his mother to avenge her murder of his father. Such practices were not characteristic of Greek society in the Archaic Period and after. Cannibalism had long since disappeared in Greece, if it ever existed, and blood vendetta and human sacrifice were quickly disappearing. Of course a gory description of an outmoded or outrageous social practice is a good way for a storyteller to attract attention from a restless audience, as makers of modern horror films well understand.

## GREECE AND ROME

Classical myth comprises not just the stories of the Greeks, but also Roman versions of those stories, and some stories native to Rome. The Romans re-made Greek culture in their own image, and they, not the Greeks, passed the classical tradition to modern Europe.

When Alexander "conquered the world" in 336–323 BC, he did not con-quer Italy or any other region west of the Adriatic Sea. The western lands were still remote, although Greek cities had flourished in Italy and Sicily since the eighth century BC. But even in Alexander's day a small tribe of Indo-European speakers south of the Tiber river, living in and near the city of Rome and pos-sessing a superior political and military organization, had begun a course of re-lentless expansion without parallel in human history. Controlling perhaps a few hundred square miles in the sixth century BC, by the time of Christ the Ro-mans governed virtually the entire Mediterranean world and large territories to the north and east of the Mediterranean. Greece itself became a Roman province in 146 BC, as did Asia Minor in 133 BC, and Syria in 63 BC, but the Roman Period in ancient history, as distinguished from the Hellenistic Period, may conveniently be dated from 31 BC, when Egypt, the Hellenistic cultural center, fell into Roman hands. The western Roman Empire crumbled in the fifth century AD, but its Greek-speaking eastern part lasted until AD 1453, pre-serving virtually all the records we have of ancient Greece.

As Rome was in early times surrounded by hostile peoples speaking differ-ent languages, so she was isolated by geography. Greece is made up of innu-merable islands, large and small, and, on the mainland, coastal pockets suited to seaborne commerce and international exchange with the East and its extra-ordinary cultures. Italy, by contrast, is a long boot-shaped peninsula, split down the middle by the rugged Apennine range that cuts off Italy from the East. Seas to the east and west of Italy are noted for their sudden storms, and the whole peninsula had few good harbors, only one on the coast facing Greece. To cross the peninsula from east to west, one had to cross high bandit-ridden moun-tains, and traffic from north to south by land was slow and dangerous until the construction of the famous Roman military roads; the first, the Appian Way, was not built until 312 BC. We need not be surprised, then, that Italy remained so long on the periphery of ancient Mediterranean culture.

Italy was a melting pot of diverse peoples who spoke many languages. The Romans spoke Latin, an Indo-European language, but there were many other Indo-European Italic dialects whose speakers could scarcely understand each other. North of Rome lived the powerful and influential Etruscans, who, like the Greeks, resided in independent city-states.[7] Their origin is unknown, but some think they emigrated from Asia Minor sometime in the twelfth century BC. The culturally powerful Etruscans spoke a non-Indo-European tongue of unknown affiliation, but took over the Greek alphabet from Greeks living near the Bay of Naples, almost within decades of the alphabet's invention around 800 BC. The Etruscans gave this writing to the Romans and the Romans gave it to us. With the alphabet came the riches of Greek culture and, above all, Greek myth.

The Etruscans ruled the city of Rome during the sixth century BC, bequeathing a rich legacy to Roman society, government, and religion; the very name *Roma* may be Etruscan. The Roman gladiatorial games developed from Etruscan funeral games in which prisoners were killed in honor of the dead as a form of human sacrifice. The unique genius of the Roman people was to absorb cultural achievements from foreign peoples, and yet remain Roman; in the fourth century AD they even took over the Christian church, of Jewish origin. While other peoples made things of beauty, the Roman destiny was to rule, as the Romans often explained to themselves.

In early times Rome was an oligarchy, ruled by a council of aristocrats, the Senate ("body of old men"); this period is called the *Republic* (from the Latin *res publica,* "public business"). The Republic broke down after a hundred years of civil war between competing factions within the oligarchy, and Augustus Caesar, the grand-nephew of Julius Caesar, defeated his rivals and took power about the time of Christ. Augustus, pretending that the Republic still existed, modestly called himself *princeps,* "first citizen" (the source of our *prince*), and *imperator,* "commander" (or "emperor"). Henceforth Rome was in reality a monarchy, ruled by one man.

Although the Romans had their own religious heritage, they had few traditional stories, as far as we know. They adopted Greek legends, which they learned mostly from Greek poets of the Hellenistic Period. No legend was more important than the story of Aeneas, a Trojan hero in Homer's *Iliad.* By accepting Aeneas as their actual progenitor, the founder of their race, the Romans aggressively laid claim to the rich and prestigious cultural tradition of Greece. Still, as we will see in chapters 13 and 14, myth functioned rather differently among the Romans than among the Greeks.

---

[7]The name of the modern territory of Tuscany is derived from the ancient name Etruria.

# FURTHER READING

Beard, M., *Classics: A Very Short Introduction* (Oxford, 1996). Classics today, in 100 pages, organized around the temple of Apollo at Bassae.

Boedeker, D., and K. Raaflaub, eds., *Democracy, Empire and the Arts in Fifth-century Athens* (Cambridge, MA, 1998). Excellent collection of essays by established scholars.

Cartledge, P., *The Greeks* (Oxford, 1993). Fine essays on history and myth, men and women, citizens and aliens.

Cartledge, P., ed., *The Cambridge Illustrated History of Ancient Greece* (Cambridge, 1998).

Chadwick, J., *The Decipherment of Linear B*, 2nd ed. (Cambridge, England, 1990). Fascinating account of the unraveling of the mysteries of this syllabic script. Chadwick collaborated with Michael Ventris in deciphering Linear B.

Chadwick, J., *The Mycenaean World* (Cambridge, England, 1976). Overview with excellent illustrations.

Drews, R., *The Coming of the Greeks* (Princeton, 1988). Discusses the arrival of the Indo-Europeans in the Aegean and the Near East.

Finley, M. I., *The Ancient Greeks* (New York, 1987). An overview by a leading historian.

Murray, O., *Early Greece* (Stanford, 1983). Reflections of Homer's own time in the *Iliad* and *Odyssey*.

Pomeroy, S. B., Stanley M. Burstein, Walter Dolan, and Jennifer Tolbert Roberts, *Ancient Greece: A Political, Social, and Cultural History* (Oxford, 1998). Superb overview, covering historical and cultural topics.

Snodgrass, A. M., *Archaic Greece: The Age of Experiment* (Berkeley, 1980). Superior analysis of the formative period of Greek classical civilization.

Vermeule, E., *Greece in the Bronze Age* (Chicago, 1972). Scholarly review, with rich bibliography.

# CHAPTER 5

# THE DEVELOPMENT OF CLASSICAL MYTH

MYTH BEGINS in the primordial past; it is possible (although it cannot be proved) that features of myth found in the Classical Period first appeared 10,000 or even 100,000 years ago, long before the Greeks and Romans existed. In thinking about the beginnings of myth, we can try to peer beyond our earliest written records to reconstruct myths, or religious beliefs, that may have been current in prehistoric times. Comparative material, archaeological and linguistic, may offer some opportunity to do this, as does the study of just how myth was transmitted before writing. In this chapter we review the earliest information we can infer about the history of myth, then review how myth developed through the historical periods in the pre-Hellenic cultures of the ancient Near East, and in Greece itself. Surprisingly, the Greeks seem to have owed little to the indigenous cultures of the southern Balkans and a great deal to Mesopotamian culture; more and more, scholars prefer to view Greek culture as an offshoot of the Mesopotamian, rather than as an independent development, very much as Roman culture was an offshoot of the Greek.

## ROOTS OF *MUTHOI* IN THE BRONZE AGE AND THE ANCIENT NEAR EAST

Of great interest to students of the origins of classical myth are names found on Linear B tablets of numerous gods, named as the recipients of offerings, who are familiar from later Greek literature: Zeus and Hera, Poseidon,

Athena, Artemis, Hermes, Enyalius (an alternate name for Ares), Paean (an alternate name for Apollo), and Eileithyia (the birth goddess) are all found on tablets. Dionysus, a deity long thought to have entered Greek religion after the Bronze Age, is also mentioned (or it is a man named after him). Potnia, "Lady" as in *Potnia Thêrôn,* "Mistress of the Wild Animals," an epithet of Artemis in classical times, seems to be a separate deity, perhaps the name of a Mycenaean mother-goddess. Deities completely unknown in classical times also appear. We may be sure, therefore, that some of the classical Greek gods did exist in the Mycenaean Age, but as far as we know, only as objects of religious cult. We have no stories or hints of stories preserved in the Linear B records. Although interesting frescoes representing a sea battle and other activities have been found on the island of Thera in the Cyclades, perhaps a Minoan outpost, we cannot identify one single Minoan or Mycenaean myth.

Whereas such myths as those of the Trojan War appear to be Greek in origin and to go back to the Bronze Age or earlier, other very important stories had their origin in the non-Indo-European Near East. The Greek myth of the origin of the present world-order in a battle of the gods was certainly of Mesopotamian origin. Such stories may have come to Greece in the Bronze Age, but far more likely were imported from eastern ports in the late Dark Age at the same time that the Greeks invented the alphabet on the basis of the earlier Phoenician writing (c. 800 BC), or they may have been learned from Semitic peoples residing in Greece at this time.

Until about three hundred years ago, Western Europe knew very little about the ancient Near East, and most of what was known came from the Old Testament, preserved in its original Hebrew and Aramaic (closely related to Hebrew) and in translations into Greek (c. 300 BC) and Latin (c. AD 400). There are also many references, usually inaccurate, to the Near East in Greek and Latin authors and in the fathers of the Christian church. Reliance on the literal accuracy of the first five books of the Bible, the Pentateuch (**pen**-ta-took), led to a telescoped notion of the length of history: In 1654 Archbishop James Ussher of Armagh, Ireland, dated the creation of the world at 4004 BC! Ideas of historical change assumed either decay from a Golden Age or a cyclical process of development followed by recession.

Then in the seventeenth century European travelers began to enter the lands of the ancient Near East and bring back firsthand reports. Pietro della Valle, an Italian nobleman, journeyed to Constantinople, Egypt, Palestine, and Syria, and in Persepolis, the ancient capital of Persia (559–332 BC), copied from the palace doors several inscriptions written in three different forms of an unknown script. In 1700 an Oxford scholar, although unable to read the script, gave the name *cuneiform* ("wedge-shaped") to the writing. From this time onward a stream of archaeological material from the Near East poured into Western European museums, including many inscribed clay tablets, and the languages of the region were gradually deciphered. The British scholar George Smith in 1872 reported that he had deciphered a fragment of a tablet with a description of a universal flood that had destroyed all humankind. The next year, in Iraq, Smith found the text of the Babylonian story of creation, the *Enuma elish*. The much later composer of Genesis, the biblical book of creation, evidently borrowed such stories, so that Genesis could no longer be regarded as an original and divine revelation. Not surprisingly, these and similar discoveries forced a reconsideration of the meaning of myth.

Some related myths, but with their own innovative features, come from the non-Semitic Hittites, one of the most powerful and important peoples of the Bronze Age, who controlled central Anatolia (Asia Minor) from about 1600 to 1200 BC, then enjoyed a revival in the ninth and eighth centuries BC in northern Syria and southeastern Anatolia, near to trade routes that led to the Mediterranean and points west. Their myths were preserved on clay tablets in cuneiform writing (and in their own special hieroglyphic writing) from the thirteenth century BC, found in the archives at their capital city of Hattussas in modern north-central Turkey. Although the Hittites were Indo-European speakers—the earliest attested—they too inherited cultural traditions first formulated among the Sumerians of southern Mesopotamia and later refined by the Sumerians' Semitic successors.

Non-Semitic ancient Egypt, too, had myths, but they were not nearly so rich or varied as those from Mesopotamia.[1] Literary texts from Egypt are mostly collections of wise sayings, reports of a man's important achievements, hymns that praise gods (without, however, telling stories), and sophisticated and amusing tales for scribal instruction and entertainment. Occasional folktales survive. The most important myth by far in ancient Egypt told of the murder of the god Osiris and his resurrection, but nowhere do the Egyptians themselves tell the complete story; we must depend on an account in Greek.

## THE SINGERS OF *MUTHOI*

In archaic Greek culture, between Homer and the Persian wars (c. 800–500 BC), the authoritative utterances, the *muthoi,* of greatest interest to the Greeks told about two great wars fought in an earlier time around the walls

---

[1]The Egyptian language belongs to the Hamitic family (after Ham, son of Noah), now usually called the Afro-Asiatic family; similar in structure to Semitic languages (with words built on triliteral consonantal roots), ancient Egyptian shares almost no common vocabulary with Semitic languages.

of Troy and Thebes. Such stories, which we call myths, were the stock in trade of professional singers called *aoidoi*, "singers" (singular *aoidos*, a-**oi**-dos, related to our "ode"). *Aoidoi* composed in a unique rhythmical language as they performed in aristocratic courts, and perhaps elsewhere. The American classical scholar Milman Parry established the existence of these singers in famous studies from the 1930s. The *aoidoi* accompanied their songs by playing on a four- or seven-stringed lyre. Few in number, highly trained, and attendant in halls of petty kings, the *aoidoi* were the myth-tellers of preliterate Greece.

Early in life an *aoidos* learned through association with a master, through unconscious absorption, a special language of poetic composition. As ordinary language is shaped by unconscious grammatical patterns, this one was shaped by an unconscious rhythm, which we analyze in written versions as *dactylic hexameter:* that is, there were six ( *hex-*) units (-*meter*) in each line, each of them consisting of one heavy and two light beats ( *dactylic,* "like a finger") or of two heavy beats. [2] The special language contained many preset rhythmical phrases such as "swift-footed Achilles" and "the wine-dark sea," which helped the *aoidoi* to compose a poem as they sang it to the accompaniment of the lyre. Although *aoidoi* were illiterate, the Greek alphabet was used from the time of its invention around 800 BC to record *aoidic* songs.

Homer was such a poet, and Hesiod was another. Homer himself gives us an account of the blind *aoidos* Demodocus (de-**mo**-di-kus, "favored by the people") in Book 8 of the *Odyssey.* At an assembly in the morning, the king tells a messenger, "Summon the glorious *aoidos* Demodocus, on whom a god immortal has poured great skill at reciting. / His song will surely delight us, whatever subjects he fancies" (8.43–45). In the course of the festivities, Demodocus sings and plays several times including a song of the quarrel between Odysseus and Achilles. After an interval, Demodocus is called on to accompany a group of expert young dancers; he is evidently a skilled musician as well as a singer of songs. He now sings the racy story of the trapping of adulterous Ares and Aphrodite in bed while having intercourse (to Greek moralists one of the most troublesome myths because of its content). After another interval, Odysseus gives Demodocus a token of honor and requests a new song. Demodocus invokes the Muse and sings of the Trojan Horse. Many think that Demodocus is a self-portrait of Homer himself, and most of what we know about the social context of Homer's own singing comes from these descriptions.

Although making use of traditional stories and motifs, *aoidoi* must always have spoken to contemporary concerns and, of course, had no concept of

---

[2]An example in English: "Thīs ĭs thĕ |fŏrēst prĭm|ĕvǎl, the |mūrmŭring|pīnes ănd thĕ|hēmlŏcks," the first line in the once-famous poem *Hiawatha* by Henry Wadsworth Longfellow (1807–1882).

history. Real warriors are interested in hearing about real wars, especially if they themselves fought in them or if their fathers or grandfathers did. For this reason it is likely that the great cycles of myth surrounding the Trojan War and the war against Thebes do go back to campaigns waged in the Late Bronze Age (c. 1600–1200 BC), passed on by generations of oral poets. Homer, however, never calls the songs of the *aoidoi* either *epea* or *muthoi*.

The mystery remains how such oral songs, whose contents we call *myths,* ever came to be written down—certainly not by *aoidoi* themselves, who were entertainers singing for their keep in wealthy households, according to Homer's descriptions. In any event, our written version of Homer preserves only one aspect of his original song. Gone are the music, gesture, emphasis, voice, and charisma which are essential aspects to the performance of any oral song. All that remains is some rough and ready information about the sounds of Homer's ancient *epea.*

By recording *aoidic* songs on papyrus, the early alphabet-possessors of the eighth and seventh centuries BC created the first texts in the Western literary tradition, the poems of Homer and Hesiod. Such recordings of *aoidic* texts formed from the first the basis for Greek education, the learning of the alphabet well enough to decipher such texts, memorize them, and perform in the symposium or sometimes at public festivals. Not only did the Greek alphabet preserve the rudimentary features of the sound of human speech, but it was easily learned so that no special schools existed to transmit knowledge of it. In the Near East, by contrast, special schools provided aspiring scribes with a lengthy education, which led to a life of privilege and leisure. Nor did Greek alphabetic writing serve the interests of the state, as it had in the Near East; rather, it served the social interests of the Greek aristocracy, who achieved status and recognition through their ability to perform memorized song.

The most favored texts in Greek education, remarkably, were not the *Iliad* and the *Odyssey* or the poems of Homer's near-contemporary Hesiod, but the *Cyclic* ("circle") *Poems,* now lost. They were called "cyclic" because they told stories "in a circle" around the *Iliad* and the *Odyssey,* the events before and after the Trojan War. We know something about their contents from much later summaries. The popularity of the Cyclic Poems probably depends on their being far shorter than the immensely expansive *Iliad* (16,000 lines) and *Odyssey* (12,000 lines). From the Cyclic Poems, pot-painters and tragedians preferred to take their subjects; they were a compendium of Greek *myth.*

The recording of *aoidic* song in alphabetic writing popularized Greek legend and vastly extended its currency, because anybody who could read could imitate in public representation Homer and other poets, if they possessed the physical object, the text. Because alphabetic writing, unlike all earlier writings, made a material thing out of the sound of speech, which otherwise is ephemeral, it enabled the Greeks to approach speech, and its contents, analytically. Such texts enormously encouraged the analysis of thought couched in writing and led directly to the discovery of philosophy.

Those who possessed alphabetic technology were not themselves singers, but cultural heirs of the man who had invented the alphabet. Specialists in the public performance of memorized texts were called *rhapsodes,* probably "staff-singers," because they held a staff as they recited.[3] Rhapsodes were the first actors. They depended on a written prompt and generated their effects through dramatic gesture and costumes. *Aoidoi,* by contrast, recreated their poems afresh with each performance, did not depend on a written text, and played a lyre while they composed. Rhapsodes are like classical musicians who have memorized a composition by Beethoven; *aoidoi* are like jazz musicians who play the same tune, but never twice in the same way.

When recorded in writing, the contents of *aoidic* texts, once transient utterances, *muthoi,* had become potentially immortal physical objects, *myths.* If we ignored theoretical considerations, we might define classical myth as simply "all the plots of all the poems sung by the illiterate *aoidoi,* taken down by dictation," a definition coming close to myth as "a traditional tale," a definition we examined earlier.

## *MUTHOI* IN THE GREEK ARCHAIC PERIOD

Although many Greek myths may have taken shape during the Bronze Age in Mesopotamia and in the Mycenaean and Dark Ages of Greek history, it was not until the Archaic Period, c. 800–480 BC, that myths were actually committed to writing. Consequently, we derive most of our knowledge of Greek myth from writings of this and later periods. Additional information from the Archaic and Classical Periods also comes to us from the 50,000 pictured Greek vase paintings that survive and occasionally from sculpture. Scholars estimate surviving pictured vases to represent about one percent of the original production, giving us some idea of the explosion of images that flooded ancient Greece and Italy in this period, for which there is no parallel in the ancient world.

The earliest written texts are the *Iliad* and the *Odyssey,* recorded some time in the eighth century BC. We know nothing for certain about Homer's life. Later tradition has him born somewhere in Asia Minor, in the city of Smyrna or on the island of Chios, but his poems show wide knowledge of the Aegean and Greece. The absence of descriptions of writing in Homer is one of the principal reasons for placing him in the eighth century BC, when the

---

[3]A popular etymology, which began already in the ancient world, explained the word as "song-stitcher," as if the poet sewed together the strands of older tradition.

alphabet was new and unfamiliar.[4] It would have been impossible to record Homer in the earlier Linear B or Phoenician syllabic scripts because the complex rhythms of his poetic line depended on the alternations of long and short vowels, which these scripts were incapable of notating.

The *Iliad* is set in a period of several weeks during the ninth year of the Trojan War. Its principal theme is the wrath of Achilles, his anger over being mistreated by the leader of the expedition, Agamemnon. Within this frame Homer includes a wealth of subordinate myths. The somewhat shorter *Odyssey* narrates the return of Odysseus to his home after an absence of twenty years. The *Iliad* and the *Odyssey* define what we mean by *epic*, a long narrative poem celebrating the deeds of heroes. To judge from Homer's own descriptions in the *Odyssey* of the *aoidoi*, his audiences seem to have been all or mostly male; the only woman mentioned as present at a poetic performance is a queen (but Penelope, too, overhears a performance of oral song). Under what conditions Homer may have sung songs as long as the *Iliad* or *Odyssey* remains unclear. These poems were probably never presented orally in the form in which we know them, the result of artificial conditions created by the writing down of the poems, when the poet could sing slowly, without an audience to entertain. For these reasons he could greatly expand his narrative.

Views have differed widely about the "reality" of the world Homer portrays. The archaeologist Heinrich Schliemann thought that Homer was describing the Bronze Age (Chapter 9), but in fact Homer knows little or nothing about the Bronze Age. For example, in Homer the dead are cremated on a large pyre, then their ashes gathered and buried in an urn. But the Mycenaean Greeks interred the bodies of the dead in graves lined with stone slabs or, if royalty, in enormous underground beehive-shaped tombs. Homeric society consists of petty chieftains, each ruling a small territory; in the Bronze Age great centers of power kept careful watch over a controlled economy by means of a professional bureaucracy. Although Homer mentions a certain kind of helmet made of boars' tusks and several other objects familiar only in the Bronze Age, such objects may have been preserved as heirlooms long after the destruction of Mycenae. Others think that the conditions Homer describes are those of the Dark Age, c. 1150–900 BC, or that Homer's world is an imaginary mixture of details from different periods. Yet the *Odyssey*'s description of dangerous seafaring in the far west must depend on real Greek exploration there beginning about 800 BC. On balance, it seems most plausible that Homer incorporated various features from earlier periods preserved through the oral tradition, but that his poems, and

---

[4]On a single occasion Homer refers to writing (*Iliad* 6.168), but seems not to understand it. The many problems surrounding the genesis of the Homeric poems, still hotly debated, are called the Homeric Question.

especially the social and religious values that move the actors, reflect Homer's own age, the eighth century BC.

The influence of Homer's poems on Greek and later culture is inestimable. Less influential, but perhaps more important to the study of myth, is Hesiod. Unlike the anonymous Homer, who conceals his personality behind his poems, Hesiod tells us something about himself in his two surviving poems, the *Theogony* and *Works and Days*. His father had lived in Asia Minor, then moved to mainland Greece to a small forlorn village at the foot of Mount Helicon near Thebes, where Hesiod lived. Like Homer, Hesiod became an *aoidos*. We have seen how, while he tended his flocks on Helicon, the Muses, inspirers of poetry, came to him in a vision and gave him the power of song (Chapter 1).[5] In his remarkable description of the Muses, Hesiod identifies himself: He is the first European *author* (Homer never identifies himself), gives the first definition of a *poet* (= "maker"), and provides the justification why a poet can speak with authority about past, present, and future (because the Muses inspire him). In *Works and Days*, Hesiod also tells us that he was a singer at funeral games in honor of a dead prince on the nearby island of Euboea.

The *Theogony*, a description of the creation of the present world-order, owes a great deal to Mesopotamian myth, telling how Zeus overcame an earlier generation of gods and monsters in battle and established his own power (see Chapter 6). The *Works and Days* describes a bitter dispute between Hesiod and his brother over the disposition of their father's property, a theme that allows Hesiod to range widely over issues of right and wrong, which he illustrates by telling such myths as the story of Pandora. This is "wisdom literature," a well-established genre in the Near East and another sign of Hesiod's closeness to Eastern sources.

We have already mentioned the important lost Cyclic Poems. Another important source from the Archaic Period is a collection of poems known as the *Homeric Hymns*. Like the poems of Homer and Hesiod, most of them were composed orally and, in antiquity, were believed to be by Homer himself. In fact they are from a later date, mostly from the seventh and sixth centuries BC. Four are several hundred lines long: those to Demeter, Apollo, Hermes, and Aphrodite. A hymn is a metrical address invoking a god or goddess by listing cultic names and telling an important story about the deity. The *Homeric Hymns* are a literary elaboration of this old tradition and very unlike Near Eastern hymns in their focus on mythic narrative. Whereas epic seems to have been performed before elite male audiences, hymns may have been performed in public places, at festivals that may have included women and a broader range of social classes. Yet, like epic, they were composed in performance by specially trained *aoidoi*.

---

[5]Thus Helicon is synonymous with poetic inspiration in the Western literary tradition.

In Homer's poems, action is always described in the third person. From the sixth century BC comes a small body of personal lyric poems (including the fragments of Sappho's work), on a wide variety of topics, but celebrating notably the individual's pain in love, politics, and the uncertainty of war. Many of these poems touch on mythical themes. Unlike the Homeric, Hesiodic, and Cyclic Poems, however, this poetry was not composed in performance and recorded by dictation, but was composed directly in writing, meant to be memorized by others and represented orally. This shift in the way literature was created was to have epoch-making consequences.

## *MUTHOI* IN THE GREEK CLASSICAL PERIOD

We must remember that there never was an agreed-upon version of any Greek myth, because there was no text (like the Bible) with sacred authority and no organization (like the Christian church) to establish an official version. As the Muses in Hesiod explained, they were capable of disseminating lies as easily as the truth: The gods were in any event not a source of truth. In the absence of divine revelation, the Greeks invented *ethics,* a way to tell right from wrong without divine authority, and *secular law,* rules of behavior not sanctioned by divine revelation. Ethics and secular law together make up humanism. The poets gave form to Greek myths, but no one poet, not even Homer, could claim to promulgate an official version.

The *rhapsodes* rapidly popularized Greek myths, previously confined to the immediate small aristocratic audiences of *aoidoi,* who could never have been many in number. One often hears, or assumes, that myths were also told by mothers to their children or in other family contexts, but the evidence for this is slight; such stories seem to have been of the bogeyman variety and were certainly not what we think of as Greek myth.

The *aoidoi* continued to exist in Greece through the Archaic Period and continued to perform and to dictate their songs, or perhaps in some cases to write them down themselves, but by the early fifth century BC, when composition in writing had become the rule, the *aoidoi* disappeared. In addition to lyric poetry, the new technique of composition in writing made possible *choral song,* memorized for public presentation by a group of twelve or more boy or girl dancers (Greek *choros* = "dance"). Often the chorus would speak for itself in the first person singular, a fact that has created great confusion because until recently readers equated the "I" of such poetry with the personality of the poet. Greatest of the choral poets was Pindar (518–438 BC), some of whose verses we examined, in Chapter 1. Much of his poetry is lost, but a large body of victory odes to athletes survives. These odes ordinarily contain a myth that in some way reflects on the glory of the athlete being praised. Some of our earliest versions of Greek myths are found in Pindar and in surviving poems by his contemporary Bacchylides (ba-**kil**-i-dēz) from the island of Ceos, who also wrote choral poetry.

By far our most important source from the Classical Period is the tragic plays, performed in Athens during the fifth century BC. The origin of tragedy is obscure. The word *tragoidia* may mean "goat song." Because the goat was an animal associated with Dionysus at whose spring festival in Athens tragedies were staged, perhaps the name is taken from the song sung during the sacrifice of a goat in the god's honor. Composed in writing, the script of a tragic play was like a modern screenplay, not meant to be read, but to serve as a prompt book for a live performance. Although afterwards the texts could be studied by students and quoted by intellectuals, all of Greek literature was meant to be heard, not read silently as we are reading this book and the literary selections within it.

The actors were always male (as the audience probably was) and never more than three in number. They wore masks with stereotypical features to distinguish their roles (for example, old man, young girl, or king). They could communicate emotion only through the use of words and gestures, not by facial expression. Tragedy was a form of popular entertainment, directed to the complex concerns of the Athenian citizen, including his taste for patriotic propaganda, horror, violence, and conflict between the sexes: themes that still command an attentive audience. Dionysus, the divine patron of tragedy, was a god of the *demos,* the "people" (i.e., the adult male citizens). Pisistratus, an Athenian tyrant of the sixth century BC, encouraged production of the plays, no doubt to favor the emerging mercantile class who had placed him in power.

Aristotle attempted to explain the function of the violent plots of many tragedies by suggesting that, in beholding the dramatization of the destruction of a noble man or woman, the audience was cleansed "through pity and fear" (*Poetics* 6.2): *pity* for the protagonist (= "first actor") and *fear* that the same fate might become one's own. Tragedy, then, allowed the audience to experience intense, sometimes disturbing emotions that could not be experienced in real life without terrible cost. Tragedy painlessly expanded one's experience as a human being. No more effective answer has ever been offered to the censors who, throughout human history, have policed public entertainment to make it conform to preconceived notions of what is proper.

Aristotle also discussed the structure of Greek tragedy, noting how the protagonist is greater than we, rises to high fortune, then in a "turning around" (*peripeteia*) comes to a "down-turning" (*katastrophê,* our word "catastrophe") as the result of a "missing of the mark" or "mistake." The Greek word *hamartia,* "mistake," was early mistranslated as "flaw," leading to a misunderstanding of Greek tragedy that is still encountered today. Other explanations of the protagonist's misfortune attribute it to *hubris,* often translated as "pride," but really *hubris* means "violence" and only by extension the thoughtless behavior that encourages violence. Surely *hubris,* "violence," is punished in Greek myth—Clytemnestra killed her husband Agamemnon because he had killed their daughter, and the gods hated him because he had burned the temples of Troy—but neither "tragic flaw" nor "pride" are useful categories for understanding Greek myth.

Aeschylus (525–456 BC) is the earliest tragedian whose works survive. We have seven plays of the more than eighty he wrote. Aeschylus loved long and elaborate descriptions, especially of foreign lands, and high-flown metaphorical language. He used myth to explore such grand moral issues as the conflict between individual will and divine destiny, and his characters tend to be types or to embody some principle. Aeschylus lived when Athens basked in its greatest glory, and in his epitaph, which he himself composed, he mentioned only that he fought at Marathon. Aeschylus' play, the *Persians*, about events of his own time, is the only surviving tragedy that does not have a mythical theme (others did exist, however).

The career of Sophocles (496–406 BC) exactly coincides with the political and cultural dominance of Athens. Born six years before the battle of Marathon, he died two years before Athens' humiliation by Sparta at the end of the Peloponnesian War. Of the 123 plays he wrote, seven survive. The vivid characters of his tightly plotted dramas are typically locked in bitter conflict. Sophocles likes to show the dignity of human beings in conflict with superior, often divine forces, a noble individual caught in an overwhelming crisis. His heroes are lonely and unbending. They learn too late how they should act. He is deeply influenced by folklore, especially by the theme of "how the oracle was fulfilled": In all his plays a prophecy or oracle predicts an unexpected outcome.

From Euripides (485–406 BC) more plays survive than from Aeschylus and Sophocles combined, nineteen from the more than ninety he wrote. Euripides was a poet of great range who subjected the traditional myths to rigorous scrutiny and sometimes severe criticism. His characters are often deflated heroes, mere mortals caught up in some all-too-human squabble. His characters often veer off into abnormal mental states. Aristotle remarked that Sophocles showed men as they ought to be, but Euripides showed them as they really are (*Poetics* 1460b). He reflects contemporary Athenian rhetoric; most of his plays center on a long debate. He has been called an irrationalist because he likes to celebrate the power of emotion over reason.

In Aeschylus, the inherited curse and divine will motivate the action; in Sophocles, fate stands behind events; in Euripides, passionate, often erotic, and especially female emotion drives the action. He is the most modern of the tragedians. His plays were often revived in antiquity and are commonly performed today.[6] Euripides loved sensational bloody scenes and was not above happy endings.

---

[6]During the Vietnam War, the *Trojan Women*, an antiwar play, ran for over ten years in New York City.

The myths in tragedy are a web of interlocking family histories. Of the thousand tragedies performed between the end of the sixth century BC and the end of the fifth, not a single one was concerned exclusively with the doings of gods and goddesses, as far as we know. Tragedy shows little interest in the sort of large mythic cycle Hesiod describes, of creation, the battles of Titans and Olympians, and the births and loves of the gods (the *Prometheus* of Aeschylus stands almost alone). Although gods and goddesses appear on stage and have important roles, the focus is always on the men and women of the Greek legendary past, and often on the passions and horrors of family life. No possibility is omitted: Sons kill their mothers, wives kill their husbands, sons kill their fathers, mothers kill their children, a father kills his daughter or son or all his children, a daughter kills her father, brothers kill each other, sons kill their stepmothers, mothers expose their infants to die, men and women kill themselves. Every chord is struck on the theme of sexual trespass: A son sleeps with his mother, a father rapes his daughter, adultery is rampant, lustful women seduce honorable men (never the reverse), husbands desert their wives and mistresses. Complementing such extreme dishonesty are family relations characterized by intense love and devotion: between brother and sister, brother and brother, father and son, husband and wife, father and daughter.

In their loves and hates, the characters in Athenian drama can be extreme cases, and in no sense do such tales reflect ordinary life. Yet the audience must have experienced corresponding emotions, although more muted, in their own lives, even as we experience the same emotions today. At precisely the same time as the tragedies were performed, with their gory scenes and exaggerated emotions, Greek philosophy and Greek science were coming into being. Some intellectuals, for example Anaxagoras, already in the fifth century BC subjected myth to a rigorous criticism, denying its validity as a means to achieve understanding.

## MYTH IN THE HELLENISTIC PERIOD

The conquests of Alexander the Great spread Greek culture throughout the eastern Mediterranean and deep into Asia. In 331 BC he founded Alexandria in the western delta in Egypt; ironically, for the next 300 years the center of Greek culture was to lie outside Greece. At Alexandria was established the first real library, the *Mouseion,* "Hall of the Muses," where the classics of Greek literature were gathered together and edited in standard editions. For the first time, scholars appeared in the modern sense, who established critical principles to determine the original form of texts corrupted through repeated copying. All Greek texts that survive today passed through the hands of the Alexandrians, who pursued many other branches of learning, too, especially mathematics, astronomy, and medicine.

While *aoidoi* composed their poems in performance, and *rhapsodes* and tragic actors memorized their parts from a written prompt to display in public, literature in the Hellenistic Period seems to have been read aloud from the actual papyrus scroll, probably to a small audience of friends. The psychological effect of this shift was enormous. Literature was now written to be read, not performed, and as a result it became more and more self-conscious and learned; it was often extremely abstract and difficult. The Alexandrian librarian-scholars, keenly interested in myth, produced highly complex poems on mythical topics.[7] Such learned, allusive poetry is called *Alexandrian*. The great scholar Callimachus (c. 305–240 BC), author of the first scientific history of literature, wrote mythical poetry of this kind. Although most of his work is lost, Callimachus profoundly influenced the Roman poets, and through them all subsequent Western literature. Another example is his learned pupil Apollonius of Rhodes (third century BC), who wrote an epic poem on Jason in the style of Homer, the *Argonautica*, our most important treatment of this myth.

The Hellenistic Greeks were also keenly interested in the essential truth of myth; influenced by the philosophical school of Stoicism founded by Zeno of Citium (a town in Cyprus), they refined the allegorical method of interpreting the ancient stories. As early as the fifth century BC, Greek scholars called mythographers began to gather into collections traditional stories about the doings of gods and heroes. In the Hellenistic Period these efforts increased. The most important survivor is the *Library*, attributed (mistakenly) to Apollodorus, a scholar of great distinction of the second century BC. The *Library* is not a work of art, but a straightforward account of mythical events from the creation of the world to the death of Odysseus. It is one of our best sources of information about many Greek myths, especially those told in the lost Cyclic Poems. Another handbook, a geographical survey of Greece by Pausanias (c. AD 150), also preserves much mythical material otherwise unknown. One of the founders of modern anthropology, classical scholar Sir James Frazer (1854–1941), author of *The Golden Bough,* derived many of his theories about the nature of myth from his study of Pausanias, on whom he wrote a famous commentary.

From the Hellenistic scholars and poets, the Romans acquired their own knowledge of Greek myth. As we will see in the next section, their contribution was substantial.

---

[7]One such poem, the *Alexandra* (= the Trojan princess Cassandra) by Lycophron, contains about 3,000 words, of which 518 are found in no other extant texts!

## THE ROMAN APPROPRIATION OF GREEK MYTH

Careful students of Greek culture from an early date, the Romans eventually took over the whole body of Greek myths, with minor modifications, substituting similar Roman divinities for the Greek gods and goddesses (see chart on page 230). Catullus (84–54 BC), a contemporary of Julius Caesar, is best known for his love poems, but also wrote on mythical themes. Vergil (70–19 BC), the greatest Roman poet, told the story of Aeneas in his epic, the *Aeneid*. This poem has one of our fullest descriptions of the underworld and our most vivid account of the sack of Troy. The poem also preserves the legends of Dido, queen of Carthage, and of Hercules' battle against the monster Cacus.

The poetry of the Roman Ovid (c. 43 BC–AD 17), a generation younger than Vergil, is our most important source from the period of the early Roman Empire. Ovid was a man-about-town in Rome, of good birth, famed for his clever and witty verse. He moved in the highest society. Implicated in a sexual or political scandal that touched the emperor Augustus' own house (we know no details), he was exiled in AD 8 to the town of Tomis (now Costanza) on the Black Sea—remote, lonely, and cold—and there he died. Ovid left behind a large body of poetry, but none more influential than the *Metamorphoses* (met-a-mor-**fō**-sēz), by far the most substantial and influential repertory of Greek myth (see Chapter 13). This highly original work is a handbook in its own right, a compendium of over two hundred stories ingeniously united by the theme of the transformation of shape. The poem is itself ever-changing, beginning with the transformation of chaos into cosmos and ending with the transformation of Julius Caesar, Augustus' great-uncle and father by adoption, into a star.

The Roman historian Livy (59 BC–AD 17), Ovid's contemporary, wrote an enormous work describing the history of Rome from the beginning down to his own time, about a fourth of which survives. The early books of Livy give legendary accounts that belong more to the study of myth than to history. Seneca, tutor to the emperor Nero (ruled AD 54–68) and defender of Nero's crimes before the Roman senate, wrote voluminously, including several tragedies on mythical subjects. Characterized by extreme violence and savage emotion, these plays made a deep impression on the authors of the Renaissance, and on Shakespeare above all.

So long as myths were transmitted orally, they were subject to endless change and local variation; written versions also introduced change, to fit the concerns and conditions of the day. Eventually, however, and certainly by the Hellenistic Period, standard versions began to emerge of certain myths because of their treatment by Homer or Sophocles. A difficulty we face in studying Greek myth is to separate the myth from the work of literature in which it is embodied. A focus on the myths alone would give us a bare-bones listing of all the extant variations of, say, the story of Oedipus. A literary analysis, on the other hand, might concentrate on how Sophocles portrays character in his play *Oedipus the King.* Although this book is primarily about myth, which exists independent of any specific version, we touch on literary features of works that have made some myths better known than others. After all, we care about Achilles not because he fought at Troy, but because Homer described his personal torment in a way that speaks to us all as human beings.

## FURTHER READING

Baldry, H. C., *The Greek Tragic Theatre* (New York, 1973). What the Athenian stage looked like, how the actors performed, the Athenian tragic contests, and related topics.

Bonnefoy, Y., comp., *Mythologies,* 2 vols. (Chicago, 1991). An English translation of the French encyclopedia *Dictionnaire des mythologies et des religions des sociétés traditionnelles et du monde antique.* Essays by French scholars on myths from around the world, with an extensive section on Greek myth (in Volume 1).

Easterling, P. E., ed., *The Cambridge Companion to Greek Tragedy* (Cambridge, England, 1997). Various essays focused on performance and reception, especially productions of tragedy on stage and in film since the Renaissance.

Gantz, T., *Early Greek Myth, A Guide to Literary and Artistic Sources* (Baltimore, 1993). A modernization and rewriting in English of the nineteenth-century German *Griechische Mythologie* by C. Robert and L. Preller, this invaluable handbook lucidly traces in detail the historical development of each myth, giving original ancient sources for each variant and including references to many ancient artistic representations.

Graf, F., *Greek Mythology, An Introduction* (Baltimore, 1993). Readable and learned overview.

Huxley, G. L., *Greek Epic Poetry* (Cambridge, MA, 1969). Reconstructs the contents of lost epic poems.

Lesky, A., *Greek Tragedy* (London, 1976). Astute literary analyses of the surviving plays.

Lewis, D. M., and A. Pickard-Cambridge, *The Dramatic Festivals of Athens,* 2nd ed., ed. J. Gould. (Oxford, 1989). The standard scholarly study of the festivals at which tragedy was performed, tragic costume, how the prize was awarded, makeup of the audience, training of actors.

Lord, A. B., *The Singer of Tales* (New York, 1965; reprinted 1976). The theory that Homer was an oral poet who composed without the aid of writing, by a student of M. Parry.

Parry, M., *The Making of Homeric Verse,* ed. A. Parry (Oxford, 1971). The introduction is the best presentation of Parry's views.

*The Perseus Project,* <http://www.perseus.tufts.edu/>. Has thousands of links to texts, works of art, maps, lexica, and other aids to understanding myth and the classical world.

Rose, H. J., *A Handbook of Greek Mythology: Including Its Extension to Rome,* 6th ed. (New York, 1959). The standard English-language handbook of Greek myth for many years, it is still valuable, although old-fashioned in style and interpretation.

Simpson, M., *Gods and Heroes of the Greeks: The "Library" of Apollodorus* (Amherst, MA, 1976). A translation of an ancient Greek handbook of mythology. The notes and introduction are invaluable compendia of scholarship.

Tripp, E., *The Meridian Handbook of Classical Mythology* (New York, 1974). Excellent desktop reference work to Greek myths, if you just want to know the stories. Useful references to primary sources.

# CHAPTER 6

# MYTH AND CREATION: HESIOD'S *THEOGONY* AND ITS NEAR EASTERN SOURCES

I N THE FIRST CHAPTER, we examined the use of the word *muthos* and saw how Homer's "emphatic utterance" and the "true and lying things" of Hesiod's Muses became the true or false *muthoi* of Pindar, depending on moral content. Then Aristotle defined the typical plot patterns in *muthoi*. In a different approach, anthropological comparisons of Homer's texts with similar ones from the southern Balkans suggest that myth was something passed on by oral singers, a traditional tale, leaving some to think that myth was coterminous with oral song, that one was the other.

Another valuable approach to understanding myth is to look past rigorous definitions and examine the stories that most agree are myths, whatever they are, and attempt to place them into general categories. We may distinguish between several types of myth, based on the nature of the principal characters and the function that the story fulfilled for listener and teller. In this chapter let us examine *divine myths,* stories in which supernatural beings are the main actors. Such stories generally explain why the world, or some aspect of it, is the way it is. Divine myths are closest to religion because they attempt to answer basic questions about human nature and destiny. Such stories satisfy the requirement of seriousness that some expect in a myth (hence divine myth is sometimes called *true myth* or *pure myth*). In subsequent chapters, we will examine two other categories, *legends* (or sagas) and *folktales,* although in practice it is often difficult to separate one type from another, at least when we focus on structural elements and not on the social background of the stories. Stories that appear to be legends, for example, often turn out to incorporate elements of folktale or to explain the nature of things, as do divine myths. Such categories nonetheless allow us to isolate and study various aspects of myth.

## DIVINE MYTH

The supernatural beings who are the principal characters in divine myth are depicted as superior to humans in power and splendor. Sometimes they can take on human or animal shape. They control awesome forces of nature—thunder, storm, rain, fire, earthquake, or fecundity. When these beings appear in their own form, they are often enormous in magnitude and of stunning beauty or ugliness. Conflicts between them can take place on an immense scale and involve whole continents, high mountains, and vast seas.

Sometimes the supernatural characters in divine myth are little more than personified abstractions without clearly defined personalities. In Greek myth, for example, Nikê (**nī**-ke), "Victory," is just the abstract concept. In other cases, the supernatural beings are gods, goddesses, or demons with well-developed and distinctive personalities of their own. Zeus, the sky-god in Greek myth, is much more than a personification of the sky; he is depicted as a powerful father, an often unfaithful husband, and the upholder of justice in human communities.

The events of divine myth usually take place in a world before or outside the present order where time and often space have different meanings from those familiar to human beings. For example, one Greek myth explained how Zeus came to rule the world: He fought against the Titans, an earlier race of gods,[1] defeated them in a terrible battle, and established his empire on the ruin of theirs. It would be pointless to ask when these events occurred, even within the context of the story, because they are set in a time before human chronology has meaning. Moreover, many divine myths of the Greeks are set in a place far removed from the familiar world of human beings—on Mount Olympus, far away and unapproachable.

Understandably, many of the gods about whom traditional tales were told were both actors in the stories and the objects of religious cult. Zeus is a character in Greek myth, but he was also a god for whom the Greeks built temples, carried out sacrifices, and celebrated festivals. Because of this dou-

---

[1]The word *God* (capital G) should be limited to a single all-powerful being, in any religion—Jewish, Christian, Muslim, or other. A small *g* shows that you are talking about one of many immortal powers in a polytheistic ("many gods") system. A *demigod* is the offspring of a god and a human, who sometimes becomes a *god* at death. *Deity* covers all these concepts.

ble function of the gods, divine myth is easily confused with religion, but the two must be clearly distinguished (see Chapter 7). Myths are traditional *stories;* religion is belief and the course of *action* that follows from *belief.* Belief is "what you accept (with or without proof) as a basis for action." For example, the Greeks believed that Zeus caused the rain to fall; therefore, they sacrificed animals in time of drought to persuade him to bring rain. Myths often justify a religious practice or a form of religious behavior, but we can retell a myth, even a myth about divine beings, without engaging in religious behavior. Although the relationship between myth and religion is complicated, and we will say more about it in the next chapter, we must remember at the outset that myth is a story, whereas religion is a set of beliefs that motivates a course of action.

Divine myths served a function in ancient cultures analogous to that of theoretical science in our own: They explain why the world is the way it is. Many of these myths tell of the origin and destruction of grand things: the universe, the gods, and ourselves; the relationships of gods with one another and with human beings; and the divine origin of such human economic and social institutions as the growing of crops, the cycle of the seasons, the making of wine, and prophecy and oracles. Many divine myths deal with limited matters, the origin of local customs and practices.

In more technical language, we can describe such explanatory myths as *etiological,* from the Greek word *aition,* "cause." A creation myth is an example of an etiological tale because it explains the causes that brought the world into existence. An etiological myth explained the origin of Mount Etna, a dangerous volcano in Sicily: Beneath it Zeus imprisoned the fire-breathing monster Typhoeus (tī-**fē**-us), who continued to spew forth smoke and lava. Another example may be the myth of Persephonê, daughter of the wheat goddess Demeter. Persephonê must spend four months of the year in the underworld, and Demeter refuses to let anything grow during those months—the hot, barren summer. The change of seasons is "explained," according to many, by the myth. Another etiological myth made clear why Demeter was worshiped in one part of Greece in the form of a mare. According to the story, Demeter changed herself into a mare in an unsuccessful attempt to escape the amorous attentions of Poseidon, god of the sea. Of course, an etiological tale such as this does not explain the real cause of a practice. In reality, Demeter was probably represented as a mare because at some stage in the evolution of her cult horses had a special importance. The etiological tale expresses a conjecture about the cause of something that existed long before the explanation.

Both divine myth and modern science offer explanations of why the world is the way it is, but they do so in very different ways. Greek divine myth explains, in general terms, why the male is in charge and why there are generations of displaced former deities still active in the universe. We learn, too, that humankind is present but unexplained, and that there looms the threat that a later generation might overturn the present order. Such explanations are couched in the form of stories. Scientific explanations, by contrast, are based on impersonal general laws and statistical probabilities discovered, or at least verified, by repeatable quantitative experiment. Mythic explanations, expressed in traditional tales, assume that supernatural beings control the world through the exercise of personal will. Thunder is an expression of Zeus's anger, not the necessary result of impersonal physical forces. Greek myth could thus blame sudden and puzzling deaths on the will of the gods, as in the story of how the gods Artemis and Apollo struck down the fourteen children of Niobê. Modern scientists may be puzzled by death from cancer, but they do not blame such death on a divine and irrational agent. The modern world was born from the struggle of scientific thought against mythical explanations for why and how things happen in the world and why the world is the way it is.

## HESIOD'S *THEOGONY*

Hesiod's 1,000-line poem, the *Theogony,* offers some of the clearest examples of divine myth in ancient Greece. It tells how the world we know today came into being. In contrast to the familiar story told in the biblical book of Genesis, where God stands outside his creation and exists before it, Hesiod tells of the origin of the universe through succeeding generations of gods; *theogony* means "origin of the gods." Especially, he wishes to show how Zeus, who rules the world today, came to power. Hesiod's poem is in external form an elaborate hymn to Zeus. We have already examined Hesiod's invocation to the Muses, who grant him the power to sing this song: "true things" (*etumea*) about the beginning of things (Chapter 1).

Hesiod tells how first there was Chaos, then came Gaea (**jē**-a), "Earth," and her husband Uranus (**yur**-a-nus), "Sky." But Uranus would not allow their offspring, the Titans (**tī**-tans), to be born. He thrust them back into a cranny of Gaea, who in exasperation conspired with her son Cronus to overthrow the tyrant. Cronus took a sickle of steel, waited for his father, then castrated him. But Cronus too proved a tyrant, who swallowed his own offspring, the future Olympians. Only Zeus escaped, because Cronus' wife gave him a stone wrapped like a baby to swallow. Zeus grew up in secret, overthrew Cronus, and instituted a new realm, the present one, in concert with his brothers and sisters. He overthrew all who threatened his power, including the monstrous Typhoeus, a child of Gaea, and the race of giants (= "earthborn ones"). At last his power was secure.

Scholars once thought that Hesiod's story of Zeus's war and ascendancy over the Titans must reflect a historical conflict between the Greek Indo-European invaders with their new gods (especially Zeus) against the indigenous peoples, of unknown stock, with their (mostly female) deities. The recovery of ancient Near Eastern myths, however, leaves no doubt that the story of war in heaven, and other features of Hesiod's Greek account, are taken from earlier Eastern cultures.

## THE TRIUMPH OF MARDUK

In general, myth in the ancient Near East was divine myth, not legend or folktale, and many see a historical connection between Hesiod's poem and Near Eastern creation myth as found in the Babylonian poem *Enuma elish,* "When on high." *Enuma elish* was recited on the fourth day of the New Year's festival in Babylon in honor of the god of the city, Marduk. We are not sure how such Eastern stories crossed barriers of language and culture to enter Greece, but cross they did.

The text of *Enuma elish* reached its present form well before 1100 BC, although it preserves far older material. Telling of the first days of the creation, the story had the magical power to renew the world at the critical joining of one year with the next. There is little drama or suspense. It is our best example from Mesopotamia of a myth we know to have been told during a religious ritual.

The poem opens with the gods of the primordial waters, male Apsu, fresh water, and female Tiamat (**tē**-a-mat), salt water, mingled together in an indeterminate mass:

> When on high heaven was not yet named,
> nor was the hard ground below called by name—
> there was nothing but primordial Apsu, the begetter,
> and Mother Tiamat, she who gave birth to everything.
> The waters of Tiamat and Apsu were mingled together as a single body.
> No one had woven a reed hut. There was no marsh land.
> It was a time before the gods had come into being,
> or were called by name, or their destinies determined—
> this was when the gods took form within them.°
> Lahmu and Lahamu° were brought forth, called by their names
> Before they had grown.
> Anshar and Kishar° took form, greater than the others.
> They made the days long, added on years.°
> Anu was their heir, rival to his own fathers.

*. . . within them:* That is, the waters of Apsu and Tiamat. To name is to create, for the essence of a creature resides in the word that designates it.     *Lahmu and Lahamu:* perhaps "Mr. and Mrs. Mud," the primordial slime.     *Anshar and Kishar:* probably Heaven and Earth, Up and Down, to judge from the roots *An* (sky) and *Ki* (earth). *. . . added on years:* i.e., time passed.

With Lahmu and Lahamu, "mud," the creation has begun, even as Gaea, "earth," appeared out of Chaos. From Apsu and Tiamat came four generations of gods, Anu (sky) and Ea (ē-a), the water god, among them. The new gods came together to dance. Their activity and noise disturbed Apsu's rest, and with his officer Mummu, Apsu went to Tiamat to complain:

> I cannot stand their ways!
> The day brings no respite, and the night no rest.
> I will ruin their ways and drive them away!
> Then may peace come again, and sleep!

Although the loving mother Tiamat vigorously opposed Apsu's wish to destroy their troublesome offspring, Mummu urged it, and his advice so pleased Apsu that Apsu's face grew radiant and he kissed his officer.

When the younger gods heard of the plan to destroy them, they fell into a panic. Only Ea, "who knows everything, the skillful, the wise," kept his head. He cast a spell over Apsu and Mummu, sending them into a deep sleep. He killed Apsu, strung a rope through Mummu's nose, and imprisoned him. On top of the dead Apsu, Ea built his house, into which he moved with his wife. She soon gave birth to the real hero of the poem, Marduk, god of Babylon, in every way an extraordinary being:

> He sucked from the teats of goddesses.
> His nurse filled him with glory.
> His body was charming, sparkling his eyes.
> He was born fully developed, mighty from the start.
> When his father Ea looked upon him,
> he rejoiced and beamed; his heart was gladdened.
> He made him perfect, a god twice over.
> Exalted above them all, he was superlative in every way.
> His limbs were well made, impossible to describe,
> beyond comprehension, hard to perceive.
> Four were his eyes, four were his ears.
> When he opened his mouth, fire shot forth.
> His four ears were huge,
> his four eyes saw all that was.
> His limbs were immense, he was enormously handsome.

His grandfather Anu was so proud that he fashioned four winds as Marduk's playthings. The winds blew constantly to and fro, once more stirring the waters of Tiamat, and again the older gods complained. Tiamat, who earlier defended the younger gods, was now determined to destroy them, and begot an army of monsters to help her:

> She set up the snake with horns, the dragon, the lahmu-hero,°
> the lion demon, rabid dog, and scorpion-man,

savage *ûmu*-devils,° fishman, bullman.

*lahmu-hero:* It is not clear what is meant.     *ûmu:* A word of unknown meaning.

To lead the horde, she chose a new husband, Kingu, "her only lover." She placed him on a throne and armed him with the mysterious Tablets of Destiny, which give power over the universe.

When Ea heard of the fresh preparations, he lost his nerve and ran to the god Anshar. In consternation Anshar bit his lip and slapped his thigh and demanded that Ea war against Tiamat. At this point the tablet is broken, but apparently Ea was unsuccessful, for when the text resumes, it is Anu who attacks Tiamat. But she put her hand against him, and Anu ran away in terror. At the moment of crisis, the gods lost all hope and sank into despair, as they do in many Mesopotamian myths.

Then Anshar remembered Marduk, whose moment has come. He kissed Marduk on the lips, and Marduk agreed to fight Tiamat and her army of monsters, but only on condition that he be given absolute power as reward:

> "My word alone shall establish fate, not yours!
> What I fashion shall last forever!
> What my lips decree, shall never be changed, never altered!"
> Hastily, the gods agreed.
> They gave him a scepter, a throne, a royal robe.
> They gave him relentless weapons to overwhelm the foe:
> "Go slice the throat of Tiamat!
> Let the winds bring her blood, tidings of joy!"

Taking bow and arrows, a mace and net, with lightning flashing before him, with seven winds at his back, Marduk mounted his chariot—the image of a thunderstorm. The chariot's team were named Killer, Ruthless, Racer, and Flyer, and their teeth dripped poison. Radiant with power, he roared down the road toward Tiamat, but when he saw her, he (like Ea and Anu before him) lost his nerve and had to endure the taunts of Tiamat. But he soon regained his courage and rebuked her, so that she was seized by uncontrollable rage, let out a roar, and attacked:

> Tiamat and Marduk, the wisest god, locked together.
> They tangled in the hand-to-hand, clasped in battle.
> Marduk spread out his net to catch her.
> The storm that followed behind him, he splashed in her face.
> When Tiamat opened wide her mouth to swallow him,
> he drove down the storm so she could not close her lips.
> The savage winds swelled her belly,
> her body puffed up and her mouth opened wide.
> He fired his arrow, it burst her belly,
> carved through her guts and split the heart,

wrecked and extinguished her life.
He threw down the corpse and trod upon it.

The army of monsters tried to flee, but Marduk caught them in his net, fixed them with nose-ropes, and bound their arms. He imprisoned Kingu and took control of the Tablets of Destiny. Then

Marduk trod on Tiamat's legs.
With his mighty mace he smashed her skull.
When he had sliced open the arteries of her blood,
the North Wind bore it to places unknown.
When the gods saw what had happened, they were joyous, radiant.
They brought gifts of homage to Marduk.
But the lord paused to look at her corpse,
so that he might divide the monster and fashion clever things.
He split her like a clamshell into two parts.
Half he raised up high, calling it sky.
He lowered the bar and set up watchmen.
He commanded them never to let her waters escape.

On top of the corpse Marduk built a large temple and cult centers for the sky-god Anu, the storm-god Enlil (**en**-lēl),[2] and the water-god Ea. He made the constellations, set up the calendar, put the north star in its place, and brought forth the sun and moon. From Tiamat's spittle he made the surging clouds, the wind, the rain; from her poison, the billowing fog. He heaped a mountain over her head and pierced her eyes, from which flow the rivers Tigris and Euphrates. Other mountains he heaped over her breasts, then bent her tail into the sky to make the Milky Way. With her crotch he held up the sky.

Marduk returned home in triumph, delivered the Tablets of Destiny to Anu, and presented his captives before the gods. He washed off the gore of battle, dressed in royal attire, and sat on a high throne to receive homage from the gods. He proclaimed that he would build a great temple, a luxurious dwelling for himself and for all the gods, when they came to visit. He announced another plan:

"I will mash blood together and bones
and make a primeval man: Man shall be his name.
His purpose will be to serve the gods,
that they might be at ease!"

He brought the rebel Kingu before the assembly:

---

[2]Probably Enlil was the original hero in the story, replaced later by the local Babylonian god Marduk; each is a storm-god.

They tied him up and dragged him in before Ea.
They carried out the execution, severed his arteries.
From his blood they made man.
Ea made labor to be man's lot, but the gods he set free.

Marduk then divided the gods into those who live in the sky and those beneath the earth. The grateful gods eagerly began to build the palace of which Marduk had spoken, and after two years completed the great ziggurat (an artificial mountain) of Babylon. A banquet was held, and Marduk was proclaimed lord of the universe. The story ends with a long list of the fifty names of Marduk (over one fourth of the total poem), with detailed explanations of each name. In this way was the world made, and the same order of kingship established among the gods as in Babylon itself.

In *Enuma elish* and other Mesopotamian myths, the original creative element is watery, feminine, and ambivalent, both life-giving and life-destroying. Above the earth the waters may descend as life-giving rain, but below the earth they bound the land of the dead. The same ambivalence as that of the original, primeval element of the universe is displayed by female deities, who both nurture and destroy. The dangerous, chaotic waters may be represented by a monster or dragon who is overcome by a hero who fashions the cosmos. There is a complex association among water, chaos, monsters, and death. Dragon-combat and cosmogony ("origin of the ordered world") can be one and the same. The hero establishes the world order and his own permanent reign over the corpse of the monster.

Mesopotamian divine myths, like the story the Greek Hesiod tells in his *Theogony,* envision the formation and organization of the world and of human society as a result of process and change. The world has not always been the way it is now; its initial unity in the primeval waters has moved to diversity. Creation is not from nothing, but, as in Hesiod, from a primordial chaos by means of sexual reproduction and a series of successively more powerful generations. A younger generation opposes, overcomes, and controls or destroys an older, until the present world order comes into being. This general pattern is called the *succession myth.*

## THE HITTITE *KINGSHIP IN HEAVEN* AND THE *SONG OF ULLIKUMMI*

Other Eastern divine myths important to the later classical tradition come from the mighty Indo-European Hittites, who ruled the central Anatolian plain in the Late Bronze Age (their powerful capital was near modern Ankara), whose art and culture was strong well into the eighth century BC in what is today southeastern Turkey and northern Syria. Only small portions of a poem called *Kingship in Heaven* survive, but the myth has clear relevance to Hesiod's Greek cosmogony:

In earlier years, Alalush was king in heaven.
Alalush sits there on his throne.
And strong Anush [= Anu], first of the gods, is his servant.
He bows to him at his feet.
He always gives him great cups
to drink into his hand.
For nine years of rule, Alalush was king in heaven.
After nine years, Anush made war against Alalush.
He defeated Alalush
who fled under the dark earth,
but Anush sat on the throne.
Anush is there on his throne
and strong Kumarbi always gives him food to eat
and he always bows at his feet
and always gives him great cups into his hand.
For nine years Anush ruled as king in heaven.
In the ninth year, Anush made war with Kumarbi.
The eyes of Kumarbi he could not defeat.
He slipped from Kumarbi's hand and fled.
Anush the eagle flew in the sky
and Kumarbi closed in behind him,
grabbed his feet
and pulled him down from the sky.
He [Kumarbi] bit off his genitals.
His sperm went into Kumarbi's stomach.
He swallowed Anush's sperm
and was happy and he laughed.
    And Anush turned back to him
and began to speak to Kumarbi:
"You are really pleased about your stomach.
It swallowed my sperm.
You should not rejoice!
I have placed a burden in your middle.
First, I have made you pregnant with the storm-god;
second, with the river Aranzakh°
third, with the heavy Tasmishu.°
And I placed the burden, the terrible gods into your middle!
You will perish, hitting your head on the mountain Tashshu!"
When Anush finished speaking, he disappeared.
Then Kumarbi went high into the heavens.
He spit from his mouth.
The stricken king spit from his mouth upwards.
That which had been ingested, Kumarbi spit out.[3]

*Aranzakh:* The Tigris.    *Tasmishu:* An attendant of the storm-god.

[3]Translated by Frederick W. Schwink.

There the tablet breaks off. When it resumes, we learn that Anush argued with the storm-god, who was still within the body of Kumarbi, over how the storm-god should escape from Kumarbi's body. Kumarbi felt dizzy and asked Aya (= Ea) for something to eat. He ate something, which hurt his mouth. At last the storm-god, warned not to come forth through various openings, especially not through Kumarbi's anus, came out of the "good place," apparently Kumarbi's penis. The rest is lost, but somehow the storm-god, called Teshub in other texts, escaped from Kumarbi's body, overthrew him, and became king of heaven.

Another Hittite tale, the *Song of Ullikummi,* tells us more about the celestial kingship and Kumarbi's struggle for ascendancy. Kumarbi planned destruction for the storm-god Teshub, who seems to be Kumarbi's own son. Kumarbi "took wisdom unto his mind," rose from his chair, took a staff, put sandals on his feet, and set out to a place called Cool Pond. There Kumarbi had intercourse with a huge rock, "five times he possessed it, and again ten times he possessed it."

The rock became pregnant and gave birth to a stone child. The child was placed on Kumarbi's knees and Kumarbi named him Ullikummi (= "destroyer of Kummiya," the city of Teshub). Kumarbi then delivered the child to Ubelluri, a giant who, like the Greek Atlas, carried heaven and earth. Ubelluri placed the child on his shoulder. Soon Ullikummi, who grew an acre each month, was so big that the sea came only to his waist and his head reached the sky. Teshub learned of the monster and, to get a better look, ascended Mount Casius in northwestern Syria. Realizing the danger, he marshaled his forces and attacked. Teshub was temporarily defeated, but Aya obtained the very tool by which heaven and earth had first been separated and with it cut away Ullikummi from Ubelluri, reducing Ullikummi's power. Teshub took heart and mounted his chariot, prepared to fight again. Here the tablet breaks off, but certainly Teshub, highest god of the Hittite pantheon, did overcome the dragon Ullikummi to become king of heaven.

## THE DIVINE MYTH OF SUCCESSION IN HESIOD AND THE NEAR EAST

In *Enuma elish,* first came a theogony, the generation of Apsu and Tiamat and their descendants. These new gods bring a principle of movement into the world (their dance), which contrasts sharply with the older forces of chaos, which stand for inactivity and inertia (symbolized by their desire to sleep). The primordial gods' resistance to change leads to a battle of the gods in which newer gods overthrow the older. This succession motif is important in Greek myth as well.

In the first round of the battle of the gods, the wise and clever Ea over-comes wicked Apsu by a spell; his magical power resides in the spoken word. Ea's wisdom and cleverness are contrasted with Apsu's brutish lust to destroy, a common folktale motif; the dragon-slayer is clever and tricky, his opponent dull and stupid. Tiamat, like Gaea, manages to be both beneficent and malevolent. She first opposes her husband's destructive designs, but when Apsu is killed she herself becomes the destructive monster. Later, in a repetition of the succession motif, Tiamat is destroyed by her grandson Marduk, who becomes ruler of the world.

The Hittite *Kingship in Heaven* is similarly based on the succession motif: First Alalush was king, then Anush, then Kumarbi. The *Song of Ullikummi* carries the conflict one generation further: Now Kumarbi must be overthrown. To defend his power, Kumarbi, like Tiamat, begets a terrible monster against which the storm-god Teshub must contend for supremacy.

In both *Enuma elish* and Hesiod's *Theogony* the first generation of gods is made up of primal pairs: Apsu, the male sweet waters, and Tiamat, the female salt waters, and Uranus and Gaea. The fathers Apsu and Uranus hate the first children, who are begotten within the mother. In an initial round of conflict the clever sons Ea and Cronus overthrow their fathers. In a second round of conflict gods of the third generation—Marduk and the storm-god Zeus—revolt against an earlier divine generation. Terrible monsters are overcome: Tiamat and her army in *Enuma elish;* the Titans, Typhoeus, and the Giants, all children of Gaea, in the Greek story. The storm-god is then made king. Mesopotamian and Greek myths alike report a cosmic history that begins with mighty powers of nature and ends in the organization of the universe as a monarchic, patriarchal state. Both mythical traditions make use of the motifs of succession and dragon-combat.

Similarities between the Hittite and Greek myths are equally striking. According to *Kingship in Heaven,* first a primordial god (Alalush) was ruler, then the sky-god (Anush) ruled, then another god (Kumarbi), and then, probably, the storm-god (Teshub). The same sequence of generations appears in Hesiod: First came Chaos (= Alalush?), then Uranus/Sky (= Anush), then Cronus (= Kumarbi), then the storm-god Zeus (= Teshub). Both Anu ("sky") and Uranus ("sky") were castrated by their sons, and gods were born from the severed organs. As long as heaven and earth are locked in sexual embrace, forming a solid whole, there is no space within which the created world can appear. Castration was a real practice imposed on enemies taken in war, but in the logic of the myth, castration is separation, and separation is creation. Both males, Kumarbi and Cronus, have children within themselves. The children of each, Teshub and Zeus, both storm-gods, overcome their fathers to win victory in heaven.

According to the Hittite *Song of Ullikummi,* the Hittite storm-god Teshub must defend his reign against a dragon of chaos, Ullikummi, even as Zeus takes on the formidable Typhoeus. The Hittite Aya/Ea uses the weapon by which heaven and earth were separated to cut the enormous Ullikummi, born from a rock, away from Ubelluri, the giant who holds up the world; Zeus too (according to Apollodorus 1.6.3) uses a sickle against Typhoeus, just as Cronus castrated Uranus with a sickle. Teshub takes his stand on Mount Casius in Syria to view Ullikummi, the same mountain on which Zeus' war against the Titans, the Typhonomachy, takes place (Apollodorus 1.6.3).

There are differences in detail and profound differences in tone between the Eastern and the Greek stories: The writing systems of the Mesopotamians and Hittites, unlike the Greek alphabet, were unable to record the suppleness and color of spoken language. Nonetheless, there are enough similarities to place beyond doubt that transmission has somehow taken place. The Greek divine myths of theogony and cosmogony are old and have passed across linguistic, cultural, and racial lines. Greek theogonic and cosmogonic myth partly reflects the Greeks' own attitudes, but its basic structure, and many of its cultural assumptions, come from non-Greek peoples.

## FURTHER READING

Athanassakis, A. N., *Hesiod: Theogony, Works and Days* (Baltimore, 1983). Good translation with valuable notes.

Black, J. A., and A. Green, *Gods, Demons and Symbols of Ancient Mesopotamia* (Austin, TX, 1992). Excellent compact reference to images and names.

Brown, N. O., *Theogony. Hesiod* (New York, 1953). A lucid prose translation prefaced by one of the best essays on the *Theogony* in English.

Burkert, W., *The Orientalizing Revolution: Near Eastern Influence on Greek Culture in the Early Archaic Age* (Cambridge, MA, 1992). Demonstrates the direct influence of Eastern myth on Greece.

Caldwell, R. S., *Hesiod's Theogony*, translated, with introduction, commentary, and interpretive essay (Cambridge, MA, 1987). Readable, literate translation with comprehensive commentary and general interpretation (but along Freudian lines).

Frankfort, H., et al., *The Intellectual Adventure of Ancient Man* (Chicago, 1946). Exciting and penetrating account of myth and culture in Egypt, Mesopotamia, and Palestine in the Bronze Age. See also *Before Philosophy* (New York, 1949), a shortened edition of the same book.

Friedman, R. E., *Who Wrote the Bible?* (New York, 1989). Lucid summary of two hundred years of biblical scholarship, explaining how our present text may have come into being.

Hoffner, H. A., and G. M. Beckman, eds., *Hittite Myths* (New York, 1998). Up-to-date treatment.

Jacobsen, T., *The Treasures of Darkness: A History of Mesopotamian Religion* (New Haven, CT, and London, 1976). A survey of Mesopotamian, Sumerian, and Semitic myth, organized chronologically, with sophisticated analyses of individual myths.

Kramer, S. N., ed., *Mythologies of the Ancient World* (New York, 1961). Contains a valuable essay on Hittite mythology by H. G. Göterbock, as well as other useful essays on Egyptian, Mesopotamian, Canaanite, Greek, Indian, Persian, Chinese, Japanese, and Mexican myth.

Lamberton, R., *Hesiod* (New Haven, CT, 1988). A compact survey of the poet, his times, and his work.

MacQueen, J. G., *The Hittites and their Contemporaries in Asia Minor,* revised edition (London, 1986). Excellent general survey.

McCall, H., *Mesopotamian Myths* (Austin, TX, 1990). The best short introduction to the topic.

Penglase, C., *Greek Myths and Mesopotamia* (New York, 1994). Parallels and influence in the *Homeric Hymns* and Hesiod.

Pritchard, J. B., ed., *Ancient Near Eastern Texts: Relating to the Old Testament,* 3rd ed. (Princeton, 1996). The standard collection of translations by many experts, with commentary, of original texts written in the many languages and scripts from the ancient Near East; a book of incomparable scholarly value.

Walcot, P., *Hesiod and the Near East* (Cardiff, 1966). Review of the comparative evidence between Hesiod and Near Eastern literature.

West, M. L., *The East Face of Helicon: West Asiatic Elements in Greek Poetry and Myth* (Oxford, 1997). West argues that Greek culture is really an offshoot of West Asiatic culture; massive documentation to support a radical thesis.

West, M. L., *Theogony* (Oxford, 1966) and *Works and Days* (Oxford, 1978). These scholarly editions of the Greek text contain invaluable introductory essays and commentary on all aspects of the poems.

# CHAPTER 7

# GREEK MYTH AND GREEK RELIGION: PERSEPHONÊ, ORPHEUS, AND DIONYSUS

Ałthough the Greeks owed very much to their Eastern forebears in the imaginative worlds they inhabited, the Mesopotamians and Egyptians lived in a world of gods, kings, and chronologies whereas the Greeks lived in a world of *myth*. Everywhere, in both worlds, are gods and spirits, constantly bringing their power to bear. One common definition of myth even requires the presence of gods, spirits, and demons, as we have seen, but such beings belong properly to religion.

*Religion,* like myth, is a word used in many ways with different meanings to different people. For one raised a Christian, for example, religion is a faith, divorced from the demand for particular practices among its adherents. Christian faith does not rigidly prescribe any action; Jesus even opposed traditional religious practice. The stories in the gospels are extremely important to Christian faith, but they are not viewed as myths. In the pre-Christian world, religion was not a faith and, except for special cases, did not espouse or promulgate a doctrine. We may define such a religion as "a set of practices based on belief in invisible, often superhuman beings." By contrast, myth, whether telling of nonhuman beings or not, is always a story. Myth entertains, thus is often humorous, and it offers moral instruction to humans. Thus myth may depict the gods in ways that illuminate the human situation rather than the divine. These distinctions are critical to our understanding of myth, because myth and religion are always intimately combined, closely related, and easily confused. In the rest of this chapter we will explore various ways in which these two realms of human behavior, ancient religion and ancient myth-making, closely intertwine.

## RELIGION: GENERAL

Christians, Jews, and Muslims believe that there is one God who made the world. He stands outside it, yet dwells in the human heart. His nature is love, and he works for good in the world. His plan for humans is revealed through sacred writings, which specialists (priests, rabbis, and mullahs) interpret to the masses within buildings set aside for this purpose (churches, synagogues, and mosques). Christian clerics are usually paid and devote their lives to interpreting God's will. God demands of his followers love, faith, and adherence to a strict code of moral behavior, including sexual behavior. Christians (not Jews) who follow his commandments can expect to be rewarded in another world after death. These religions once had, and to some extent still have, important social and political missions.

The Greeks, by contrast, had many gods, who did not make the world, but dwelled within it. Zeus was their leader, but Void (Chaos), Earth (Gaea), Night (Nyx), and other gods existed before him and his brothers and sisters; they continued to exist even after Zeus, by force, achieved ascendancy. No Greek god was all-powerful, but each controlled a certain sphere of interest, which sometimes overlapped with that of other gods. The Greek gods had personalities like those of humans and struggled among one another for position and power. This is *anthropomorphism* ("in the shape of humans"). They did not love humans (although some had favorites) and did not ask to be loved by them. They did not impose codes of behavior. They expected to be given respect and honor, but even so might act contrary to human needs and desires. They did not reveal their will in writing; their priests, having no writings to interpret, were required only to perform appropriate rituals. Because there were male and female gods, there were male and female priests to perform such rituals.

The appropriate ritual was always a form of sacrifice, the killing of an animal or many animals, or the offering of foodstuffs. Greek myths contain countless references to such sacrifices, and the disastrous consequences that can follow when they are ignored, abused, or perverted. Although human sacrifice is often mentioned in Greek myths, it appears to have been highly uncommon during the historical period, and archaeology has produced only one clear example from the Bronze Age (from Crete).

The underlying logic of sacrifice was always the same: In order to gain the god's good will, destroy what you value most. It was a kind of insurance policy: Pay in advance and you will not suffer in the future. Sacrifice obligated the god to humans, put the gods in the humans' debt.

Sacrifice was performed outside the god's house on an altar, usually to the east of the temple; the temple was not itself a place of worship. There was no official priestly organization with social or political missions. Priests and priestesses came from local families or were sometimes chosen by lot. When one wished to know the god's will, one went to a seer or to an oracle. Religious activity—appropriate  sacrifice—could help in this life, but had no effect on one's lot in the next world (the mysteries at Eleusis were a notable exception). Notions of guilt or sin, which arise from disobeying God's rules of universal application, were unknown; there were no such rules to obey.

The Greek gods were capricious and terrifying, not to be taken lightly, Yet the Athenian comedians made fun of them, and Greek intellectuals criticized them for the immoral behavior reported in Greek myth. A small minority even questioned the existence of the gods and sought other than divine causes behind the phenomena of the world. The thinking of these radical intellectuals led to the refinement of the proposition that gods do not fashion human misery or happiness, or success in war or love, or anything else. Humans make their own world, a fundamental principle of what we think of as Western civilization. Already Homer had enunciated this principle in a speech of Zeus at the beginning of the *Odyssey* (1.22ff).

## SOME RELIGIOUS EMBLEMS DRAWN INTO MYTH

Although religion has separate origins from myth and serves a different social function, its terms and its forms of expression are constantly drawn into myth. Let us consider an example to illustrate the transformation of a religious emblem into a myth.

Conspicuous in the museums of southeast Europe and the Near East are figurines that have exaggerated sexual organs and plump buttocks and breasts. Such objects are the oldest freestanding sculptures in the world. Male figurines, often with an erect penis, are also found, but in far fewer numbers. Some have wished to connect such figures with goddesses and gods of fertility known from the historical period and prominent in myth. One of the best known of these small statues, several inches high, was made c. 6500–5700 BC in Çatal Hüyük (**cha**-tal **hoo**-yuk), in south central Turkey, evidently the oldest agricultural community in the world. While seated in a throne, a woman is giving birth. Leopards, on which she rests her hands, crouch on either side. In the history of religion, she is sometimes called the Great Mother, the source of life, though it is unlikely that there ever was a single goddess from which derived local and national goddesses. By 560 BC in Greece, on the famous François vase, a similar goddess is labeled *Potnia Thêrôn,* "Mistress of the Beasts," that is, Artemis, protectress and hunter of the things of the wild. Her role in Greek religion was to promote the abundance of game (the name *potnia* appeared already on the Linear B tablets). In this case, the historic cult of the goddess Artemis, who protected wild game, appears to be many thousands of years old; therefore perhaps elements of her myths, too, reach back into the very distant past. Unfortunately, we can never be sure which details in the stories preserved to us are old and which are recent, and prehistoric idols are after all religious artifacts, whereas myth is a story. The relationship between the archaeological and written record is always difficult, but never more so than when dealing with prehistoric myth and religion. As religious emblems, fertility figurines are not myths.

A story, however, was told how Heracles, commanded by the evil Eurystheus of Tiryns, encountered Artemis as he carried away the Ceryneian Hind. The goddess persuaded him to let it go. Here is a myth, a story with a beginning, middle, and end: Heracles pursued the hind (because Eurystheus had ordered him); he caught it (he might not have); he met Artemis and let it go (he failed to bring the hind to Eurystheus after all). How wonderful that the great hero Heracles, a man who could even conquer death, captured a deer and met the goddess! The strangely insignificant exploit, like those we examined earlier, may be based on Near Eastern representations of heroes or gods struggling with horned opponents. A Mesopotamian religious emblem, representing the fecund powers of nature, has become a story that illustrates the arbitrary power of the very dangerous Artemis. That power is religious, but the story about it is *myth*.

Another example of the incorporation of religious emblems into myth is Perseus' beheading of Medusa, one of the most discussed Greek myths. Medusa and the Gorgon were said to be one and the same, but the image of the Gorgon—the so-called *gorgoneion*, a head with large staring eyes, boars' teeth, and serpent hair—originally did not belong to the myth of Perseus at all. Homer refers to Gorgo as just a fearsome demon with staring eyes, represented on the shield of Agamemnon, leader of the Greek host, together with allegorical figures:

> Round about it ten circles of bronze, and on it twenty bosses of tin,
> shining and white, surrounding a boss of metallic dark blue.
> As a crown was the face of Gorgo, fearful for man to behold,
> glaring terribly; with her, as companions, Terror and Panic.
>
> HOMER, *Iliad* 11.33–37, trans. A. T. Murray, modified

Gorgo also appears in the *Odyssey*, when Odysseus is describing his visit to the underworld:

> Cold terror seized me
> lest noble Persephonê rise to me from the mansion of Hades
> displaying the head of Gorgo, that dreadful monster.
>
> HOMER, *Odyssey* 11.633–635, trans. A. T. Murray, modified

In the art of Homer's day, however, the *gorgoneion* is never found, and its origin is obscure. Some associate this artistic representation with Eastern monsters, while others trace it back to the Bronze Age and the Minoan cult of the snake goddess. In any event, when the *gorgoneion* appears in Greek art in the late seventh century BC, well after Homer, it seems to be used as an *apotropaic* ("turning away") device, a magical means to deflect "the evil eye," according to the magical principle that like is effective against like. Belief in the evil eye, the notion that an unfriendly look can harm, is universal, and apotropaic eyes are found in other cultures to deal with this fear.[1] For some reason the *gorgoneion* often appears on the interior of Athenian wine cups, perhaps because intoxication makes one vulnerable to magical harm. The outside of these cups sometimes have two large goggly eyes so that as the drinker raises the cup to drink, the eyes reflect back any unfriendly stare (a few examples have an erect phallus for a base, allowing the drinker to "give the finger" to his companions as he drinks!). Apotropaic Gorgons also appear on early Greek temples, as gargoyles do on medieval cathedrals.

Evidently, a folktale told how Perseus slew one of three wicked sisters, a monster named Medusa, but her appearance was not defined. Only later did Greek artists borrow the iconography ("way of representing") of Gorgo, an apotropaic bogey perhaps of Mesopotamian origin that turned away the evil eye, and attribute it to Medusa. Hesiod mentions the birth of the winged horse Pegasus and a creature named Chrysaör ("he of the golden sword") from Medusa's severed neck (*Theogony*, 280). By the time of the seventh century BC, at least two generations after Hesiod, temple sculpture from Corcyra showing a horse and a small man together with a *gorgoneion* prove that its iconography had by then been drawn into the myth.

## DEMETER AND PERSEPHONÊ

The relationship between myth and religion can be far more complex than the simple incorporation of an object of worship or a magical device into a story. Let us consider the case of Demeter and Persephonê, about whom was told one of the best known and most perplexing of all Greek myths in the *Hymn to Demeter* from the seventh century BC.

The outlines of the story are simple: With the permission of his brother Zeus, king of the gods, Hades, lord of death, sweeps away Persephonê, daughter of Demeter, and carries her to the underworld. Demeter wanders the world in mourning, stopping at Eleusis where she establishes her cult. While she mourns, nothing will grow or reproduce. At last Zeus allows Persephonê to return to the upper world, on condition she has eaten nothing. Because she ate

---

[1]Until the seventeenth century, the English word *fascinate* meant "to fix with the evil eye."

a pomegranate seed, however, she must spend two thirds of the year above ground and the other third below. Again the world was fruitful.

In ancient times the story was interpreted as an agricultural allegory in which Hades was identified with earth and Persephonê (or Korê, "maiden") with grain buried in the earth. Korê's return from the underworld was interpreted as the growth of the new wheat crop. This allegorical interpretation, which we mentioned in Chapter 2, does not, however, correspond with the facts of Greek agriculture. In the hymn, Korê returns in the springtime ("This was the day, the very beginning of bountiful springtime"), whereas in Greece the wheat seed is placed in the ground in the autumn, sprouts soon after, grows through the wet winter, then is harvested in May and threshed into late June. It does not sprout in the spring at all. What must be meant, some argue therefore, is that the seed, Korê, is placed in underground containers during the four hot, sterile summer months until it is brought forth for the autumn planting. Although this interpretation accords with Korê's spending one third of the year in the house of Hades and two thirds on earth, it disagrees explicitly with the hymn and with how the ancients themselves understood the story. But we should probably reject a strict allegorical approach and search for other ways to understand the myth.

Persephonê is a marriageable virgin and, on one level, the hymn is a human story that exemplifies the real experience of Greek girls who in their early teens were married to war-hardened men twice their age, whom they scarcely knew. The sudden loss of virginity is a death to childhood, an end to playing with friends in the sweetly scented meadow, where Hades took her; even so, Greek brides dedicated their dolls to Artemis just before marriage. Because she ate the pomegranate's seed, she can never return to her former state; Greek brides carried an apple or quince into their bridal chambers. A father had the right to give his daughter to whom he chose, even as Zeus gave Persephonê to her uncle, a common form of marital union in Greece to prevent the division of a family's property. Marriage was literal death for many Greek women, who died in childbirth.

Yet Persephonê's fate is different from real brides, who at marriage permanently entered the sphere of their husband's house, where they bore children and became mothers in their own right. Persephonê, by contrast, lives in two worlds, belonging wholly to neither. She is forever Korê, "maiden," forever childless, never fulfilled. When a Greek girl died unmarried, she was said to be Hades' bride, and a wedding vase placed over her grave as a memorial. The pomegranate seeds eaten by Persephonê are symbolic of her sexual union with King Death. He offered her seeds, she took them within her body, but the seeds will never bear fruit. Never again can she return permanently to her mother's home. She is Death's proper mate, and with him she will rule the land of the dead.

Demeter's experience more closely exemplifies the real life experience of Greek mothers, who must in the nature of things give up their daughters to a stranger's household. In many ways her grief is greater than that of her daughter; in art Persephonê is always shown consoling Demeter. Nor was the daughter entirely the innocent victim. She accepted the pomegranate. Persephonê's curiosity brought division between herself and her mother.

Viewed more broadly, Demeter represents the loss that a mother feels for any child, as Greek mothers lost so many children to war and disease. Her loss causes her first to grieve and to rage, but eventually, like mothers must, to accept that the world will go on, in spite of irreparable sorrow. In popular Christianity, the Virgin Mary, whose cult derives from pagan goddess cults, is also *Mater Dolorosa*, "the grieving mother," weeping over her dead child.

In addition to exemplifying the facts of real life as women experienced them, the myth of Demeter offers a mythical explanation, or etiology, for the presence of death in the world, explaining why the fertility of the earth cannot be separated from the inevitable presence of death. There can never be a world (except in the imagination of poets) in which there is only life and never death, because life comes out of death, one feeding on the other. Life *depends* on death. The Two Goddesses are a mythic image of the intimacy between the two realms.

The *myth* then is complex and meaningful on many levels. The primitive *religion,* by contrast, must have been simple and direct: Demeter is the female power that makes the grain to grow, powerful on this earth and, in the form of her daughter Persephonê, in the other world too. The goddess's goodwill brings good crops, and her anger brings poor. When we encounter the religion of Demeter and Persephonê in the historical period, however, the religion has been transformed by an unknown route into one of the most famous cults of the ancient world, which promised personal regeneration through the goddess.

## THE ELEUSINIAN MYSTERIES

In the seventh century BC, when the *Homeric Hymn to Demeter* was written down, the city of Athens was growing rapidly. At about 600 BC Athens absorbed the nearby village of Eleusis, and ever after the mysteries were the property of the city of Athens. Eventually they were visited by the whole Greek world, then by the Romans. The word *mystery,* which has entered our language from this Eleusinian cult to Demeter, comes from the Greek *mystês* (plural *mystai*), meaning "one who closes" (one's eyes?) in order to enter the temple or during the sacred rites. From the Latin translation of the word *initiatus* comes our word *initiate,* literally "one who has gone in," that is, into the temple of Demeter to participate in the secret ritual.

To divulge what happened within the temple, called the Telesterion ("hall of initiation"), was punishable by death, and all modern commentators on the Eleusinian Mysteries must begin by confessing that we do not know what happened there. Most of our information comes from unfriendly and unreliable sources, especially the founders of the Christian church. Yet archaeological investigation and careful examination of the surviving sources, including the *Homeric Hymn to Demeter,* have enabled us to form a more accurate picture of the events.

In origin, the Mysteries seem to have been an agrarian festival designed to promote the growth of the grain. They were certainly functioning by 1500 BC. Two principal families were in charge: the Eumolpids, whose ancestor Eumolpus, according to the hymn, received them from Demeter herself, and the Kerykes, "heralds," descendants of Eumolpus' son Keryx ("herald"). The high priest, always a Eumolpid, was called the hierophant (hī-**er**-ō-fant), "he who reveals the *hiera,* "sacred things." The Kerykes provided the torch-bearer and the herald. For their services, members of these families received a fee from the initiates. We also know that there was a priestess of Demeter, who like the hierophant lived permanently in the sanctuary.

The principal ceremony of the Mysteries was held annually in the fall. In classical times, a truce was called (and usually observed) for fifty-five days. Heralds were sent to neighboring cities inviting participation. On the day before the festival, the *hiera* were removed from the Telesterion and carried to Athens in a majestic procession led by priests and priestesses. On the next day began the festival proper, which lasted for eight days. All who could speak Greek (except murderers) were eligible for initiation, including women and slaves.

On the fifth day, following various preliminary rites, the grand procession back to Eleusis took place, bearing the *hiera.* At night, carrying torches and chanting prayers and hymns, they reached Eleusis. The initiation proper took place on the next two days. The initiates had fasted, but now they drank the *kykeon,* the sacred drink offered to Demeter, mentioned in the hymn. Although many have thought that a drug may have been taken, the *kykeon* seems to have been a barley drink mixed with pennyroyal, without psychotropic effects.

The initiates entered the Telesterion, a building unique in Greek architecture. The ordinary Greek temple, elaborately decorated with sculpture, was meant to be viewed from the exterior, while the interior merely held the cult statue. By contrast, the Telesterion was built to hold several thousand people under its great roof, supported by a forest of columns. Inside, off center, stood the Anaktoron, a rectangular stone building with a single door at the end of one of its long sides, probably representing an ancient hut from the earliest days of the cult. Beside the door was a stone chair for the hierophant, who alone could enter the Anaktoron. A huge fire burned on top of the hut, its smoke passing through a hole in the roof.

Except for the flickering light from the fire and torches, the crowd was shrouded in darkness. Terrifying things were shown. When the Anaktoron opened, the hierophant appeared in the midst of a brilliant light. More than that, we do not know, although some have thought that a dramatic reenactment of the myth took place. Evidently, the *hiera* were shown and something was said, but what the *hiera* were or what was said, we do not know. The myth speaks of the joy of reunion between daughter and mother, and the message of Eleusis, however communicated, must lie in the emotion excited by the return of the divine Korê. The initiates were blessed with hope, not for immortality as such (never mentioned in connection with Eleusis), but for a pleasurable existence after death.

The Eleusinian Mysteries advocated no doctrine, but as a group experience fostered a feeling of community among Greeks. A high moral tone surrounded the cult, which emphasized ritual purity, righteousness, gentleness, and the superiority of civilized life based on agriculture. On the one hand, in myth, you have a story about an unhappy, childless marriage, in which an accommodation is reached with the mother-in-law. Part of this story is set at Eleusis. On the other hand, in religion, you have an elaborate system of cult that serves economic and personal interests: the growth of the grain and a happy afterlife for the initiate.

The Eleusinian Mysteries were the most honored cult of Greek religion, giving hope and comfort to untold thousands from all over the Mediterranean world and commanding veneration until they were finally suppressed at the end of the fourth century AD. Some of the ideas associated with the cult, even before then, found their way into Christianity and are reflected in the words of St. Paul:

> But some one will ask, "How are the dead raised? With what kind of body do they come?" You foolish man! What you sow does not come to life unless it dies. And what you sow is not the body which is to be, but a bare kernel, perhaps of wheat or of some other grain. . . . Lo! I tell you a mystery."

> *1 Corinthians* (15.35–37, 51)

## THE MYTH AND CULT OF DIONYSUS

A god even closer to Christian ideals of resurrected life was Dionysus, whose myths and cult provide another example of how closely myth and cult can be interwoven. The Dionysian religion was quite different from those devoted to other ancient deities. The original Olympian gods were separated from human beings by a great gulf symbolized by the poetic conception of Zeus and his court as ruling from the high peaks of Mount Olympus. These gods were known through their works, helpful or harmful, but were rarely directly manifest to ordinary human beings. Dionysus was different. Most stories about him take place on earth, in the midst of human beings. The Greeks believed they could feel his presence in a direct way, and the cultivation of this experience was a central focus of his religion. Many features of the myths of Dionysus are best understood as reflections of the practices of his cult, far more so than in the case of the myths and cults of Demeter and Persephonê.

He was "the god who comes," and the myths tell of his sudden and violent arrival in Greek cities. The intense emotion felt by individual followers must have come in a similarly abrupt and decisive manner. The god's presence in his followers was called *enthousiasmos*, "being filled with the god" (the origin of our word enthusiasm). His followers experienced *ekstasis*, "standing outside oneself" (hence our word ecstasy). When Dionysus was present, his devotees lost their sense of personal identity and became one with the god. So strong was this sense of oneness that the follower was called Bacchus, another name for Dionysus. With the loss of identity came a willingness to transcend ordinary standards of decent and rational conduct. Appropriately, Dionysus was known as *lysios*, "deliverer": Through their enthusiastic and ecstatic communion with the god, his devotees were temporarily released from everyday life and united with a cosmic force.

The presence of a crowd of witnesses fostered the experience of Dionysian ecstasy, as suggested in myth by the band of followers who always surround the god: the maenads and satyrs. Continuous dancing to the beating of drums and the playing of flutes, and the consumption of wine, led devotees to direct experience of the god. So did the communal tearing apart of an animal (*sparagmos*) and the eating of its raw flesh (*ômophagia*). In prehistoric times this practice may have taken a cannibalistic form, with human beings as victims. In the myths, the god's crazed followers tear the king of Thebes, Pentheus, limb from limb (although they do not actually eat him), Dionysus' nurse Ino boils her son in a pot, and the daughters of the king of Orchomenus (the Minyads) eat their own children. The myths no doubt exaggerate the more sensational forms of the cult—cannibalism and human sacrifice were abhorrent by the Archaic and Classical Periods. Still, we have inscriptional evidence that Dionysus' followers really did practice the "eating of raw flesh" as late as the Hellenistic Period.

The cult of Dionysus appealed especially to women, whose social responsibilities were to preserve the stability of the family. Some explain Dionysus' appeal to women by saying that women are more emotional than men and thus more likely to embrace a religion centered on intense feeling; others suggest that women formed an oppressed class in Greece who longed for the ecstatic release that Dionysian religion could provide. Whatever the correct explanation, in myth Dionysus is surrounded by women—his nurse, Ino; the nymphs of Nysa, who helped to raise him; the maenads, "maddened ones," his female followers; and his wife, Ariadnê, daughter of Minos. The nymphs of Nysa in particular, as nourishers and followers of the god, were mythic models for the bands of female devotees. Although Euripides (who liked to defy his audience's expectations) describes the Bacchae's behavior as chaste in his famous play the *Bacchae* ("followers of Bacchus"), sexual profligacy was undoubtedly a feature of the real religion. It is not surprising that Hera, protectress of the family, opposed the raging god who excited married women to madness and caused them to forget their duty to husband, family, and community.

Greek and Roman religions in general lacked creeds and claimed little moral authority, but they did develop local priesthoods, who seemed to have tamed the savage features of Dionysiac religion. Nevertheless, on several occasions the worship of Dionysus was felt to be a political threat. In Rome his cult grew to such proportions during the long and painful war with Carthage that in 186 BC an alarmed senate, after many executions, brought it under severe restrictions.

From the religion of Dionysus and the cult of Pan derive the goatish qualities of popular representations of the devil in medieval Europe and the attribution to the devil of ritual indulgence in intoxicants and sex. Yet the Dionysian notion of the identification of god and worshiper was similar to Christian doctrine and is sometimes expressed in terms strikingly similar to those current in Dionysiac cult. For example, from the *Book of Common Prayer of the Church of England* (AD 1549, still used in churches of the Anglican Communion):

> Grant us therefore, gracious Lord, so to eat the flesh of thy dear Son Jesus Christ, and to drink his blood . . . that we may evermore dwell in him and he in us.

In the myths, Dionysus was twice-born, because Zeus killed his mother Semelê with a thunderbolt, then stitched the fetus in his thigh, from which the god later emerged. Paradoxically, the pagan god of drunkenness and sexual license served as one model for the early Christians in their attempts to understand their relationship to their own dying god. Sarcophagi with scenes from the stories of Dionysus were often reused for Christian burials. In the eleventh or twelfth century AD an unknown Byzantine author, no doubt inspired by parallels between Pentheus' interrogation of Dionysus in Euripides' *Bacchae* and Pontius Pilate's of Christ, put together a work called *Christus Patiens* ("The Suffering Christ"), the story of the crucifixion told as a Greek tragedy. *Christus Patiens* is made up entirely of lines taken from ancient drama, especially the *Bacchae* by Euripides.

## THE MYTH AND RELIGION OF ORPHEUS

Finally, let us consider the myth and cults that went by the name of Orphism, parallel in certain respects to the myths and cults of Demeter/Persephonê and Dionysus. In the sixth century BC, religious teachers began to claim the mythical Orpheus as the promulgator of special teachings about the nature and destiny of human beings. Like the Eleusinian Mysteries, these "teachings of Orpheus" offered ordinary Greeks hope for salvation, a means of ensuring a more comfortable life after death. Unlike other Greek religious teachings, however, the Orphic doctrines were recorded and transmitted in written form, in the so-called *Hymns of Orpheus,* a collection of writings from different times by many different authors. These hymns were supposed to contain the knowledge that Orpheus gained in the world below and later taught while he wandered through Thrace. Although these stories incorporate material from various myths, they were made up by the Orphic poets; Plato was to imitate the practice. Although most of the Orphic hymns are now lost, we can draw some conclusions about their central doctrines from surviving fragments and other sources.

Dionysus figures prominently in these myths. Our knowledge about one important Orphic myth is derived from comments by an unfriendly Christian writer from about AD 200, Clement of Alexandria, who ridicules beliefs he finds absurd and offensive:

> The mysteries of Dionysus are utterly savage. While he was an infant, the Curetes° danced around him in full armor but the Titans sneaked in, distracted the baby's attention with toys, and tore him limb from limb. The poet of initiation, Orpheus, tells the story:°
>
> > Tops and hoops and dollies,
> > With moving feet and hands;
> > Pretty golden apples,
> > From singing western lands.
>
> To make you laugh, let me list the silly symbols of that rite of yours: knuckle-bones, ball, top, apples, wheel, mirror, fleece.
> Well, Athena stole the heart of Dionysus and, because it was still palpitating, she received the name of Pallas.° Meanwhile, the Titans who had torn Dionysus to pieces set a pot on a tripod. They tossed in his limbs, which they first boiled up, then put them on spits and held them over the fire. Afterward Zeus appeared (if he was really a god, he had doubtless caught a whiff of roasting meat, which those gods of yours claim as their due). He blasted the Titans with a thunderbolt and gave the remains of Dionysus to his son Apollo to bury. Apollo would not dream of disobeying Zeus, so he took the mangled corpse to Parnassus° and buried it there.

CLEMENT OF ALEXANDRIA, *Protrepticus* 2.15

*Curetes:* "youths," referring to the young men who banged on shields outside the cave where Zeus was raised as an infant, to drown the infant's cries.    *story:* Here Clement quotes from an Orphic hymn.    *Pallas:* On the assumption that Pallas means "beating" (a possible but improbable interpretation).    *Parnassus:* That is, Delphi.

The story appears to reflect an initiation rite common in preliterate societies. A young man (Dionysus) is approached by older men (the Titans), symbolically "killed," then brought back to new life in the adult world (though this third part is missing from Clement's account). Some accounts tell how the Titans smeared their faces with gypsum, an actual practice in initiation rites where older men take on the role of the ghosts of tribal ancestors.

Other Orphic myths report that Zeus created human beings from the ashes of the blasted Titans. Thus, although human nature has an evil, Titanic aspect, it also has within it a spark of divinity, because the flesh of Dionysus, whom the Titans had earlier devoured, was mingled with the Titans' ashes. A human being therefore possesses a divine Dionysian spark encased in a gross Titanic body, and the goal of human striving should be to free the immortal soul from its bodily prison. This view is succinctly expressed in an Orphic slogan: The body is a tomb (*sôma sêma*).

The Orphics also taught metempsychosis, or the reincarnation of the soul. According to this doctrine, the souls of the dead do not remain forever in the realm of Hades, but repeatedly return to earth for a new life in a different body (Plato accepted this view and so did Vergil after him). It is only with great effort, and with the help of Orphic teachings, that the soul can at last be purified and the cycle of rebirth broken.

The soul's escape from its entanglement with matter required a life of ascetic purity, including abstention from such animal products as meat and woolen cloth, from beans (for unknown reasons), and from sexual intercourse. Magical formulas could also be useful in the world below. A number of gold plates have been found in tombs in south Italy and on Crete that contain Orphic instructions to be used by the dead.

The religious teachings advanced in the cult of Orpheus show strong influence from shamanism, a religious practice highly developed in Siberia and found across Asia down into Thrace, Orpheus' legendary homeland. The training of a shaman involves arduous rites, including a symbolic dismemberment and reconstitution of his body (remarkably similar to the Orphic story about Dionysus). In this context, the myth of Orpheus becomes more than a simple folktale, the story of a man who went to the other world and returned. Orpheus can be viewed as a shaman in his own right, returning from the underworld to teach the truth about human nature and destiny.

Although the origin and exact nature of the Orphic teachings are shrouded in mist, they seem to be connected with the doctrines of Pythagoras (sixth century BC). Pythagoras is best known for the philosophical claim that the essence of reality is to be found in mystical relations between numbers, proportions, and measures. Pythagoras also believed in metempsychosis, and he taught his followers to lead ascetic lives based on principles much like those of Orphism. Plato's dualistic conception of human nature—the soul as a divine spark entombed in an earthly body—parallels Orphic teaching and probably depends on it, as do his views on metempsychosis and the virtues of an ascetic life. Through Plato, Orphic doctrines influenced the fathers of the Christian church. Much of what we think of as Christianity is Platonic philosophy, some of it Orphic in origin. The early Christians themselves recognized the affinity, and paintings in catacombs sometimes show Christ as Orpheus.

Both Orpheus and Dionysus journeyed to Hades. Although Orpheus failed to bring back Eurydicê, he did bring back knowledge of death and its sequel, teachings spread through his followers. In his myth the master-singer drew close to Apollo, god of musical harmony and prophecy, and away from Dionysus, god of ecstasy. He finally met his end at the hands of maenads, followers of Dionysus—according to some accounts, while paying tribute at dawn to Apollo, the rising sun.

# FURTHER READING

Burkert, W., *Greek Religion*, trans. J. Raffan (Cambridge, MA, 1985). A standard scientific description of Greek religion.

Carpenter, T. H., and C. A. Faraone, eds., *Masks of Dionysus* (Ithaca, 1993). The relationship of Dionysus to tragedy and his influence on the modern world; essays by leading scholars.

Linforth, I. M., *The Arts of Orpheus* (Berkeley, 1941).

Mikalson, J. D., *Honor Thy Gods: Popular Religion in Greek Tragedy* (Chapel Hill, 1991).

Mikalson, J. D., *Athenian Popular Religion* (Chapel Hill, 1983). Both books provide an understanding of how common people, as opposed to poets and intellectuals, perceived their religion.

Detienne, M., *Dionysos at Large* (Cambridge, MA, 1989). A study by the eminent French interpreter, using the methods of comparative social science.

Dodds, E. R., introduction to *Euripides' Bacchae*, 2nd ed. (Oxford, 1960). The best short discussion of the religion and myths of Dionysus.

Dodds, E. R., *The Greeks and the Irrational* (Berkeley, 1951; reprinted 1973). A classic investigation into the importance of unreason among the Greeks, the discoverers of reason.

Else, G. F., *The Origin and Early Form of Greek Tragedy* (New York, 1972). Presents Thespis as the inventor of Greek tragedy.

Foley, H. P., ed., *The Homeric Hymn to Demeter: Translation, Commentary, and Interpretive Essays* (Princeton, 1993). Facing Greek/English text with excellent essays focused on gender.

Gimbutas, M., *The Goddesses and Gods of Old Europe 7000–3500 BC: Myths, Legends, and Cult Images* (Berkeley, 1982). This prehistorian argues that ancient Greek mythical images of goddesses go back to the Neolithic Period.

Lewis, I., *Ecstatic Religion, A Study of Shamanism and Spirit Possession*, 2nd ed. (London, 1989). Excellent general study.

Mylonas, G. E., *Eleusis and the Eleusinian Mysteries* (Princeton, 1961). The best book on the topic; a thorough summary of the literary and archaeological evidence.

Nilsson, M., *A History of Greek Religion,* 3rd ed. (New York, 1980). An English-language compressed version of his authoritative (and enormous) study in German; Nilsson was one of the great scholars of Greek religion.

Nilsson, M., *Greek Folk Religion* (Philadelphia, 1972). Religion of the common people.

Otto, W. F., *Dionysus, Myth and Cult* (Bloomington, IN, 1965; originally published in Germany in 1933). Despite its romantic style, Otto judiciously summarizes the ancient evidence and argues for Dionysus as an indigenous Greek god.

Pollard, J. R. T., "Greek Religion," in *The New Encyclopedia Britannica, Macropaedia,* 5th ed., vol. 8, pp. 406–11 (1974–1984 printings only). Superb summary, with bibliography.

Richardson, N. J., ed., *The Homeric Hymn to Demeter* (Oxford, 1974). The standard scholarly edition of the Greek text, with introductory essay in English and copious notes.

Vernant, J.-P., "Greek Religion," in M. Eleade, ed., *The Encyclopedia of Religion* (New York, 1987), vol. 6, pp. 99–118.

# CHAPTER 8

# MYTH AND THE HERO: THE LEGENDS OF HERACLES AND GILGAMESH

IF DIVINE MYTH IN ORAL CULTURES is analogous to science in modern literate Western society, *legend* is analogous to history. Both legend and modern historical writing attempt to answer the question, "What happened in the human past?" Because the human past explains and justifies the human present, the telling of legends was an important activity in the cultural life of ancient peoples, but never more so than among the ancient Greeks. In divine myths, as we have seen, the principal characters are gods and goddesses, and the events described can be of momentous importance. In legends, the central characters are human beings, heroes, not gods and goddesses. Although supernatural beings often play a part, their roles are subordinate to those of the human characters. In the legend of Orestes, the god Apollo orders Orestes to kill his mother, but the emphasis of the story is on Orestes' carrying out the order and the terrible consequences to himself.

## HEROES AND HEROINES

We use the term *hero* very broadly to refer to the principal character in a play or film, to celebrate a neighbor who saves a cat in a tree, or to express admiration, as in the phrase "my hero." For us, a hero (or a heroine) is someone who stands out from others, someone distinguished by prominence, bravery, or merit. For the ancient Greeks, however, the term *hero* had a much more specific meaning. Homer used it to mean any "noble" or "well-born" figure, but later the term was applied exclusively to noble figures from the distant past, some of whom had come to be worshiped as powers dwelling beneath the earth, both male and female. Such hero-cults, centered around tombs surviving from the Bronze Age, were an important element in ancient Greek religion, but our concern is with the myths that recounted the lives and deeds of these legendary figures.

Heroes and heroines, the principal actors of legend, are drawn from the ranks of the nobility; they are kings and queens, princes and princesses, and other members of an aristocratic elite. They have extraordinary physical and personal qualities and are stronger, more beautiful, or more courageous than we. Most Greeks had no doubt that such legendary figures really lived, and members of important families regarded themselves as descended from them. Whereas divine myth is set in a different or previous world-order, legendary events belong to our own, although they took place in the distant past, at the very beginning of human time when mighty heroes and heroines lived on earth, great cities were founded, difficult quests undertaken, monsters slain, and momentous wars waged.

The ancient Greeks, not doubting that such events as the Trojan War really did occur, pointed out the tombs of legendary heroes and the actual sites of heroes' exploits. But the Greeks had no way to compare their traditions with historical reality. Today, armed with the insights of archaeology and techniques of historical investigation, modern scholars recognize that the oral transmitters of traditional tales had little respect for historical truth. Greek myth tells us more about the circumstances and concerns of its transmitters than it does about life in the distant past.

Still, legends can contain an element of historical truth. Modern scholars have long thought that Greek legend does reflect, however dimly, major events and power relationships of a historical period now known to us through archaeological remains. Many or most of the figures in Greek legend probably did live at some time, most likely in the Mycenaean civilization of the Late Bronze Age (c. 1600–1200 BC). Their very names provide one bit of evidence. For example, the name of Menelaüs, the legendary husband of Helen of Troy, means something like "upholder of the people." This distinctive name is appropriate to the aristocracy that certainly existed during this period, and similar names actually appear in written documents of the time (the Linear B tablets, the writings of the Mycenaeans).

Further evidence is provided by archaeology. Excavation has shown that many of the places associated with important legendary events were great centers of civilization during the Bronze Age. Troy, for example, was a city of considerable importance until it was destroyed about 1250 BC. Although we have no proof that it was destroyed by Greek warriors, as Greek legends assert, there remains a tantalizing correspondence between the legend and the archaeological evidence.

Like divine myths, some legends also served a specific etiological function. Thus, one Greek story explained why, at the spring wine festival, Athenians brought their own cups, although at other festivals they drank from a
communal bowl. According to the legend, the Mycenaean prince Orestes,
who had killed his own mother to avenge her murder of his father, came to
Athens at the time of the festival. The king of Athens did not wish to send
Orestes away impolitely, but neither did he want the Athenian people to be
polluted by sharing a bowl with a man who had murdered his mother, so the
king had every man drink from his own cup. In fact, the use of separate cups
probably arose from a fear of contagion from ghosts, thought to be abroad at
this season. The practice had nothing to do with a visit from Orestes, and the
story was invented well after the custom was established.

## HERACLES, SON OF ZEUS

There is no one set of qualities that makes a hero, but no one doubted that
Heracles was the greatest of the Greek heroes. By studying his career, we can
attempt to form certain generalizations. This great hunter and warrior has
much in common with the Mesopotamian hero Gilgamesh, as we will see,
and there can be little doubt of a direct relationship across cultural boundaries. Best known of the many stories about this archetypal hero are the
twelve so-called "Labors" (really "contests," *athloi*):

1.  The Nemean Lion
2.  The Lernaean Hydra
3.  The Ceryneian Deer
4.  The Erymanthian Boar
5.  The Augean Stables
6.  The Stymphalian Birds
7.  The Cretan Bull
8.  The Horses of Diomedes
9.  The Girdle of the Amazon Hippolyta
10.  The Cattle of Geryon
11.  The Apples of the Hesperides
12.  Cerberus

Scholars have wondered when and how originally separate and disorganized
tales were organized into a group of twelve; there is nothing like it, for example, in the Gilgamesh stories. Our earliest accounts show no trace of a standard list or number. In a genealogical passage explaining the parentage of
important mythical monsters, Hesiod in the eighth century BC refers only to
Geryon, the Hydra, Cerberus (although not explicitly connected with Heracles), and the Nemean lion from the list later to become standard (*Theogony*,
287–332).

The earliest evidence for the canonical cycle of Twelve Labors is not found in literature, but on the twelve stone panels, called *metopes* (**me**-to-pēz) mounted above the columns of the Zeus temple at Olympia, built about 460 BC. The cleaning of the Augean stables was included on the temple in the twelfth position, evidently to honor Pisa, the site of the temple, in the territory of the legendary Augeas. This labor is different from the others, which pit Heracles against dangerous enemies, and cannot belong to an earlier list. The number twelve may be an accident: The sculptor had twelve spaces to fill, and the fame of these sculptures made the selection canonical. Twelve is also a magical number and suitable for a collection: There are twelve Olympians, twelve Titans, and twelve months in the year.

By Hellenistic times the same twelve adventures always appear in roughly the same order. There is a logic to their organization. The early adventures are set in the Peloponnesus in an ever-widening circle around Mycenae. Of the first seven, six are simple combat between man and animal (once again, the cleaning of the Augean stables does not fit). Subsequent adventures carry Heracles south to Crete (Cretan bull), north to Thrace (horses of Diomedes), east to the land of the Amazons (girdle of Hippolyta), and west to Erythia (cattle of Geryon), and the last are set in paradise (Garden of the Hesperides) and in the land of the dead (Cerberus). The deliberate arrangement may reflect a lost poem, although we do not know whether such a poem might have come before or after the design of the *metopes* at Olympia.

Heracles' geographical exploration ever further afield made him a natural model for the many Greeks living overseas, especially those in the distant and dangerous west, in Sicily and Italy. Ninety percent of surviving illustrated Greek pots come from graves in Italy, and the abundance of scenes illustrating the adventures of Heracles no doubt reflects the western Greeks' reverence for him. Heracles had traveled into the Atlantic Ocean and faced Death himself, and he easily overcame every foreign people. Heracles was the colonists' favorite hero, and in fact became a god. Alexander the Great, who claimed descent from Heracles, is also identified with the mythical hero. When Alexander is shown on coins wearing the skin of the Nemean lion, he is evoking the image of Heracles as he seeks to impose his will on all foreigners who might stand against him.

Heracles' name, which seems to mean "the glory of Hera," appears puzzling. Why should he be named after Hera, when she persecutes him relentlessly? In the Greek Bronze Age, when parts of this myth may have taken form, Heracles was perhaps a common name, like John or Paul, applied to the common folktale hero who suffered greatly, then was saved at the end.

His Greek origins remain obscure, and we do not know where his legends first appeared in Greece. The Argive plain, where he served Eurystheus, and Thebes, where he was born and first married, have equally strong claims. His character is complex and hard to summarize. Although often called the archetypal Greek hero, to the Greeks of Homer's day he was already very old-fashioned, evoking the image of a bygone age when violence could solve every problem. The historical period that begins with Homer was a tamer time (although still murderous) in which the stories of Heracles served as examples of the dangers of excess, if often with a humorous twist (as in the story of his having bedded the fifty daughters of Thespius in one night!).

To be a "hero," then, does not mean "heroic" in a modern sense. Heracles does everything too much. He commits terrible crimes, which are followed by humiliating expiation. He violates the most sacred human obligations, killing his wife, children, and his guest-friend Iphitus, after which he must live in degrading bondage first to the cowardly Eurystheus, then to Queen Omphalê in Lydia as her sexual plaything and slave. A passing reference in Homer speaks of the time when Heracles shot Hera in the breast with an arrow! Another passing reference in Homer mentions that he shot Hades "in the Gate, among the dead." Here is the hero's essence: reckless, fearless, sometimes tricky, getting away with things others cannot, attacking the very gods.

Of course other heroes challenge Death, a recurring feature of the hero's career—Odysseus and Aeneas descend to the underworld—but none so often or explicitly as Heracles, and no other is rewarded at the end with immortality, Heracles' reward for completing the Twelve Labors. After death, Heracles married Hêbê, "youth," on Mount Olympus: He never grew old. In life he journeyed to the underworld and brought back Cerberus. The triple-bodied Geryon lives across water (where death's realm lies) in the far west (where the sun dies daily), and from there Heracles returned. The souls of the dead often are pictured as birds: Heracles slays the death-dealing species that hovers around Lake Stymphalus. Busiris is the Egyptian lord of the dead, but Heracles kills him. The apples from the Hesperides' garden grow on the tree of eternal life; they fall, although temporarily, into Heracles' hands. In one version, his pursuit of the Ceryneian deer also takes him to this garden, for the deer is the magical but dangerous animal that appears in folktales, leading the hunter from the everyday world into a world of mystery or enchantment.

As the best loved of all Greek heroes, Heracles was *alexikakos,* "the averter of evils," summoned as a god to turn away disease, human and animal attack, and every kind of harm. A common oath in Greek was "By Heracles!"—just as we might say, "By God!" He was the paradigm of heroic tragic existence, but in many humorous tales, and on the comic stage, his reputation for womanizing and gluttony made him a figure of fun. He embodied the Greeks' naive eagerness to try anything without fear of the result, which too often proved disastrous. He destroyed evil, sinned greatly, loved unwisely, fathered a whole race, and died at a woman's hand, yet received his triumphant reward. Heracles is not a hero who fights other heroes, like the warriors before the walls of Troy and Thebes. He is the tough guy, the strongest man on earth, another folktale type, the animal-slayer who made the world safe by destroying dangerous beasts.

## THE MESOPOTAMIAN HERO GILGAMESH

Not all ancient cultures produced such heroic myths. There are no heroes (in the Greek sense of the word) in the myths of ancient Egypt, and none in the Bible except for David, who killed a giant, and Samson, who like Heracles killed a lion and was destroyed by a woman. Even the ancient Romans had no true heroes of their own devising. The ancient Mesopotamians, however, did tell a series of stories about a hero of their own, the great king Gilgamesh, and most scholars would trace stories about Heracles back to this non-Greek Mesopotamian figure. The so-called "epic" of Gilgamesh is not an oral poem, like Homer's poems and Hesiod's, taken down in dictation, but rather a scribal exercise meant to be read and studied by other learned scribes. Still, the Gilgamesh stories have many elements in common with the legends of Greece, and most scholars understand there to be a direct connection between them. Gilgamesh overcame a great bull, as did Heracles, and he destroyed a mysterious monster called Humbaba. Heracles began his heroic career as an animal-slayer, then proceeded further afield to take on new adversaries. As Gilgamesh crossed faraway waters to consult with Utnapishtim, the man who never died, so did Heracles descend to the underworld and bring back its guardian, the demonic dog Cerberus. As divine myth passed from East to West, so did basic patterns of legend.

Gilgamesh seems to have been a real king of the Sumerian city of Uruk (ū-ruk; biblical "Erech," modern Warka), remembered for building the city walls, and his example is strong evidence that legendary characters did live at one time. According to surviving king lists inscribed on clay, he lived for 126 years sometime about 2600 BC, the grandson of a certain Lugalbanda. Fragments telling of his life and deeds survive recorded in cuneiform script in Sumerian, Akkadian, and Hittite languages. On twelve tablets from the library of Assurbanipal in Nineveh (seventh century BC) survives something close to a connected tale, recording a version of the story that may go back a thousand years earlier. The story had many separate episodes, which in the tablets from Nineveh have been pieced together to form a whole.

### Gilgamesh and Enkidu

The poem begins with a summary of Gilgamesh's career:

> The man who saw everything to the ends of the earth,
> who experienced everything, considered all!
> He saw what was hidden, he disclosed the undisclosed.
> He brought back a story of times before the flood.
> He went on a long journey. He was wearied; he rested.
> Everything he did he engraved on a monument made of stone.

Many have noticed how the first lines of the Greek *Odyssey* seem to echo this very opening of Gilgamesh, a clue to continuity from East to West in the mythical narrative tradition:

> Sing to me, O Muse, of the wily man,
> who wandered far after he had sacked the holy city of Troy.
> Many were the men whose cities he saw and he learned their mind
> and many the hurts he felt in his heart upon the sea,
> trying to win his own life and the return of his comrades.
>
> HOMER, *Odyssey* 1–5, trans. A. T. Murray, modified

Described as two-thirds divine and one-third mortal (just how this is possible is not clear), Gilgamesh was destined to die. He became king of Uruk, but was proud and mighty and abused his royal power. All who challenged him he overcame, and he slept with every virgin of the city before her wedding night.

At last the people of Uruk could bear no more and begged the gods for relief. Aruru, mother of the gods, pinched off a piece of clay and fashioned a rival to Gilgamesh, someone who could temper his spirit. Her creation was Enkidu (**en**-ki-doo), a primitive man who wore his locks long like a woman. His body was matted with hair, and he lived in the wild, ran with gazelles, ate grass, and drank at the water holes.

One day a trapper saw Enkidu. Terrified, the trapper reported to the city that there was a wild man on the steppe destroying his traps and releasing his game. Meanwhile, Gilgamesh had learned in a dream about the coming of one who would be his best friend.

> Gilgamesh says to him, the trapper:
> "Go, my trapper, and take a whore with you.
> When he [Enkidu] comes to water the beasts at the water hole,
> she will pull off her clothing and lay bare her ripeness.
> When he sees her, he will approach her.
> Then will his beasts, raised on the plains, reject him!"

For two days the trapper and the whore waited beside the water hole. On the third day Enkidu came. The whore bared her nakedness. For six days and seven nights Enkidu made love to her until, satisfied at last, he arose and went back to the wild, sadly changed.

> Enkidu was lessened, he could not run so fast,
> Yet he had acquired discernment, was wiser.
> He returned, sat at the feet of the whore.

The whore explained to Enkidu that now he was like a god and that he should follow her. From the shepherds he learned how to eat bread, drink wine, and wear clothes. A report came from the city that on that night Gilgamesh would deflower a virgin about to be married. Enkidu leaped up and declared that he would challenge the tyrant.

Enkidu entered the city. Crowds gathered around him, admired his strength, and compared him with Gilgamesh. As Gilgamesh came down the alley, Enkidu threw up a challenge. The two mighty men wrestled. Walls shook, doors broke. At last Enkidu was thrown to the ground. The rivals got up and, filled with mutual admiration, embraced one another warmly and began a lifelong friendship.

## Gilgamesh and Humbaba

Gilgamesh proposed that he and Enkidu go together to the Land of the Living, also called the Land of the Cedars, ruled over by the sun god Shamash (**sha**-mash). Enkidu hesitated; he had already been there and feared Humbaba, the guardian of the forest. Gilgamesh brushed aside his friend's fears: Even if they perished, their names would live on. The heroes made careful preparations. They took with them mighty swords, axes, and bows. After crossing seven mountains, they came to the edge of the cedar forest, which extended one thousand miles in every direction.

> They stood, they admired the forest,
> stared and stared at the high cedars,
> stared and stared at the entrance to the cedars,
> where Humbaba left tracks as he paced on his rounds.
> The paths were worn, the road was good,
> they admired the Cedar Mountain, dwelling of gods.
> The cedars gleamed on the side of the mountain.
> Their shade was delicious, bringing happiness.
> The undergrowth was thick, blanketing the forest.

But when Enkidu touched the gate of the forest, his hand was at once paralyzed. Gilgamesh helped him to overcome his fear. They entered the forest and traveled far. At night they had ominous dreams, for Humbaba knew of their presence.

> Then Gilgamesh took up his ax and chopped at the forest.
> When Humbaba heard the noise,
> he was angered. "Who has come,
> who has injured the trees
> which grow in my mountains?
> Who has felled the cedar?"

The sun god Shamash urged Gilgamesh to attack Humbaba, but suddenly Gilgamesh was overcome with sleep and fell down on the ground as if dead. Enkidu could not stir him. Then Gilgamesh came to himself, stood up, and put on his armor. Overcome, with tears in his eyes, Humbaba begged for his life, even taking Gilgamesh by the hand like a friend. Gilgamesh struck Humbaba on the neck with his sword. Enkidu struck him too, and down fell Humbaba, dead. They offered his head to Enlil, the storm-god, but Enlil was furious that they had killed the guardian of the forest.

## Gilgamesh and Ishtar

When they arrived back in Uruk, Gilgamesh put away his dirty clothes and combed out his long hair. Ishtar, the sex-goddess, saw how handsome he was and promised that, if he would only pour his seed into her, she would give him rich rewards. Gilgamesh sneered at the great goddess and abused her as follows, one of the best known passages in Mesopotamian literature:

> "You are a charcoal grill which goes out in the cold!
> You are a back door that lets in the squall and the storm,
> a fortress which smashes down the brave,
> pitch which fouls its bearers,
> a siege engine that wrecks the enemy's land,
> a shoe that pinches its owner's foot!
> Which lover did you love forever?
> Which of your shepherds pleases you for all time?
> Listen, I will name your lovers:
> To Tammuz, lover of your youth,
> you have given moaning year in, year out.
> You loved the spotted shepherd-bird,
> then struck him, breaking his wing.
> Now he sits in the woods crying "Oh—my wing!"
> You loved a lion, the perfection of power;
> twice seven pits you dug for him.
> Then you loved a stallion, a charger in war;
> what is his lot? the whip, the spur, and the lash."

Gilgamesh gave other examples of those who had suffered after yielding to the goddess of love, including her father's own gardener: When he brought her baskets of dates, she turned him into a frog!

Ishtar burst into a fury and stormed off to her father, Anu, king of heaven. She demanded that Anu send down the Bull of Heaven to destroy Gilgamesh. If Anu refused, she would crack open the gates of the under-world and release the legions of the dead. Anu agreed, and Ishtar entered Uruk, leading the Bull of Heaven. The bull snorted, a chasm opened, and a hundred young men of Uruk fell in, then two hundred, then three hundred. The bull snorted again and a second chasm opened; in fell a hundred young men, then two hundred, then three hundred.

When the bull snorted a third time a chasm opened,
and Enkidu fell in,
but leaped out and seized the Bull of Heaven by the horns.
The Bull of Heaven shook spittle into his face
and with its fat tail threw dung all around.

Enkidu, blinded with dung, called out to Gilgamesh, who plunged his sword into the monster's neck. The heroes cut out its heart for the sun god Shamash. Ishtar, enraged, appeared on the towers of the city. Enkidu cut off the bull's genitals and threw them in her face. If he had the chance, he would lash the bull's guts to her body!

The two friends held a great celebration, but the gods were deeply offended by Enkidu's behavior. One of the pair would have to die. Enkidu had terrible dreams. He knew that he would die. He dreamed that he had gone down

to the house which is never left, once entered,
on the trail of no return,
to the house where the dwellers live in darkness,
where dust and clay is food.
They are clothed like birds, have wings for garments,
and never see the light, dwelling in darkness.

Enkidu fell sick and for twelve days lay in bed. Then he died. Gilgamesh mourned, hovering over the body, waiting for it to revive. On the seventh day a maggot crawled from Enkidu's nose. Gilgamesh realized that, for Enkidu, the end had come.

## The Quest for Eternal Life

Gilgamesh roamed the open country, terrified of the death that would one day be his lot as well. He decided to search for Utnapishtim (ut-na-**pish**-tim; "he saw life" = Hebrew Noah, probably "reposed," "at rest"). Utnapishtim and his wife were the only mortals to have survived the flood, for the gods had transported them across the sea to a place where they enjoyed everlasting life. Gilgamesh set out to question Utnapishtim about the living and the dead.

On his long journey Gilgamesh (like Heracles) killed ferocious lions lurking in the passes, then came to the high Mountains of Mashu, where the sun rises. At the gate of the mountain, Scorpion Men, whose glance was death, stood guard. Somehow (the tablet is broken here) he persuaded them to let him pass. He entered a tunnel of darkness, where no one could see ahead or behind. For twelve leagues of darkness Gilgamesh traveled on the path of the sun. At last he saw light and emerged into the garden of the gods at the edge of the sea (perhaps the Phoenician coast of the Mediterranean). Gorgeous plants made of precious stones grew there.

In the garden lived Siduri (si-**doo**-rē), the divine beer maid. Siduri advised Gilgamesh to give up his search, to accept mortality, to eat good food and drink strong liquor, to wear fine clothes and love his family; no one, except Shamash, had ever crossed the lethal waters of the sea. But she could not persuade him and Gilgamesh set off, punting across the waters of death. On the other side, Utnapishtim came up, complained about Gilgamesh's uncouth appearance, then delivered a speech about death:

> No one sees Death,
> No one sees the face of Death,
> No one hears the voice of Death.
> Brutal Death just cuts you down.
> We may build a house, we may build a nest:
> our brothers divide it when we die.
> There may be hostility in the land,
> but then the river rises in flood.°
> Dragonflies drift upon the water,
> they turn their gaze upon the sun.
> From the beginning there has been no permanence.
> The sleeping and the dead are the same,
> There is no picture of Death.

*rises in flood:* That is, death settles all disputes.

How did Utnapishtim escape the lot of other mortals? Utnapishtim answered this question by relating the story of the flood. He and his wife had escaped death because of the storm-god Enlil, but who would intercede for Gilgamesh?

To prove Gilgamesh's innate mortality, Utnapishtim suggested a trial. Let Gilgamesh stay awake for six days and seven nights, the length of time of the flood. If he could not conquer Sleep, the brother of death, how could he conquer Death himself? Gilgamesh thought the trial easy, but promptly fell asleep and awoke seven nights later. Although he denied that he had slept, Utnapishtim pointed to seven loaves in progressive stages of decay that his wife had baked and placed, one each day, at the hero's side.

There was still a chance that Gilgamesh might escape at least the ravages of old age. Utnapishtim told him of a prickly herb that grew deep in the sea. Its flower, which looked like a rose, would restore youth to an old man. Gilgamesh tied stones to his feet and dropped down deep into the water, found the plant, and plucked it, although its thorns tore his hands. He cut the ropes that held the stones, bobbed to the surface, and came ashore. Gilgamesh set out for home. On the way he stopped to bathe in a cool well. A serpent that lived in the well emerged and ate the plant. That is why serpents can renew their youth.

Gilgamesh realized that immortality could never be his. He sat down and wept. He returned to Uruk and admired its great city walls, his true achievement. He engraved his tale on a stone, grew old, and died. He was given a splendid burial.

## THE WAY OF THE HERO

The Gilgamesh epic, which seems to stand behind stories about Heracles, is the longest and most ambitious literary epic recorded in the complex Mesopotamian cuneiform writing. A central theme is the contrast and hostility between the natural world and the cultural world of humans. Enkidu is the "natural man"—his hair is long and he eats grass with the beasts of the field. After intercourse with a woman, he becomes "wise" and is separated from the natural world, the lot of all humankind. Similarly, Adam and Eve, after eating from the Tree of Knowledge, see that they are naked (discover their sexuality) and must leave the Garden of Eden (the natural world). When Enkidu is dying, he bitterly blames the world of culture for his undoing. He blames the trapper who found him and the whore who tamed him. Sympathizing with Enkidu's resentment, Gilgamesh puts on animal skins and wanders through the wild on a quest to the ends of the earth. When the quest fails, he returns from nature to the world of culture, dons clean clothes, and rejoices in the city walls, the symbolic divide between the human and natural worlds.

Although gods occasionally die, their ordinary lot is to live forever. Only a mortal like Gilgamesh can suffer anguish from speculating on the meaning of action and of life, and on his hopeless future in a stale, dank afterlife where clay is food and good people and bad, kings and ordinary mortals, are treated alike. This very torment is an essential part of his nature as a hero and explains our interest in him: We too live between nature and culture, and we too are destined to die.

The deep concerns and speculations that underlay this story developed specifically in Mesopotamia, a dangerous land with mysterious beginnings. Egyptians did not fear death, and so did not seek a way to escape it; they had already found that way. The hostility toward the female stands out strongly in this story: Heirs of this attitude will appear in the biblical story of Adam and Eve, in Hesiod's story of the first woman Pandora, who released evils into the world, and in the story of Heracles' destruction at the hands of his wife. Ishtar embodies the irresistible force of sexual attraction and death, wrapped into one. Here for the first time appears the story of the journey in search of truth; Heracles too was a great traveler, slaying monsters and journeying to the land of the dead. The immensely influential Greek *Odyssey,* another version of the wandering hero, has given the West its self-image as a restless inquiring being, spinning restlessly across the prairies, even into space, but the story is not Western in origin.

We know nothing about the historical Gilgamesh or his reign, but we can imagine that the real king Gilgamesh might have been a great ruler who accomplished much in his lifetime. It is easy to believe that he or his followers would have been eager to see his reputation enhanced and his memory preserved for posterity (just as the story itself tells of Gilgamesh's longing to be remembered in reputation and in words graven on stone). The Mesopotamian legend of Gilgamesh, like many ancient Greek legends including those of Heracles, probably began in such a wish to preserve a memory of the words and deeds of a real man who accomplished great things during his lifetime.

In the fluidity of oral tradition, however, such stories about heroes easily mix with other elements having no real connection to any particular historical figure. The hero's name is preserved, but the stories told about him come to incorporate patterns drawn from other stories, many of them motifs known to us from folklore (see Chapter 10):

- The hero's birth is miraculous or unusual, but of his childhood we know little (Gilgamesh was partly divine, Heracles was the son of Zeus).

- The hero has great strength and is a menace to his compatriots as well as to others (Gilgamesh abused the people of Uruk, Heracles murdered his music teacher and slept with the fifty daughters of a certain King Thespius).

- The hero's truest companion is another male (Gilgamesh's friend Enkidu is like Heracles' nephew Iolaüs, who accompanies him on some adventures).

- The hero falls under an enemy's power and is compelled to perform impossible labors (Gilgamesh is forced to fight the Bull of Heaven, Heracles obeys the evil Eurystheus in the performance of his labors).

- The hero breaks a taboo, and a terrible price is demanded (Enlil was angry that Gilgamesh and Enkidu killed Humbaba, lord of the forest; Heracles killed his wife and children and so was sold into slavery as a sexual toy to Queen Omphalê).

- The hero faces the temptations of an irresistible but dangerous woman (Gilgamesh resists this temptation and insults Ishtar; Heracles, by contrast, always gives in to woman's temptation: The difference tells us something about the Greeks).

- The hero is responsible for his best friend's death (Enkidu dies after he and Gilgamesh kill the Bull of Heaven; the motif is absent from the Heracles cycle, but prominent in the story of Achilles and Patroclus).

- The hero goes on a long journey to discover the secret of eternal life (the deathless Utnapishtim lives beyond the waters that separate this world from the next; Heracles goes to the underworld, and from the edge of the world secures apples from the Tree of Life).

- The hero returns home and accepts his limitations (Gilgamesh returns to rule Uruk; Heracles, by contrast, continues his aggression to the end, perhaps reflecting unsettled conditions in the Greek world when myths were being formulated there).

- The hero is rewarded with something of great value (at his death Gilgamesh receives full honors; Athena leads Heracles into heaven where he lives forever, married to Youth).

Similar elements can easily be found in the stories of such other heroes as Odysseus, Perseus, Bellerophon. We might think of these elements as plot-devices, contributing to a good story, filling it with tension, struggle, danger, ambition, defeat, and reward. They appeal at deeper levels to every human's struggle with existence and hopes for survival. Still we must beware of thinking that a single pattern can explain the career of every "hero." Menelaüs, Agamemnon, Hector, Priam, and Paris, important in Homer's *Iliad,* are heroes, but their careers do not follow this pattern at all. *Hero,* we must remember, is a word meaning a famous man of olden times, and famous men could be very different.

## FURTHER READING

Brommer, F., *Heracles: The Twelve Labors of the Hero in Ancient Art and Literature,* trans. and enlarged by S. J. Schwarz (New Rochelle, NY, 1986). The best succinct review of Heracles in literature and art.

Conacher, D. J., *Euripides' Alcestis* (London, 1988). Introduction is good.

Dale, A. M., ed., *Euripides: Alcestis* (Oxford, 1954). The introduction to the Greek text has a good analysis of the myth and how Euripides used it.

Dalley, S., *Myths from Mesopotamia: Creation, the Flood, Gilgamesh, and Others* (Oxford, 1989). The most recent translations, with commentary, of the Mesopotamian myths of Atrahasis, Gilgamesh, the descent of Ishtar, and other important myths.

Galinsky, K., *The Heracles Theme* (New York, 1972). Surveys the development of the figure of Heracles from ancient through modern times.

George, A., *The Babylonian Gilgamesh Epic* (Oxford, 1992). New research on the Gilgamesh epic, including previously unpublished fragments.

Heidel, A., *The Gilgamesh Epic and Old Testament Parallels* (Chicago, 1963). Scientific study of great value.

Sandars, N. K., *The Epic of Gilgamesh* (Baltimore, MD, 1972). Readable, inexpensive compilation, with a good introduction, of the many fragments (written in several languages) that make up the epic.

Slater, P. E., *The Glory of Hera: Greek Mythology and the Greek Family* (Boston, 1968). A psychoanalytic interpretation of Heracles' career and other Greek myths.

# CHAPTER 9

# MYTH AND HISTORY: CRETE AND THE LEGEND OF THE TROJAN WAR

HOMER'S *ILIAD* TELLS the story of a great campaign that the Greeks waged against a stronghold in northwestern Asia Minor sometime in the long-ago past. The Greeks never doubted that this war took place, but in modern times the question "Was there a Trojan War?" touches on complex questions about historical truth that the Greeks themselves defined. The Greeks' greatest intellectual achievement, together with their discovery of philosophy, was the discovery of *history*. Philosophy is the reasoned search for truth in the world, most familiar to us as modern science, until recently called natural philosophy. Herodotus (c. 484–420 BC) invented history, the reasoned search for truth about the past based on fact, and Thucydides, who lived a generation later, refined his methods to create something close to modern theories of historical truth. To explore the question "Was there a Trojan War?"—and by extension every question about the historicity of myth—we must gain some understanding of the achievements of these two seminal thinkers.

## HERODOTUS, FATHER OF HISTORY

Herodotus lived one generation after Pindar. The origin of our word *history* is *historia*, the third word in Herodotus' very long book about the Persian wars against Greece in the early fifth century BC. In Greek the word means "inquiry," that is, into the causes of conflict between East and West.

Herodotus must have read out loud his story about the Persian wars, reading from a papyrus manuscript in some context we can only imagine. By Herodotus' time *aoidoi* like Homer and Hesiod were mostly gone. Panyassis of Halicarnassus, a relative of Herodotus to whom epic songs about Heracles were attributed, seems to be the last known *aoidos*. Herodotus did not memorize a written text, a transcript of a poem orally composed and taken down by dictation, as did the rhapsodes, but he himself had created the written text from which he read aloud. Already, experiment in Ionia had fashioned the first Greek prose, a practice on which Herodotus seems to depend, and in any event he had no need for a hexametric rhythm. Yet to a fifth-century Athenian, Herodotus would have seemed similar to a rhapsode when he declaimed aloud the highly involved tale about a war he had not himself seen, but only heard.

His sources were uneven and shallow, not reaching back much more than three generations, into the sixth century BC; in America today families preserve information about grandfathers and sometimes great grandfathers, but rarely anything beyond. He seems to have traveled widely and talked to men actually involved in the war against Persia, as if today we were to write a history of the Second World War from men, now old, who had vivid memories of it. Herodotus' sources were mostly oral, then, but in no sense the same as Homer's "oral tradition," wherein one generation of singers replaced another in succession, each passing on a timelessly ancient tale of "the man who returned home after a long journey" or "the war of the gods in heaven."

Herodotus' purpose, like Hesiod's and Pindar's, was nonetheless to celebrate *alêtheia,* "that which should not be forgotten." Here is how his book opens:

> This is the display of the inquiry [*historia*] of Herodotus of Halicarnassus, so that things done by humans be not forgotten in time, and that great and marvelous deeds, some displayed by Greeks, some by non-Greeks, not lose their glory, including among other things the cause of their waging war on each other.
>
> HERODOTUS 1.1.1, trans. by A. D. Godley, modified

The essential difference between Herodotus and what preceded is that, in glorifying the deeds of his fathers, Herodotus sought to discover the *causes* of the Persian war, along with its *meaning*. History, like science, is a search for causes, but causes can be evaluated only in relation to whether they are true, based on fact. As we have seen, the truth or falsity of traditional tales is important already in Hesiod, but now in the fifth century BC, the distinction will generate *history* out of *myth*. Herodotus identifies the ultimate origin of the war between East and West in stories about Io, Jason, and the Trojan War, what we call *myths*. First, however, Herodotus must launder the myth and discard *pseudea,* "false elements," so that only *alêtheia,* "that which is not for-gotten," "truth," remains.

According to the myth, Zeus fell in love with Io, a young woman from Argos, priestess of Hera and daughter of the river-god Inachus. Zeus and Io made love in a cloud of mist that Zeus the rain-god lowered around them. Hera knew, nonetheless, and to save Io from Hera's anger, Zeus turned Io into a cow. Hera then sent a gadfly that tormented the poor animal, who wandered across the Hellespont to Asia, Palestine, and finally to Egypt, where Io regained her human form.

Herodotus, without apology, presents a very different version, and gives to the historical Phoenicians—Semitic sailors from the coast of the Levant—Zeus' role as sexual predator:

> Among other places to which the Phoenicians carried Egyptian and As-syrian merchandise, they came to Argos, which was at that time preemi-nent in every way among the people of what is now called Hellas. The Phoenicians came to Argos, and set out their cargo. On the fifth or sixth day after their arrival, when their goods were almost all sold, many women came to the shore and among them especially the daughter of the king, whose name was Io (according to Persians and Greeks alike), the daughter of Inachus.° As these stood about the stern of the ship bar-gaining for the goods they liked, the Phoenicians incited one another to set upon them. Most of the women escaped: Io and others were seized and thrown into the ship, which then sailed away for Egypt. In this way, the Persians say (not the Greeks), Io came to Egypt, and this, according to them, was the first wrong that was done.°
>
> HERODOTUS 1.1.1–4, trans. by A. D. Godley, modified

*Inachus:* in the myth, a river god.     *that was done:* that is, between East and West.

The myth has become fiction ("something shaped") in the modern sense, presented in the guise of history (= a true story about the past). Herodotus has preserved the mythical fact that Io traveled from Greece to Asia, but explains it as an instance of woman-theft, surely a common practice in the real world. He has thrown out the window all interference by gods, when in the myth the story was about the gods' behavior. He has made a rig-orous separation between the human realm and the divine, if he admits the existence of the divine at all. Precisely in his idiosyncratic preference for rea-sonable explanations that do not invoke divine will, he betrays his essentially Greek character: No Egyptian, Hebrew, or Assyrian could have excluded di-vine will from an explanation of human events. Herodotus has made up out of whole cloth his story about Io's abduction (with a little help from similar realistic descriptions in Homer's *Odyssey*), and we might fairly compare his invention with Pindar's explanation of the reason for Pelops' disappearance (Chapter 1). Pindar's story is a kind of "new myth," because gods are prominent, while Herodotus' account of Io is a kind of "fake history," because although untrue, it might have been true.

Next, Herodotus turns to two other myths. According to the myth, Zeus loved Europa, daughter of Cadmus, a Phoenician king. He appeared to her in the form of a beautiful bull as she played on the seashore with her companions. Seduced by the bull's gentleness, she climbed on its back. The bull plunged into the sea and swam across the sea to Crete, where Zeus possessed her. Europa gave birth to Minos, king of the Cretans. Another myth told of the expedition of Jason, prince of Iolcus, to Colchis at the ends of the Black Sea to obtain the Golden Fleece, guarded by a dragon that never slept. Only with the help of the unscrupulous witch Medea, daughter of the Colchian king, did Jason and Medea succeed in returning to Greece. But in these complex traditional tales Herodotus finds only further examples of woman-theft. He attributes his account to "the Persians," but it is hardly likely any Persian was so well-versed in Greek myth. These are Herodotus' own explanations:

> Next, some Greeks ... landed at Tyre in Phoenicia and carried off the king's daughter Europa. These Greeks must, I suppose, have been Cretans. So far, then, the account between them was balanced. But after this (the Persians say), it was the Greeks who were guilty of the second wrong. They sailed in a long ship to Aea, a city of the Colchians, and to the river Phasis: and when they had done the business for which they came, they carried off the king's daughter Medea. When the Colchian king sent a herald to demand reparation for the robbery and restitution of his daughter, the Greeks replied that, as they had been refused reparation for the abduction of the Argive Io, they would not make any to the Colchians.
>
> HERODOTUS 1.2.1–3, trans. by A. D. Godley, modified

As if the Greeks and the Men of the East were single peoples, each keeping track of which side had snatched the most women!

Herodotus goes on to offer a new explanation for the origin of the Trojan War to replace the story known to Homer and the whole world: that Paris of Troy, also called Alexander, received Helen as the reward for choosing Aphrodite over Hera and Athena in a beauty contest (= the Judgment of Paris). Here is Herodotus' revised account:

> Then (they say), in the second generation after this, Alexander [= Paris], son of Priam, who had heard this tale, decided to get himself a wife from Hellas by capture; for he was confident that he would not suffer punishment. So he carried off Helen. The Greeks first resolved to send messengers demanding that Helen be restored and atonement made for the seizure; but when this proposal was made, the Trojans pleaded the seizure of Medea, and reminded the Greeks that they asked reparation from others, yet made none themselves, nor gave up the booty when asked.

> So far it was a matter of mere seizure on both sides. But after this (the Persians say), the Greeks were very much to blame; for they invaded Asia before the Persians attacked Europe. "We think," they say, "that it is unjust to carry women off. But to be anxious to avenge rape is foolish: wise men take no notice of such things. For plainly the women would never have been carried away, had they not wanted it themselves! We of Asia did not lower ourselves to notice the seizure of our women; but the Greeks, for the sake of a Spartan woman, recruited a great fleet, came to Asia, and destroyed the power of Priam. Ever since then we have regarded Greeks as our enemies."
>
> HERODOTUS 1.3.1–1.4.3, trans. by A. D. Godley, modified

Again, it is not likely that the Persians had any account whatever of Greek predations against Eastern women, or that Herodotus could have known about them if they did. His story is a kind of joke, a Greek invention making fun of Greek tradition, allowing Herodotus to make a snide remark about the sexual motives of women, pleasing to his all-male audience.

To generalize, scientific accounts are either *reductive* or *structuralist*. We will examine structuralism in Chapter 14 (also Chapter 10, on the *Odyssey*, is an example of structuralist interpretation). In reductionism, one thing is said *really* to be something else, by far the predominant mode of interpretation. Here Herodotus has reduced what we would call myths to "history" by removing gods and nonhuman powers, as if such beings did not exist or were not effective. Instead, he invokes the human motivations of lust and resentment. Such is Greek rationalism, as if it were irrational to think that gods and nonhuman powers are effective in human affairs (as maintained by all religions). *History* begins, then, in the reduction of *myth*.

Herodotus in general avoids the word *muthos* to designate the stories he tells, and prefers instead *logos,* an "accounting" as in finance, but Herodotus is also the first to use *muthos* to mean "an implausible story." The story is implausible, in Herodotus' view, because it conflicts with reason's demand that contradictory facts cannot both be true at the same time:

> And the Greeks say many other ill-considered things, too; among them, there is a silly *muthos* which they tell about Heracles, that when he came to Egypt the Egyptians crowned him and led him out in a procession to sacrifice him to Zeus. And for a while (they say) he followed quietly, but when they started in on him at the altar, he resisted and killed them all. Now it seems to me that by this talk the Greeks show themselves altogether ignorant of the character and customs of the Egyptians; for how should they sacrifice men when they are forbidden to sacrifice even beasts, except swine and bulls and bull-calves, if they are unblemished, and geese? And furthermore, as Heracles was alone, and still only a man, as they say, how is it natural that he should kill many thousands?
>
> HERODOTUS 2.45.1–3, trans. by A. D. Godley, modified

Here his usage of *muthos*, although casual, is identical to our own use of the word *myth*.

## MYTH AND HISTORY IN THUCYDIDES

Thucydides (thu-**sid**-i-dēz), of Athens (c. 460–401 BC) brilliantly refined Herodotus' preference for reason over tradition. Thucydides must have heard readings from Herodotus' *Inquiry* while he was a young man, for Herodotus seems to have resided in Athens, a small town by modern standards, during the mid-fifth century BC. We do not know how the writings of Thucydides and Herodotus were circulated in Athens. Thucydides was a general in the great war between the Athenian and Spartan alliances, which broke out in 431 BC and continued off and on until 404 BC, when Athens was defeated disastrously. He was a general in Athens early in the war, but was not present in Athens for the duration of the war, because he was exiled as punishment for his role in a military action that went badly.

Herodotus wrote about events in which his father might have participated, but Thucydides wrote of contemporary events, in which he himself participated. Nonetheless, Thucydides wished to place contemporary events within the context of the past. Herodotus assumed as a matter of course that there was a Trojan War and saw in it the Persians' justification, many hundreds of years later, for the invasion of Greece. Thucydides also never questioned whether there was a Trojan War, but believed that the poets had not told the truth about it.

An old story told how Tyndareus, father of Helen, feared to marry his daughter, the most beautiful woman in the world, lest the angry unsuccessful suitors harm the groom, whoever he should be. Therefore Tyndareus compelled the suitors of Helen to swear that they would band together and avenge any harm done to the successful suitor—little did he foresee what the gods held in store. Tyndareus had feared the anger of an unsuccessful suitor, but when the foreigner Paris, prince of Troy, stole Helen from Menelaüs, to whom Tyndareus awarded his daughter, Menelaüs and his brother Agamemnon invoked the oath to force the former suitors to gather in an expedition against Troy.

Thucydides rejects this explanation in favor of one based on his experience of power in his own world, but still based on the same story about Pelops that had inspired the moralizing reforms of Pindar:

> What enabled Agamemnon to raise the armament was more, in my opinion, his superiority in strength, than the oath of Tyndareus, which compelled the suitors to follow him. In fact the inhabitants of the Peloponnesus, who have received the most believable tradition, say the following. First of all Pelops, arriving among a needy population from

Asia with vast wealth, acquired such power that, stranger though he was, the country was called after him; and this power fortune saw fit materially to increase in the hands of his descendants. . . To all this Agamemnon succeeded. He had also a navy far stronger than his contemporaries, so that, in my opinion, fear was quite as strong an element as love in the formation of the confederate expedition. The strength of his navy is shown by the fact that his own was the largest contingent, and that of the Arcadians was furnished by him; this at least is what Homer says, if his testimony is considered adequate.

THUCYDIDES 1.9.1–4, trans. R. Crawley, modified

In Thucydides' view, military power, which is an expression of worldly wealth, stands behind military events, not sentimental tales about brides and their suitors; such was his own experience of his own world. The one is history, the other is myth. Thucydides is in an awkward position, however, in trying to establish the truth of his position by citing Homer while at the same time he attempts to disprove Homer's description of events. He is trying to extract history from myth by accepting the general version of events—Pelops did settle in Greece, there really was a Trojan War, Agamemnon did lead the expedition—but he rejects the old explanation for the causes of these events. Humans cause human events in Thucydides' view and in our own (we could be wrong). Although it is not implausible that in the Bronze Age wars really were fought over women, such was unthinkable in Thucydides' own modern world of power politics. Hence, in his view, it was unthinkable in earlier times. Thucydides "historicized" myth, as many do today.

As Thucydides sees it, the fact, reported by myth, that Troy fell after ten years, must be explained according to contemporary experience with the realities of maintaining an army in the field, which Homer never discusses. The long unsuccessful campaign, therefore

. . . was due not so much to scarcity of men as of money. Difficulty of subsistence made the invaders reduce the numbers of the army to a point at which it might live on the country during the prosecution of the war. Even after the victory they obtained on their arrival—and a victory there must have been [although Homer never mentions it], or the fortifications of the naval camp could never have been built [which Homer describes]—there is no indication of their whole force having been employed; on the contrary, they seem to have turned to cultivation of the Chersonese [= the Gallipoli peninsula, opposite Troy] and to piracy from want of supplies. This was what really enabled the Trojans to keep the field for ten years against them, the dispersion of the enemy making them always a match for the detachment left behind. If they had brought plenty of supplies with them, and had persevered in the war without scattering for piracy and agriculture, they would have easily defeated the Trojans in the field, for they could hold their own against them with the division on service. In short, if they had stuck to the siege, the capture of Troy would have cost them less time and less trouble. But as want of money proved the weakness of earlier expeditions, so from the same cause even this one too, although more famous than its predecessors, must have been inferior to what people say about it and less than the current opinion about it formed under the tuition of the poets.

THUCYDIDES 1.11.1, trans. R. Crawley, modified

The war is a fact, then, but Homer's description of its conduct is a myth. The poets—Thucydides means principally Homer—have falsified the past in their efforts, through exaggeration, to tell a good story.

Thucydides appears explicitly to criticize Herodotus, victim to the same fault as Homer, in the following passage. Although Herodotus and other "*logos*-writers" (= *logographoi*) admired the importance of reason in reconstructing the truth about the past, they allowed a "myth-like quality," which always adheres to old stories, to distort the truth. Hence, Thucydides concludes, the Trojan War cannot have been as big an undertaking as Homer implies, and in any event was inferior in scale and scope to the present war between the Athenians and the Spartans, to which Thucydides will devote the rest of his long book:

On the whole, however, the conclusions I have drawn from the proofs cited may, I think, safely be relied on. Certainly my conclusions will not be disturbed either by the songs of a poet who fancies things up to make them seem greater than they are, or by whatever the *logos*-writers° say who are more interested in telling a good story than keeping to *alêthes* ["truth"]. For their subjects are quite out of the reach of evidence and their *muthôdes* [= "myth-like quality"] has made them untrustworthy. Instead we have drawn adequate conclusions about what happened long ago on the basis of the clearest data. As for the present war° in spite of the fact that people always think that the biggest war is that one they are engaged in at any moment, but when it is over to think that ancient wars were greater, yet when you look at the facts you will realize that this war was in fact much greater than any which preceded it.

THUCYDIDES 1.21.1–2, trans. R. Crawley, modified

logos-*writers:* like Herodotus.      *present war:* between the Athenians and the Spartans.

Many modern historians agree with Thucydides about the historical basis for stories about the Trojan War (as do I, with qualifications). Myth is not history, but there must be some history in myth, if we could only find it. Thucydides' approach is reductionist in that it too attempts to reach the truth in myth by stripping away such fantastic elements as gods and their doings and to force what remains into patterns of social behavior familiar from contemporary life.

## HEINRICH SCHLIEMANN AND TROY

The German Heinrich Schliemann (1822–1890), who single-handedly founded Bronze Age archaeology, was certain that the story of the Trojan War was "true," in spite of scholars' views, who thought it was "only a myth." He devoted his life to proving his views. Working at his own expense, he rediscovered the Greek Bronze Age. He tells his own story (although in mythical form!) in his autobiography and in three great books, *Ilios, Mycenae,* and *Tiryns.*

Born in poverty and without formal schooling after age fourteen, Schliemann made a fortune while young by cornering the trade in indigo dye to Russia. During the Gold Rush, he was in Sacramento, California, where he made enormous sums trading in gold and in 1850 became an American citizen by being in California when it became a state. He controlled the Russian market for gunpowder in the Crimean War (1854–1856) and dealt in contraband cotton during the American Civil War (1861–1865). Schliemann claimed he could learn any language in six weeks, and his surviving correspondence confirms his facility in twelve. Tired of business, enormously wealthy, and determined to satisfy his childhood curiosity about the Homeric poems, which he claimed to know by heart, he began in 1871 to dig a low hill called Hissarlik (Turkish for "place of the fort") behind the plain that leads up from the Hellespont. Persuaded by an Englishman who had long lived nearby that this mound was Homer's Troy, Schliemann attacked it with a crew of 160 men, digging an enormous (and destructive) trench to find the lowest levels.

Nothing so complex had ever been excavated. Schliemann was baffled by the intricacy of the forty-six separate strata, which fell into ten major layers. He identified the second layer from the bottom as the Troy of Homer (we now think "Homer's Troy" is more likely to have been the sixth or seventh layer). Although later excavations conducted by German archaeologist Wilhelm Dörpfeld, followed by American archaeologist Carl Blegen, were to uncover walls from the sixth layer worthy of Homer's poetic description, Schliemann could produce a site only 100 yards across, whose small size hardly fitted Homer's description of a city "wide-wayed," heavily populated, and rich.

Contemporaries first ridiculed Schliemann and dismissed him as a charlatan. But in the second layer (which we now know to belong to the Early Bronze Age, c. 2600 BC) he discovered a fabulous hoard, the "Treasure of Priam": copper cauldrons; cups in gold, silver, electrum (a natural alloy of gold and silver), and bronze; copper lanceheads; several thousand small gold rings; and wonderful jewels, including a diadem of over 16,000 pieces of gold threaded on wire. Schliemann wrote, "This treasure of the supposedly mythical King Priam, of the mythical heroic age, which I discovered at a great depth in the ruins of the supposedly mythical Troy, is at all events an event which stands alone in archaeology."

The very early date of the second layer was not then realized, and to many scholars the find justified Schliemann's work. In 1876 he turned to Mycenae, the reputed home of Agamemnon, whose Lion Gate and high bee-hive tombs were visible above ground, objects of wonder to earlier travelers. Inside the Lion Gate, Schliemann immediately uncovered a grave circle from the Middle Bronze Age (about 1600 BC). In five rectangular grave shafts lay the remains of nineteen men and women and two infants covered in gold, surrounded with weapons and other objects of exquisite workmanship. The mask on the face of one skeleton was so distinctive that Schliemann was certain he had found the body of Agamemnon himself. A famous (but false) story reports that, on seeing the mask, he sent a telegram to the king of Greece, proclaiming, "I have gazed upon the face of Agamemnon!" In fact, the grave dates to about 1600 BC, four hundred years too early for Agamemnon, according to mythical chronology. Still, Schliemann had made one of the most sensational archaeological discoveries of all time. The National Archaeological Museum in Athens today has a whole room displaying the objects from these tombs.

Schliemann went on to dig at Orchomenus in Boeotia, home of the mythical Ino, nurse of Dionysus, and Athamas, her ill-fated husband, and "strong-girt Tiryns," as Homer described it, home of Heracles near Mycenae, and at Troy again. Hundreds more Mycenaean sites, as they are now called, have since been found, and excavations at Cnossus and elsewhere in Crete have revealed the power and importance of the Bronze Age civilization there. We have learned to read the tablets found at Cnossus and Pylos, written in the script called Linear B, which have helped form a remarkable picture of Bronze Age Greece.

Schliemann's attempt to connect myth to history caught the attention of the world. He thought that he had found the historical foundations for stories before considered myths. Schliemann claimed to have found the city of Troy, but had he also found the *myth* of the Trojan War? Had there not been a myth of the Trojan War, he would not have looked at the hill of Hissarlik in the first place. Schliemann seemed to prove a historical basis for the Trojan War, but what is meant by the "Trojan War"? Did Paris elope with Helen, and did Menelaüs and Agamemnon lead the Greek expedition? Did Hector kill Patroclus? Did Achilles kill Hector? Is not that what *we* mean by the Trojan War?

Four hundred years had passed between the burning of Troy and the days of Homer, when Greek myth is first recorded, and during that time the narrative of myths was in the hands of poets who constantly altered their material. A queen named Helen *may* have run away with a prince named Paris, and a great war *may* have followed, but on our present evidence we can hardly know this as historical fact. On the one hand we have silent objects in the ground, and on the other we have words preserved in writing that reveal the mind and the soul. It is never easy to see how one fits with the other.

Thucydides' approach, supported by Schliemann's excavations, has remained strong in classical studies to this day, for example, in attempts to retrace the route that Odysseus took in sailing home. The myth told how the Greeks sacked the city through the trick of the Trojan Horse. Carl Blegen, the great modern excavator of Hissarlik in the 1920s, revealed that a great earthquake destroyed the layer called Troy 7a in the twelfth century BC, about the same time given by many ancient commentators for the Trojan War—as if ancient commentators could really know such things about a time from which no records survived, when no recorded chronology existed. The layer of Troy 7a must be "Homer's Troy," Blegen thought, because its destruction by earthquake would explain the myth of the Trojan Horse: In Greek myth (really, religion) Poseidon was god of earthquake *and* of horses. The story, Blegen thought, must have begun in the observation by witnesses that "Poseidon destroyed the city." Blegen's theory is not far from the "disease of language" of Max Müller or the ancient theories of Palaephatus (chapters 2 and 3), according to which a story began through a misunderstanding of language. In any event, the story of the Trojan Horse was the very sort of *myth*-like poetic elaboration that Thucydides decried, whose historical basis in an actual earthquake Blegen thought he had recovered.

## ARCHAEOLOGY AND CRETAN MYTH

A tantalizing parallel example of myth entangled with archaeology is found in stories about the long island of Crete, which lay at the intersection of trading routes that crisscrossed the Mediterranean from all directions: Egypt to the southeast, Cyprus, Phoenicia, and all of Asia Minor to the east, Greece to the north, and Sicily and Italy to the west. Peoples from many different lands had settled in Crete during its long history (and still do), bringing their religions, myths, and legends with them. According to modern archaeological research, the principal population, whom we call Minoans, may have come from Anatolia as early as 7000 BC, with a second wave of immigration about 3100 BC. They used several scripts. The two earliest were pictorial, perhaps modeled on Egyptian hieroglyphic writing. Later these pictographs were schematized into the (still undeciphered) Linear A and then into Linear B, used to keep tallies and inventories of commodities.

Minoan power evidently came to an abrupt end about 1450 BC, when palaces all over the island were destroyed. From this catastrophic period comes archaeological evidence of ritual cannibalism of children and of human sacrifice, no doubt in an attempt to stave off the impending disaster. Some of the native Minoans escaped to mountain retreats or, perhaps, left the island. Many scholars have thought that an enormous volcanic explosion on Thera caused the universal destruction, but recent evidence indicates that the explosion took place about 1630 BC, too early to have caused the catastrophe.

After 1450 BC only Cnossus was rebuilt, to be destroyed again by fire about 1375 BC. Still a third and final destruction came at about 1200 BC. The conflagration that accompanied the second and third destructions accidentally preserved thousands of the clay tablets inscribed in Linear B writing.[1] In 1953 British architect Michael Ventris deciphered the complicated writing and proved, to the surprise of all, that the language behind the writing was Greek. This is how we know that Mycenaeans from the mainland—Greeks—were living in Crete at this time. Mycenaean Greeks seem to have taken over Cnossus after the earlier destruction of c. 1450 BC, which indeed they may have caused. No details are known, nor do we know what caused the second and third destructions of Cnossus in c. 1375 and c. 1200 BC: insurrection, perhaps, or internecine struggles among the Mycenaeans themselves. The biblical Philistines, who settled in five cities on the coast of Palestine south of modern Tel Aviv in about 1200 BC seem to have been Mycenaean Greeks from Crete; Palestine takes its name from this people.[2]

In thinking about Cretan myths, and about Crete, we must remember that "Cretans" before about 1450 BC were Minoans, racially, linguistically, and culturally distinct from "Cretans" after about 1450 BC, whose leaders were Mycenaean Greeks, presumably invaders. Gradually, Greek language and culture replaced the indigenous Minoan culture, and Greek is spoken on Crete today, but the influence of the complex older world was profound. We do not have any Minoan myths; we have Greek, especially Athenian, myths *about* Crete.

Even in the ancient world, intellectuals tried to distinguish historical truth from myth in stories about Crete, and scholars continue today. Thucydides had himself commented on this problem in the introduction to his history, arguing from mythic accounts that the kingdom of Minos was the first *thalassocracy*, a political order having "supremacy over the sea":

> Minos was the first whom we know—granted, only by hearsay—to build a navy. He was able to take control of most of the Aegean Sea, to govern the islands we call the Cyclades, and to start colonies in many of them. First of all, he had to drive out the Carians.° He then set up his own sons as rulers, and, as far as he could, wiped out the pirates, no doubt in the hope that their income would thereafter flow into his own pockets.

THUCYDIDES 1.4, trans. R. Crawley, modified

*Carians:* A people of Asia Minor, whom Thucydides assumed to have ruled these islands.

---

[1] Only recently has it been shown that the Linear B tablets come from two different destruction levels.
[2] By c. 600 BC they spoke a Semitic language as proven by recent inscriptional finds.

The archaeological record behind myths about Crete lay buried until 1899 when Englishman Arthur Evans, inspired by Heinrich Schliemann's discoveries of Troy and Mycenae on the mainland, purchased with his own funds part of the north-central plain of Crete, where a low mound showed promise of concealing ancient remains. There he gradually uncovered the ruins of ancient Cnossus, an enormous palace complex dating from the earliest European civilization, which flourished from about 3100 BC to 1000 BC. Evans applied the term Minoan (after the legendary Minos) to this culture and to the people who fashioned it. Since Evans's day, archaeologists have enlarged his excavations at Cnossus and explored many other palace sites on Crete.

Excavations suggest that the Minoans were a vigorous, pleasure-loving, seafaring people with a taste for vibrant, naturalistic art and elegant, sophisticated living. Their palaces were rarely fortified; they must have had no enemies. Frescoes recently discovered on the nearby island of Thera, a Minoan outpost, show grand flotillas of ships and armed warriors, confirming Thucydides' description of them as the first thalassocracy. In 1992, to the amazement of the scholarly world, Minoan frescoes from about 1800 BC were found in the Nile delta, further testimony to the far-reaching power of this extraordinary people.

The tales of Theseus and the Minotaur and the doings of Daedalus are also connected intimately with Athens. Those who trust myth to preserve real history see in these stories a memory of hostilities between Athens and Crete at some time before c. 1450 BC, when the Cretan thalassocracy could have exerted direct influence on the mainland. We have never understood how the Greeks came to take possession of the island, and perhaps the story preserves a recollection from a time of actual hostilities. We can neither prove nor disprove the thesis.

Most features of the myth certainly belong to a later time. Athenian supremacy in artistic production after about 900 BC must have increased the popularity of stories about an Athenian artist named Daedalus, and the exploits of Theseus are in large part Athenian propaganda generated in the late sixth and fifth centuries BC, when the sea power of Athens grew until it was unrivaled anywhere. The Athenians were glad to draw mythical parallels between their own sea empire and that of Minos, especially when such a parallel allowed them to show Theseus defeating the Minoan king in a contest requiring intelligence, bravery, and superior moral commitments, and especially chivalry towards women, as he does in a surviving poem of Bacchylides (fifth century BC).

In addition to possible historical elements, we can occasionally identify Cretan religious practices in the Cretan stories, although interpretations of Cretan religion are difficult; no contemporary texts illuminate the archaeological evidence. Most scholars agree, however, that the Cretans worshiped a mother goddess represented as a bare-breasted woman with snakes twining up her arms. Ariadnê, whose name means "the very holy one," may have been a name for this goddess, reduced in legend to a folklore heroine. Her original function as goddess would be reflected in her cult on Cyprus as Ariadnê Aphrodite, in which a young man would lie down and pretend to give birth. The bull was central to Cretan cult and figured in an acrobatic bull game often illustrated in Minoan art. The game was certainly dangerous and may underlie the legend of the man-devouring Minotaur, which means "the bull of Minos," as does, perhaps, the ritual cannibalism for which we have evidence during the period of Crete's collapse. The bull is an embodiment of divine power and in historical religion was the animal of Zeus, to whom the bull was sacrificed in bloody ritual.

Another Cretan religious emblem, often found in shrines, was the double ax, which many scholars take to represent the sacrificial tool by which the bull was felled. A Greek grammarian tells us that the Cretan word for a double-edged ax was *labrys,* so that Labyrinth would mean "place of the double ax," the place of sacrifice, where in legend Athenian youths were fed to the bull-man.

Sexual surrender of a female victim as a substitute for her sacrifice is perhaps reflected in the story of Zeus's possession of Europa in the guise of a bull, and some speculate that some such ritual may have been performed in Minoan Crete. A similar pattern appears in the tale of Pasiphaë, who couples with the "bull from the sea" sent by Poseidon, in a sense Poseidon himself, lord of the sea, with whom the Minoans had a special relationship. According to this explanation, young women once were sacrificed to gods; later, as a substitute for their life, they surrendered their maidenhood in a "sacred marriage" (*hieros gamos*) to a priest or king, who may even have worn a bull's mask.

If such a ritual gave rise to the stories of Europa and of Pasiphaë, the religious background had long since dropped away by the Greek Classical Period, when the focus falls on Pasiphaë's bizarre lust, who entered a model cow to have intercourse with a bull. Unfortunately, no classical works treating the House of Crete have survived, but we should suspect a humorous origin to principal features of the myth—Pasiphaë, a queen, inside a cow, waiting for the bull to possess her, can only be pornographic or ludicrous and conforms to a classical Greek stereotype of women as hopelessly lustful and unashamed. Similar patterns of abhorrent or excessive sexuality characterize the House of Crete in general, also appearing in Ariadnê's willingness to betray family and country to satisfy her passion, in Minos' assault on an Athenian maiden en route to Crete (in the poem by Bacchylides), and in the incestuous love of Pasiphaë's daughter Phaedra for her stepson Hippolytus (in Euripides' play *Hippolytus*). For the Athenians of the fifth century, the Cretans had become a type—the lustful, incestuous, violent, tyrannical cousins who live over the hill, who never tell the truth about anything. Already in the *Odyssey* Odysseus tells lying tales, pretending that he is a Cretan.

The overall pattern of the story of Theseus belongs to folktale (see chapter 10): A wandering hero (Theseus) comes to a strange land (Crete) oppressed by a wicked king (Minos), in league with a man-eating monster demanding human sacrifice (the Minotaur); the daughter of the king (Ariadnê) falls in love with the hero; assisted by her and a trickster-magician (Daedalus), the hero kills the monster; the wandering hero and princess flee, but the hero, abhorring her treachery, abandons the princess and returns to his home, where he becomes king (Ishtar, too, was rejected by Gilgamesh because of her treacherous nature). The prominence of such standard traditional narrative elements forces us to be extremely cautious in searching for historical events behind the myth.

Important in Cretan legend is Daedalus, the trickster-inventor so common in folklore: He invented the tools of carpentry, built the wooden cow for Pasiphaë, designed the Labyrinth, and threaded a conch shell with a thread attached with honey to an ant. He is the prototype of the passionate artist, so jealous of his powers that he murdered Perdix, his nephew and only rival. Imprisoned within the maze of his own making, according to the story, he is the emblem of the artist captivated by his own creation. Although many explain his origin as a relatively late personification from the common Greek adjective *daidalos,* which means "skillfully made," his name may appear on a Linear B tablet from Cnossus, and he is mentioned already in the *Iliad,* where Homer describes the design on a wonderful shield that Hephaestus, Daedalus' divine counterpart, makes for Achilles:

> The god of the brawny arms, displaying the skill of the artist,
> modeled a dancing floor, as Daedalus once did in Cnossus,
> for Ariadnê, the maiden of lovely soft-flowing ringlets.
>
> HOMER, *Iliad* 18.590–592, trans. A. T. Murray

Greek writers of the Roman Period attributed to Daedalus the invention of realistic sculpture and the construction of many famous buildings, including the Bronze Age conical towers on Sardinia and various temples in Egypt. Early Greek sculpture is still sometimes called Daedalic.

## FURTHER READING

Bloom, H., ed., *Homer's The Iliad* (New York, 1987). Collection of essays by leading scholars.

Cottrell, L., *The Bull of Minos* (London, 1955). Exciting popular account of the discovery of Minoan Crete.

Doumas, C. G., *Thera, Pompeii of the Ancient Aegean* (London, 1983). Popular description of the volcanic eruption that destroyed Thera, thought by many (until recently) to have caused the destruction of Minoan civilization.

Edwards, M., *Homer, Poet of the Iliad* (Baltimore, 1987; reprinted Ithaca, 1990). Readable, sensible, up-to-date analysis of Homer's poem of war.

Evans, A. J., *The Palace of Minos at Knossos* (London, 1939; reprinted 1964). The basic book on Bronze Age Crete, by the man who discovered the civilization.

Griffin, J., *Homer on Life and Death* (Oxford, 1980). Always interesting examination of major themes.

Kirk, G. S., *The Songs of Homer* (New York, 1962). A follower of the Parry-Lord school, Kirk brings many of his own original insights to the complex problems raised by the Homeric poems.

Luce, J. V., *Homer and the Heroic Age* (London, 1975). Astute comparison of the poems with archaeological data, with excellent illustrations.

Marinatos, S., and M. Hirmer, *Crete and Mycenae* (London, 1960). Lavish illustrations of the archaeological finds on Crete and the mainland, with an excellent text.

Morris, S., *Daidalos and the Origins of Greek Art* (Princeton, 1992). Thorough study of the myths and origins of Daedalus, tracing him back to Near Eastern prototypes.

Owen, E. T., *The Story of the Iliad* (New York, 1946; reprinted Waukonda, IL, 1989). Admirably analyzes the plot of the *Iliad*, book by book.

Page, D. L., *History and the Homeric Iliad* (Berkeley, 1959; reprinted 1972). A major study of the relationship between historical records and the world of the poems.

Powell, B. B., and I. Morris, eds., *A New Companion to Homer* (Leiden, Belgium 1997). The most up-to-date scholarly review of all aspects of Homeric studies.

Redfield, J. M., *Nature and Culture in the Iliad: The Tragedy of Hector* (Durham, NC, 1993, expanded edition of first edition, Chicago, 1975). Studies the relationship between the *Iliad* and the society that produced it.

Schein, S., *The Mortal Hero: An Introduction to Homer's Iliad* (Berkeley, 1984). Synthesis of the vast scholarship, especially German, on the *Iliad*.

Traill, D. A., *Schliemann of Troy: Treasure and Deceit* (New York, 1997). Calls into question many of Schliemann's claims and shows him to have acted dishonestly on some occasions.

Weil, S., *The Iliad: The Poem of Force*, trans. by Mary McCarthy and often republished. Insightful essay written against the backdrop of the Second World War.

Whitman, C. H., *Homer and the Heroic Tradition* (Cambridge, MA, 1958; reprinted New York, 1965). Close analysis of themes and plot.

# CHAPTER 10

# MYTH AND FOLKTALE: THE LEGEND OF ODYSSEUS' RETURN

V IEWED AS A WHOLE, the *Odyssey* is the story of a hero who came home after a long absence, found his household in the hands of usurpers, and killed them to reestablish his ascendancy. The older generation—tough, smart, and wise in the need for just behavior—is triumphant over the younger—brash, indolent, and self-indulgent, taking what it wants. Modern feature films, by contrast, ordinarily show the younger generation respectful of the environment and in love, triumphant over the older, which is politically corrupt and sexually predacious. Entertainers know their audience, then as now.

Because the youthful usurpers threaten traditional property rights, the poem appears to be a simple tale of revenge, of human justice triumphant over wrong. Not the gods' enmity, but their own thoughtless behavior brings about the suitors' destruction, as Zeus points out in nearly the opening lines of the poem. Such stark patterns of right and wrong, crime and punishment, and morals for all is typical of folktale, to which the *Odyssey* owes a great deal not only in its overall pattern, but in the individual episodes, especially during the wanderings. To understand myth in the *Odyssey*, we need to understand folktale.

## FOLKTALE

*Folktale* is more difficult to define than is divine myth or legend because of the variety of traditional stories grouped together under this heading. Some scholars would describe a folktale as any traditional story that is not a divine myth or legend. This category would encompass such familiar fairytales as "Cinderella" and "Snow White," which are among the many German stories written down from oral sources (although much revised) in the early nineteenth century by the brothers Jacob and Wilhelm Grimm. Likewise, the beast fables attributed to the Greek writer Aesop (sixth century BC), such as "The Tortoise and the Hare," could be considered folktales, as could a story like "Sinbad the Sailor" from the *Arabian Nights.* Most oral tales recorded in North America and Africa during the last two hundred years are folktales.

Within this diversity we can still discern common traits. As in legend, the central characters in folktales are human beings, even though gods and spirits appear and play important roles. But in folktales the main characters are usually ordinary men, women, and children rather than kings and queens and others of exalted personal qualities or social status; hence the term *folktale,* a story by and about common people, not by and about the power-possessing classes, as Homer's poetry was. Even in fables, a kind of folktale where the characters are animals, the animals speak and act as though they were ordinary humans.

Unlike legends, folktales do not pretend to tell us what happened in the human past. No one believes that Snow White or Cinderella or Hansel and Gretel or the American Indian trickster Crow really existed, as the Greeks believed that Achilles or Helen or Orestes did exist. Often the main characters in folktales have low social status, at least at the beginning of the story, and are persecuted or victimized in some way by other characters. The folktale hero may be an outcast whose intelligence and virtue are not recognized by those in power. The hero is often the youngest child, the third of three brothers or sisters, abused by siblings or by a wicked stepmother. Very often the end of the story brings a reversal of fortunes, the happy ending for which folktales are well known. Initially taken to be stupid or ineffectual, the folktale hero triumphs over all obstacles and receives an appropriate reward. Obviously, such stories have wide appeal.

Whereas divine myths explain why the world is the way it is and legends tell what happened in the human past, the primary function of folktales is to entertain, although they may also play an important role in teaching and justifying customary patterns of behavior. Folktales draw on such universal human experiences as the child's place in the hierarchy of the family and appeal to such universal human instincts as the belief that good is rewarded and evil punished, eventually. In modern literate culture, the novel and the feature film have functions analogous to that of the folktale in oral society.

Although few pure folktales have come down to us from the Greeks and Romans, whose literature is aristocratic in origin and bias, this type of traditional tale is of central importance to the study of Greek myth. To understand why, we must take note of a distinctive aspect of the folktale: the regular appearance of identifiable folktale *types,* even in stories from cultures widely separated in space or time. Folktale types are made up of smaller elements called *motifs* that can be recombined in endless variety. We might think of folktale motifs as the cells that make up the body of a tale. Common examples are the dragon that guards a spring or a magic object that protects against attack. Modern scholars have exhaustively described and organized the bewildering variety of folktale motifs, which number in the thousands.

Scholars recognize over seven hundred folktale types in traditions around the globe. Sometimes a folktale type is named after a famous example. The "Cinderella" type, for example, is any story in which an abused younger sister, assisted by a spirit, appears in fancy dress at a ball, disappears from the prince's admiring glance, then is later recognized and marries the prince. A general type often found in Greek myth is the quest (e.g., that of Theseus: Chapter 9). Compelled to seek some special object, the folktale hero journeys to a strange, terrifying, or wonderful land. There he must face a powerful antagonist—dragon, monster, ogre, or a thoroughly wicked man. To overcome his antagonist, the hero needs the assistance of animals, ghosts, or divine beings, or of magical weapons or devices. The hero is often a clever trickster, whereas his adversary is brutish, stupid, and cruel. The adversary succeeds in imprisoning, enchanting, or even killing the hero, but at last, often through a trick, the hero escapes, overcomes the enemy, and dispatches him in some cruel or gruesome way. Taking the object he sought, the hero returns to his native land, where his reward is the hand of a princess in marriage, or a part of the kingdom, or a great treasure.

In general, we may describe much of Greek myth as legend strongly colored by folktale. The main characters in these stories often have names appropriate to men and women who might really have lived, members of a social elite whose stories are attached to prominent Greek towns. Yet their adventures are of a sort we expect to find in folktale. Such distinctions are of great value in organizing our thinking about myth, but we should remember that our distinctions are the result of intellectual analysis; they would not have been recognized by the ancients themselves.

## THE FOLKTALE OF POTIPHAR'S WIFE

The best way to understand folktale is to examine an actual example, and none is older or more widespread in the ancient world than the story type about family life called "Potiphar's Wife," named after the biblical story of Joseph. The same basic story also appears in Egyptian guise, surviving in a Nineteenth Dynasty Egyptian papyrus (about 1250 BC), called by modern scholars the "Story of the Two Brothers." It is the oldest recorded folktale on planet Earth, far older than the biblical version.

In the Egyptian story, the wife of Anubis (a god's name) propositioned her husband's handsome brother Bata, and when Bata refused, she used fat and grease to make it appear as if she had been beaten. She told Anubis that

Bata had wished to sleep with her and, when she refused, had beaten her. Anubis hid behind the door of the shed, intending to kill Bata when he returned from the fields, but Bata ran away. Here the story drops its realistic guise and becomes an exploration in symbolic form of ever-renewed vitality, especially that of pharaoh, who embodied the life of Egypt. Repeatedly Bata dies and is symbolically reborn. Repeatedly death is brought by a woman's treachery, but always overturned through pharaonic vitality. The folktale is reshaped as a political myth.

The later biblical tale, perhaps about 600 BC in the form preserved to us, reads like a historical account, moralizing how with God's help the Jewish Joseph survived the foreign devil:

> Joseph was taken down to Egypt, and Potiphar, an officer of Pharaoh, the captain of the guard, an Egyptian, bought him from the Ishmaelites who had brought him there. The Lord was with Joseph, and he became a successful man in the house of his master the Egyptian, and his master saw that the Lord was with him . . . and left all that he had in Joseph's charge . . .
>
> Now Joseph was good-looking and attractive. After a time his master's wife cast her eyes upon Joseph, and said, "Lie with me." But he refused and said to his master's wife, "Lo, having me, my master has no concern about anything in the house, and he has put everything that he has in my hand . . . . How then can I do this great wickedness, and sin against God?" And although she spoke to Joseph day after day, he would not listen to her, to lie with her or to be with her. But one day, when he went into the house to do his work, and none of the men of the house was present, she caught him by his garment and begged him, "Lie with me." But he left his garment in her hand, and fled and got out of the house. And when she saw that he had left his garment in her hand . . . she called to the men of her household and said to them, "See, he [Potiphar] has brought among us a Hebrew to insult us; he [Joseph] came in to me to lie with me and I cried out with a loud voice; and when he heard that I lifted up my voice and cried, he left his garment with me, and fled and got out of the house. . . ." Then she laid up his garment by her until his master came home, and she told him the same story. . . . And Joseph's master seized him and put him into the prison.

*Genesis 39* (Revised Standard Version)

Joseph is finally freed when he interprets Pharaoh's dreams: Now the folktale is a religious myth, glorifying Yahweh's protection of his people.

An example of the same folktale type appears in Homer's *Iliad* (6.155 ff.), told about the Corinthian hero Bellerophon (bel-**ler**-o-phon). After Bellerophon rebuffed the wife of a King Proteus while residing at Corinth, the king sent him to his father-in-law in Lycia in southern Asia Minor, carrying sealed tablets with instructions "kill the bearer" (the only reference to writing in Homer). The king of Lycia sends Bellerophon on impossible tasks. First, he must kill the dread Chimera, but Bellerophon mounts the winged horse Pegasus, which sprang from the neck of Medusa as Perseus beheaded her, and kills the monster. Then he must fight the Amazons and perform other tasks, but he is always successful and in the end marries the princess and receives a portion of the kingdom: The folktale is now a heroic myth, with the familiar ingredients of dangerous woman, treacherous king, conquest of a monster, victory, marriage, and kingship. But Bellerophon came to a bad end. Arrogantly flying to heaven on Pegasus, he fell to his death.

Finally, the story appears as a tragedy by Euripides, the *Hippolytus,* where Phaedra, the wife of Theseus, falls in love with her stepson Hippolytus. When he rebuffs her advances, she commits suicide, leaving a note that Hippolytus had made advances to her. The furious Theseus lays a curse upon his son, who dies horribly, dragged to death entangled in the reins of his chariot.

The story type, given such different meaning by Egyptians, Jews, and Greeks, appeals to the same male fear of woman's power that underlies Mesopotamian tales about the vindictive Ishtar who attempted to seduce Gilgamesh, then sent the Bull of Heaven as a terrible punishment when he rebuffed her. When a respectable woman charges rape, the man, guilty or innocent, will pay a terrible price—this moral of the tale remains constant.

## THE GREEK HERO PERSEUS AND FOLKTALE

Sometimes our distinctions between folktale and heroic myth blur irretrievably. Heroic myth, after all, is defined by the nature of its actors—bold powerful men greater than we—while folktale is a way of telling a story. So folktale and heroic legend are readily combined. We usually think of Perseus as a hero, but the stories about him are like children's tales, with hideous monsters, ugly hags, magical implements, and distressed maidens. In the end, Perseus and his bride Andromeda live happily ever after. One of our earliest representations of Perseus and his enemy Medusa, the dread monster whose look turned one to stone, is on a large pot (at Eleusis) that contained the body of a child, as if the Greek child might enjoy the story even after death.

The heroic stories about Perseus actually begin with his mother, Danaë, whose fate follows a folktale pattern sometimes called *the girl's tragedy,* which contains these elements: prohibition, seclusion, violation of the prohibition, threat of punishment or death, and finally liberation. Because of an oracle, Danaë is forbidden to marry (*prohibition*). She is locked in a chamber to keep her from men (*seclusion*), but nonetheless becomes pregnant by Zeus, who comes to her as a rain of gold (*violation*). A wicked relative, her father Acrisius, places her and the child in the box and casts the box into the sea (*threat of death*), but she is saved by the fisherman Dictys on the island of Seriphos (*liberation*).

Perseus' own story follows closely the folktale pattern of the quest, which may contain these elements: A member of a family is threatened, the hero is sent on a quest, he acquires the use of a magical agent, he reaches his goal in a faraway land, he combats a villain, he is temporarily overcome, he vanquishes the enemy, he is pursued but escapes, he arrives home and is recognized, the villain is punished, and the hero is married and ascends the throne. In the case of Perseus, the tyrant Polydectes, king of Seriphos, wants to marry Danaë (*threat*), which leads to Perseus' boast that he will bring back Medusa's head (*quest*). The hat of invisibility that Hades gives him, the winged sandals of Hermes, and Athena's gift of a special wallet and scimitar make his task possible (*magical agent*). Perseus reaches the river Ocean that surrounds the world (*faraway land*) and beheads Medusa (*combat and victory*). Conspicuously missing from this story is the hero's temporary defeat. The immortal Gorgons come after Perseus (*pursuit*), but he escapes. On Seriphos (*arrival home*) he proves his greatness by holding up the Gorgon's head (*recognition*) and petrifying Polydectes, whose name meaning "Receiver-of-Many" may tie him to Death's realm (*villain punished*). He frees Andromeda and takes the kingship of Tiryns (*marriage and ascent to throne*). Perseus' victory over the sea monster Ceto who threatens Andromeda, which he kills on the way home, and his petrifying of Andromeda's threatening relatives repeat some of these motifs.

Folktale is a system of patterns and motifs, whereas heroic myth is a story about a great man. In the stories of Perseus, the hero himself has little or no personality; He is just someone who does special things. There is no internal conflict. Conspicuously absent is the hero's conflict with woman, but that is an adult theme and of no interest to children. Perseus is a children's story and was never the subject of epic poetry, as far as we know.

## ODYSSEUS AND FOLKTALE

Homer's *Odyssey* follows a related pattern, but we can analyze it in greater detail and complexity because of the richness of the narrative in the very long surviving poem (about 12,000 lines). Milman Parry showed how Homeric poetry is a kind of special language. In it, as in all language, the *aoidos* depends on unconscious linguistic patterns in the construction of his narrative. Thus does he organize words within the hexameter line by means of formulas; thus does he build action within such type scenes as a warrior's arming according to a definite sequence.

An analogous process is at work in the poet's selection and presentation of the thematic elements by which he creates his story. Having once chosen his subject—in the *Odyssey,* the wily man's journey to the other world and victorious return—Homer develops the grand narrative by fashioning a long series of episodes, each of which is generated from a single folktale pattern many times repeated. There are many ways to approach the *Odyssey,* one of the richest literary creations in the world, but one way is to understand how this pattern works, an invisible constant beneath a versatile surface identical to the pattern that supports the grand narrative: Odysseus, held by a deathly antagonist, returns to life and is "recognized." Of great interest is to discover how any episode's central figure, Odysseus' antagonist, can change from dangerous to benevolent in swift order (as Circê first wishes to castrate Odysseus, then is his obedient bedmate); or remain wholly evil (as the devouring Laestrygonians); or be wholly good (as the young and marriageable Nausicaä); or be sweet and sour at once (as the Sirens are beautiful to hear, but ordinarily fatal to the audience).

The following schema generalizes the shape of the about thirty-three episodes or tales-within-a-tale of which the *Odyssey* is composed:

I. The hero, lost on the high seas, makes a stop (a) usually on an island, (b) often just after a storm.
II. He sees smoke in the distance.
III. He encounters someone well disposed, life-giving: (a) a mother-figure, or (b) potential wife; he "tests" the figure.
IV. Or the figure he encounters and "tests" is hostile, death-dealing, even a demon of death characterized by

(a) boorishness, stupidity, and ignorance of civilized arts;
(b) huge size or unusual, nonhuman shape;
(c) gluttonous or man-eating nature;
(d) residence in a cave or place of concealment;
(e) association with earth, water, or underworld;
(f) association with wind, storm, mist (a chaotic condition of nature);
(g) absence of want and strife;
(h) the power to render unconscious, association with sleep (brother to Death).

V. There is a sacrifice or banquet.
VI. The hero is temporarily overcome.
VII. He is betrayed.
VIII. The hero overcomes the enemy through (a) trickery, or (b) strength.
IX. He has a special weapon.
X. He has a helper.
XI. He is recognized, usually by a token; the token can be (a) a tangible object, (b) a story, (c) a change of state, (d) a feat of cunning or strength.
XII. His victory or appearance is the fulfillment of prophecy.
XIII. He is purified.

XIV.   The hero (a) gets the girl who has been threatened by the demon, or (b) receives a treasure.
XV.   He celebrates his victory.

These thematic folktale motifs, organized in an unconscious structure that allows Homer to build his story, have an extraordinary way of melding into one another or of assuming a curious or inverted significance. They do not necessarily appear in this order, or all appear at once.

Let us examine two episodes from the *Odyssey,* the story of Polyphemus' cave and the story of Circê, to illustrate how this folktale structure works. The number of the relevant element of the schema is indicated in parentheses.

## The Folktale of Polyphemus

An island lies offshore from the land of the Cyclopes (= plural of Cyclops)(Ia); here Odysseus' antagonist will be the fearsome ogre well known from folktales of every land. He is Polyphemus, "Creature of Many Tales" or "The Famous One," an epithet of Hades (IV). Gigantic in size (IVb), Polyphemus lives in a cave (IVd) where he devours men whole (IVc). The intermediate island on which Odysseus first lands would be a perfect place for human habitation. Its meadows are watered, there is level plow-land, the harbor is right, game is plentiful (IVg). But the island is undeveloped, for the Cyclopes do not know ship-building, a primary human art (IVa). The mainland opposite knows little cultivation either, for there the earth yields wheat, barley, and the grape of itself (IVg). Nor do the Cyclopes possess laws or assemblies (IVa).

The circumstances of Odysseus' arrival underline the otherworldly atmosphere of this adventure: "Some god led us through the murky night, nor was there any light to see, for a mist lay deeply about the ship; nor did a moon shine forth from the sky, but was shut in by clouds" (9.142–5) (IVf). When he and his crew awake, they make a meal of wild goat, then pass the day in feasting (V).

The Greeks see smoke across the water (II). The next morning Odysseus announces his intention "to make trial of those men" (9.174), to find out who and of what sort they are (IV). Not that the wily man is ignorant of danger—"My haughty spirit thought that a man clothed in enormous power was soon to come, a savage knowing nothing of justice or law" (9.213–15). His comrades urge a wise course, that he steal the cheeses, kids, and lambs, then depart posthaste. But Odysseus wishes "to see the man himself, and whether he might give me friendship-tokens" (9.229). Trained in modern techniques of characterization, we find Odysseus' daring to be strange, or stupid, but trickery has no use in the absence of adversity, and Odysseus must go up against the beast.

Trapped in the cave (VI), the band enjoys a new kind of banquet (V): They themselves are the fare. Odysseus tricks the stupid ogre by saying his name is "Nobody" (VIIIa). Formally a recognition scene, the recognition is ironic. The false name is a disguise, parallel to the disguise by which Odysseus later will insinuate himself into his palace on Ithaca disguised as a beggar, a "nobody," to spy on and destroy the suitors: The suitors devour his livestock, as Polyphemus devours his men. Held within the darkness of the cave, Odysseus *is* Nobody; only when he emerges into light, born again, does he regain his name, which he shouts at Polyphemus, mocking him, and Polyphemus recognizes him (XId). Dramatic pressures do not prevent the ogre from recounting at length the prophecy of his undoing (XII) any more than a respect for intelligence keeps Odysseus from shouting his name and location across the water. In folktale the structure takes precedence over verisimilitude.

The magical wine that Odysseus providentially carries with him into the cave, a wine so strong that, diluted twenty times, it is yet potent, constitutes part of the trick to which Polyphemus succumbs. The olive stake is the special magical weapon (he might have used his sword) (IX). Polyphemus' sheep are a kind of treasure (XIVb) that he and the companions kill and eat in celebration of their victory (XV).

# Circê

Arrived on the island of Circê ("hawk") (Ia), Odysseus and his crew rest for two days. On the third he climbs a "rugged place of outlook" from which he sees smoke rising through the brush (II). Returning to inform his comrades, he encounters and kills a stag. In fairy-tales, witches' houses hidden in forests are regularly discovered by climbing a tall tree or by pursuing a wondrous animal, often a stag. The crew prepares a feast (V). Circê's island is a twilit world where the source of light is hidden. "My friends, we do not know where is the darkness or where is the light, nor where the sun, who shines for mortal men, goes beneath the earth, or where it rises" (10.190–2) (IVe). The companions knew the meaning of the smoke that their leader saw, for when he tells them of it, they straightaway remember Polyphemus and begin to wail and shed great tears.

Circê's means of bewitchment (like the Lotus Eaters) are baneful drugs. She administers them in order that the companions "might altogether forget their fatherland" (10.235–6) (IVh). One of his companions, Eurylochus, remains behind when the companions enter the hut, so that he might later report how the men followed the woman and "vanished altogether, nor did any of them again appear" (10.256–60) (VI). Odysseus' journey inland through the dark forest to save his comrades is comparable to the quest hero's typical decent to the underworld (cf. IVe): Gilgamesh slew the guardian of the forest.

Hermes appears to Odysseus as he goes along the path. So long as Odysseus is in the "other world," lost on the high seas, Hermes is his protector, not Athena, whose authority appears confined to the world of the living. The magical herb *moly* that Hermes gives Odysseus performs the same function (VIIIa) as the impossibly potent wine that Odysseus took with him into the cave of Cyclops, and the special stake that blinds Polyphemus has its counterpart in the sword that Odysseus holds to Circê's throat after she has failed to bewitch him (IX). In either case the weapon appears after the magical device, the wine or *moly*, has worked its effect.

Odysseus' presence within the goddess's house means, if we continue the analogy with the adventure with Cyclops, his temporary defeat, his death (VI). But he overcomes her (VIII), which brings about his recognition (XId). Curiously, the recognition here proceeds from an ironic reversal of the usual formula, from Odysseus' *failure* to change state, causing Circê to exclaim: "Why, you are Odysseus, the man of many wiles, whom Argeiphontes [= Hermes] of the golden wand always said would come to me, returning from Troy . . ." (10.330–2). As with Polyphemus, the enemy's defeat is foretold (XII). As in the Cyclops adventure, Odysseus and his men escape from darkness into light; here they are transformed from swine back to men.

After the recognition, both Odysseus and the companions receive a bath, a motif recurrent in the *Odyssey* and evidently part of the recognition formula (XIII). The effects of the bath are renewing: From Odysseus' limbs, the bath takes "the weariness that consumes the soul" (10.363).

After suppressing treachery on the part of his cousin Eurylochus with the men left at the shore (VII), Odysseus returns to the hut, where they all feast in a sort of victory celebration. The defeated antagonist is now the solicitous hostess (XV), so easily does the adversary remove its evil guise to assume a beneficent one (cf. III). Circê's behavior to Odysseus, once she is vanquished, is affectionate, considerate. She takes the hero to her bed after swearing an oath to remain harmless (XIVa). After a self-indulgent year of "marriage" passed in endless festival (IVg), his companions approach Odysseus to remind him of his purpose, which he seems to have forgotten. Polyphemus is the monstrous and masculine, the brute adversary of the folktale trickster hero; Circê is the seductive and feminine. But neither can outdo the wily man.

## THE FOLKTALE OF THE MAN WHO RETURNED

Folktale is given to moralizing on human behavior, and the powerful theme of crime and punishment is set in the beginning of Homer's poem when Zeus complains that humans blame gods for their troubles, whereas it is their own recklessness that brings them to grief (*Odyssey* 1.33–43). Zeus cites the example of Aegisthus, brother of Agamemnon who led the Greeks to Troy:

Warned not to sleep with Clytemnestra, Aegisthus did so anyway. No wonder he paid the price!

Similarly, Odysseus' foolish men dawdle in the land of the Cicones in Thrace, where five from each boat are killed. Others eat the dangerous Lotus that sends them into forgetful narcosis, open the bag of the winds that unleashes a storm, and devour the cattle of the Sun, which kills all who remain except Odysseus himself. Justice is based on restraint, on the ability to hold back and not give in to one's animal appetite. Food is good, but when forbidden by gods, on Helius' island, or when it belongs to someone else, on Ithaca, you do not eat it. Sex is pleasurable, but when your husband is absent, do without.

Sometimes, however, these simple morals, typical of folktales, are contradicted by the story itself. Although Zeus explains that humans are responsible for their own troubles, Poseidon, a god, harasses Odysseus in revenge for the blinding of Polyphemus, and Poseidon's enmity also seems to explain the destruction of Odysseus' men. The underlying structure of Homer's folktale is much older than the moral posture he gives it. We noticed earlier (Chapter 8) how the epic of Gilgamesh and Homer's *Odyssey* begin with nearly the same words. Both stories tell of a journey where deadly dangers threaten, but are eventually overcome. The hero must slay his dragon, and Odysseus overcomes many deadly enemies. Even the 108 suitors who besiege Odysseus' house are, in a realistic mode, a kind of dragon, described as voracious ("devouring his substance") and sexually threatening ("whoring with the maidservants") while seeking to marry his wife. In the same way, the folktale dragon devours everything in sight and sexually threatens a woman. In the myth of the dragon-combat, the monster is often overcome by a trick (as Perseus avoided looking at Medusa), sometimes at a banquet (where Perseus petrified Andromeda's suitors), and slain with a special weapon (as Perseus used a special scimitar given him by the gods); even so Odysseus tricks the beast with 108 mouths by entering the palace in disguise, surprising the suitors in the dining hall, then killing them with a special bow that almost no one can string (except his son, almost). As the dragon-slayer receives a princess as reward, Odysseus "marries" Penelopê.

Mesopotamian cosmogonic myth and Hesiod's stories with similar structural features describe the triumph of the ordered world over the disordered, of life and progress over death and stagnation, even as a prominent theme in Homer's *Odyssey* is the hero's victory over death—so closely interwoven are myths of creation, of the epic hero, and of the folktale hero. The enemies of Odysseus are death's allies: sleep (Odysseus falls asleep at crucial junctions in the stories of Aeolus and the cattle of Helius), narcosis (the Lotus Eaters), darkness (the cave of Polyphemus, the shadowy land of the Cimmerians), or forgetfulness of purpose (Circê). Declared by all to be dead, Odysseus travels across water, the element separating this world from the next, to the land of the Cimmerians, where he interrogates the spirits of the dead and in the underworld sees the torments of the damned. The eternal life offered him by Calypso, whose name means "concealer" and whose island is the "navel of the sea," is eternal death for the inquisitive man thirsting for experience: Death hovers in the still-central point of the boundless water, "concealing" the dead from the living. Hades means "unseen," and when someone dies, he or she will not be seen again. Water is a chaotic substance and its god, Poseidon, is Odysseus' relentless enemy. Like Polyphemus and the Laestrygonians, death devours the living in the tomb's dark and hungry maw. As dragons of death are stupid, so Polyphemus is made drunk by the wine, fooled by the trick of the name, then wounded by the pointed stake; the same pattern underlies the slaying of the suitors.

Triumph over death leads to rebirth, and Odysseus, like a baby leaving the "navel of the sea," passes through waters to emerge naked on the shore of Phaeacia. He takes refuge in a womblike hole in the dark bushes, then is welcomed by Nausicaä, a virgin who has dreamed of imminent marriage—like the marriage that unites Odysseus and Penelopê at the end of the poem. Nausicaä's role as deliverer, as new mother, is explicit as Odysseus prepares to depart for Ithaca: She says to him, "Never forget me, for I gave you life" (*Odyssey* 8.461–2).

In cosmogonic myth, the primordial being is female, like Tiamat or Gaea, who begets monstrous creatures that oppose the establishment of the ordered world; or she is herself the enemy. The female is ambiguous and may conspire with the hero to overthrow the monsters of chaos, as Gaea conspired with Cronus to defeat Uranus, or as Rhea conspired with Zeus to overthrow Cronus. The ambiguity of the female in such stories is paralleled in the extraordinary array of female types in the *Odyssey,* good and evil, who oppose or help Odysseus' efforts to return home and reestablish order. At one end of the spectrum are the dangerous seductive women Calypso and Circê, so like the seductive but deadly Ishtar in the Gilgamesh epic. Calypso, although beautiful, is a "concealer"; Circê, although beautiful, wishes to castrate Odysseus; she turns men into pigs by the irresistible female power that reduces the male to pure animal lust, snorting and groveling in the dirt. The female Scylla eats them whole; the female Sirens, like perverted Muses, lead men to their deaths through the alluring promise of secret knowledge dressed in beautiful song.

On the positive end of the scale stand Athena, Odysseus' protector; Nausicaä, the uncorrupted maid cast as potential mate for Odysseus and symbolic mother; and Penelopê, who resists sexual temptation for twenty years. In Zeus's speech about human folly, Clytemnestra is cited as an example of humans who act recklessly and pay the price. Throughout the poem Clytemnestra is the implied opposite to Penelopê (see Chapter 12). Clytemnestra is the wicked woman who gave in to sexual desire, betrayed the strict rules of wifely fidelity, and murdered her husband. Penelopê, by contrast, is the ideal woman, long-suffering, ever-faithful, ingenious in preserving the honor of her home.

Beset by a dangerous crisis, she courageously decides to take a second husband, thus setting up (unknowingly) the slaughter of the suitors. Clever like her husband, she cooly tests Odysseus with the token of the master's bed, asking the nurse to bring it from the bedroom: In its immovability, which only Odysseus knows, the bed is the symbol for their marriage, the life of the family uncorrupted by (female) adultery. In the contrasting but parallel stories of the royal houses of Mycenae and Ithaca, Odysseus is like Agamemnon, each returning from Troy to find his house in the hands of enemies; Telemachus is like Orestes, fighting to restore family right and honor. The difference between the parallel legends lies in the character of the woman. Odysseus survives because Penelopê is woman as she should be, while Agamemnon is cut down like a dog. That, too, is a moral of the tale.

## FURTHER READING

Buitron, D., and B. Cohen, eds., *The Odyssey in Ancient Art: An Epic in Word and Image* (Annandale-on-Hudson, NY, 1992) 180–85. Collects the most important representations of stories from the *Odyssey,* with interpretive essays.

Cohen, B., ed., *The Distaff Side: Representing the Female in Homer's Odyssey* (Oxford, 1995). Discusses issues of gender in the poem.

Dimock, G., *The Unity of the Odyssey* (Amherst, 1989). Excellent general study.

Doherty, L. E., *Siren Songs: Gender, Audiences, and Narrators in the Odyssey* (Ann Arbor, 1995). Discusses vanity of female types in the poem.

*Grimms' Fairy Tales.* Collection of eighteenth-century German folktales by the Brothers Grimm; established, more than any other book, what we think of as a folktale. There are many editions.

Heubeck, A. et al., *A Commentary on Homer's Odyssey,* 3 vols. (Oxford, 1988–92). A standard commentary.

Malkin, I., *The Returns of Odysseus* (Berkeley, 1999). Superb study of colonization in Italy and the origin and age of Homer's *Odyssey.*

Murnaghan, S., *Disguise and Recognition in the Odyssey* (Princeton, 1987). Thorough exploration of this theme.

Page, D. L., *Folktales in Homer's Odyssey* (Cambridge, MA, 1973). Page compares folktales in the *Odyssey* with those found in other cultures.

Powell, B. B., *Composition by Theme in the Odyssey,* Beiträge zur klassischen Philologie 81 (Meisenheim am Glan, Germany 1977). The present chapter summarizes the analysis presented in this monograph.

Thompson, S., *The Folktale* (New York, 1946; reprinted Berkeley, 1977). Still the standard survey of the nature and forms of the folktale, by the most distinguished modern scholar of the folktale.

Thompson, S., *Motif-index of Folk-literature,* 6 vols. (Bloomington, IN, 1993). The basic reference work for folktale motifs throughout the world.

Thornton, A., *People and Themes in the Odyssey* (London, 1970). Lucid and penetrating study.

Tracy, S. V., *The Story of the Odyssey* (Princeton, 1990). Summary of what actually happens in the poem.

Propp, V., *Morphology of the Folktale,* 2nd ed. (Austin, 1968; Russian original, 1928). English translation of the great Russian folklorist's seminal study of narrative pattern in folktale.

Woodhouse, W. J., *The Composition of Homer's Odyssey* (Oxford, 1930). Excellent on folktale motifs, one of the best books on the *Odyssey*.

Yohannan, J. D., ed., *Joseph and Potiphar's Wife in World Literature: An Anthology of the Story of the Chaste Youth and the Lustful Stepmother* (New York, 1968). Discusses in depth this nearly universal folktale.

# CHAPTER 11

# MYTH AND SOCIETY: THE LEGEND OF THE AMAZONS

MANY LEGENDS, or parts of legends, appear to go back to historical events. Most scholars probably agree that stories of the Trojan War descend from a real military campaign waged by mainland Greeks in the Late Bronze Age against the fortified town in northwestern Turkey, whose ruins Heinrich Schliemann exposed to modern archaeology. Other facets of myth, however, seem to have no historical roots, but to form a kind of commentary on social conditions familiar from daily life. Myths of the Amazons provide a clear example.

## AMAZONS: THE WOMEN WHO HATED MEN

The Amazons are important and recurring figures in Greek myth. Many Greek heroes fought against them. Bellerophon, at the command of a Lycian king who hoped to get rid of Bellerophon, went out against them, according to Homer (Chapter 10). According to later authorities, in action taking place later than that described in the *Iliad,* Achilles at Troy fought an Amazon invasion under the leadership of their queen Penthesilea: As he thrust a sword into her throat, their eyes met and they fell in love, a theme illustrated on some Greek pots. Even the god Dionysus, supported by his army of maenads and satyrs, defeated an Amazon host somewhere in the east.

But the myth of the Amazons was especially important in Athens, where the local hero Theseus was said to have destroyed an Amazon expedition to

Attica in revenge for Theseus' abduction of an Amazon queen. Probably, the story is based on the earlier labor of Heracles, when the evil Mycenaean king Eurystheus sent Heracles to capture the girdle of the Amazon queen, usually called Hippolyta, "looser of horses." Our oldest literary account of this exploit is in Euripides' play *Heracles Insane* (c. 417 BC):

> He gathered no mean throng of friends from Greece and came through the surge to Lake Asinê° to the mounted host of Amazons to get the gold-decked garment of the dress of Ares' daughter, a deadly hunting for a girdle. Greece received the famous booty of the foreign maid and keeps it in Mycenae.
>
> EURIPIDES, *Heracles Insane*, 408–418

*Lake Asinê:* It is not clear where this is.

The oldest artistic illustrations of Amazons, evidently of this exploit, begin on Athenian pottery of about 575 BC, where Heracles is shown with an army of heroes defeating an army of female warriors, and oddly no hint of the girdle.

A kind of consensus about the Amazons grew up in the fifth century BC. Their homeland was usually placed on the slopes of the Caucasus mountains between the eastern end of the Black Sea and the Caspian Sea or in Scythia, the southern steppe of what is today Russia, north of the Black Sea. They were descended from Ares and the nymph Harmonia. They hated men and would not tolerate them, except as slaves to perform the most menial tasks.

To preserve their race, the Amazons periodically came together with strangers and for a short time engaged in indiscriminate intercourse. When boy babies were born, they were killed or blinded and maimed. They were said to cut off the right breasts of young girls, so when they grew to maturity, they might better draw the bowstring and handle the spear, a detail constructed on the false etymology of Amazon from *a-* (= no) + *mazos* (= breast). They followed Artemis and, according to some accounts, constructed the enormous temple of Artemis at Ephesus, one of the Seven Wonders of the Ancient World.

The Greeks themselves never questioned the historical reality of the Amazons. Arian, for example, the historian of the conquests of Alexander, reported that whereas there were no Amazons in Alexander's day, they certainly had existed in the past because of the testimony of "so many distinguished authorities." In legend Alexander was said to have had an Amazon for a mistress for awhile. A clear example of accepting the Amazons to be historical is found in the fourth book of Herodotus, in describing the customs of the Sauromatians, a Scythian tribe (roughly in the modern Ukraine). Herodotus explains that the Sauromatian women could ride and shoot because they descended from a mixture of Amazons and Sauromatians. After the Greeks defeated the Amazons on the Thermodon River (near the Caucasus), Herodotus says, they boarded them on their ships, but the Amazons rose up and killed the Greeks. Because they did not know how to sail the boats, they drifted until coming onto the shore of Scythia. Here they stole horses and raided the territory. At first the Sauromatians resisted, but when they realized that their enemies were women, they sent young men to court them. At first a single couple came together and had intercourse, and then the whole tribe intermingled:

> Presently they joined their camps and lived together, each man having for his wife the woman with whom he had had intercourse at first. Now the men could not learn the women's language, but the women mastered the speech of the men; and when they understood each other, the men said to the Amazons, "We have parents and possessions. Therefore, let us no longer live as we do, but return to our people and be with them; and we will still have you, and no others, for our wives." To this the women replied: "We could not live with your women; for we and they do not have the same customs. We shoot the bow and throw the javelin and ride, but have never learned women's work; and your women do none of the things of which we speak, but stay in their wagons and do women's work, and do not go out hunting or anywhere else. So we could never agree with them. If you want to keep us for wives and to have the name of fair men, go to your parents and let them give you the allotted share of their possessions, and after that let us go and live by ourselves." The young men agreed and did this.
>
> So when they had been given the allotted share of possessions that fell to them, and returned to the Amazons, the women said to them, "We are worried and frightened how we are to live in this country after depriving you of your fathers and doing a lot of harm to your land. Since you propose to have us for wives, do this with us: come, let us leave this country and live across the Tanaïs river.°
>
> To this too the youths agreed; and crossing the Tanaïs, they went a three days' journey east from the river, and a three days' journey north from lake Maeotis°; and when they came to the region in which they now live, they settled there. Ever since then the women of the Sauromatians have followed their ancient ways; they ride out hunting, with their men or without them; they go to war, and dress the same as the men.

HERODOTUS, 4.110.117, trans. A. D. Godley, modified

*Tanaïs River:* The River Don in southern Russia, which flows into Lake Maeotis.
*Lake Maeotis:* The sea of Azov, joined to the Black Sea by the Cimmerian Bosporus.

Archaeologists have in fact found burial-mounds in Scythia of women fitted out as warriors, but to answer the question, "Were there ever Amazons?" one must decide what is meant by "Amazon" (just as we must decide what is meant by "Trojan War"). There certainly never was a tribe of warrior-women who tolerated men only as slaves and sexual tools. The myth presents a good example of *mythical inversion,* where a conspicuous feature of social behavior is turned upside down, for the lives of the Amazons are just the opposite of the lives of Greek, especially Athenian, women.

What was the relationship between the genders in ancient Greece that could produce this kind of mythical inversion? What was expected of each gender, and how did men and women understand their roles in life? To understand myth, we must understand society.

## Greek Men

Much of Greek social life revolved around the free adult males who were dominant in both the private and the public spheres. In classical Athens, there were about 25,000 such men out of a total population of around 200,000. They held final authority over their wives and the other members of their households. They alone were obligated to fight in wars, and they alone were eligible to become citizens of the *polis.* They were prepared for these roles by an education that began in early childhood and taught them not only to read and write, but also to be athletic, fearless in battle and the hunt, and in rigorous control of their appetites (more an ideal than a reality, it seems). They grew up in a small, tightly knit, relentlessly competitive community where everyone knew everyone's worth and there was no forgiveness for failure. An individual male was celebrated for victories over his enemies in war and politics, and for his wit and ability to entertain at the all-male *symposium,* "drinking party," the Greek male's principal form of social life and principal setting for the telling of Greek myths.

In Athens of the Classical Period, the first-born son in an upper-class family could expect his father to be thirty years or older. Between six and thirteen, the boy received instruction from a *pedagogue* ("trainer of boys"), who taught him how to read, write, and memorize the poetry of Homer and other poets from written texts, which he could recite before his male friends. The boy still lived in the women's quarters of the house, but every day exercised naked with his friends to harden his body against the day when, in defense of the *polis,* he would take up armor and stand against the enemy.

Isolated from the other sex, upper-class men in their twenties in Athens and Thebes (we cannot be sure about other Greek cities) gathered at the exercise ground to admire the prepubescent boys and to court them through gifts and poetry, a practice called pederasty, "love for boys." Greek pederasty has no good modern counterparts, and no other facet of ancient Greek social life seems more odd, a measure of our enormous distance from the Greeks of the Classical Period. Teenage boys also attended the symposium as cupbearers, where such courtship could continue. If the boy accepted a suitor's attentions (he need not), he would submit to kissing and fondling and, eventually, to copulation from the front between the boy's thighs, or even anal penetration. The boy was expected to derive little or no physical pleasure from his lover's attentions, in keeping with Greek moral education in self-control: In the many surviving pederastic illustrations on pots, the boy, always beardless, is never shown with an erection, while the older male, always bearded, often has one. We learn of few instances of homosexual activity between adult males, a practice held up to savage ridicule by the Greek comic poet Aristophanes (c. 450–338 BC). Pederasty was an aspect of Greek preparation for manhood and for war and was thought to enhance the refined moral qualities of loyalty, respect, affection, and courage.

At age eighteen, when many of the boys had lost their fathers in war, a male in Athens became a *citizen,* a "member of the city," able to vote in elections and speak in public. Between eighteen and twenty, he was called an *ephebe* (**ef**-ēb), "one who has come of age," and in an initiatory rite of passage he spent time outside the city practicing military procedure and honing his hunting skills. In one ephebic festival dedicated to the hero Theseus, men dressed as women, a common practice in many tribal cultures to mark the transition from youth to full manhood. Apparently, the purpose of the ritual was to identify with the female sex that had heretofore controlled the young males, then, by disrobing, to break away from women's ways forever. At this same time, the boy prepared to leave the women's part of the house.

When in his early twenties the young man sought out prepubescent boys for friendship and sexual pleasure, his marriage was still ten years away, and even when he married, pederastic attachments might continue. No longer a cupbearer at the symposium, but an equal participant in it, the young citizen reclined to eat and drink on one of the eleven or thirteen couches placed around the walls of the *andreion,* the "man's room," which had a separate entrance from that into the rest of the house. Here he competed in wit and poetry with his friends, with whom he had grown up.

The symposium is the setting for Plato's famous dialogue the *Symposium,* where drinking companions attempt to define the nature of sexual love. The topic is suitable, because in addition to the handsome boys who served wine, female courtesans called *hetairai,* "female companions," offered every kind of sexual service for pay. *Hetairai* also sang and danced and are often represented on Greek pottery, designed to be used at the symposium. They seem often to have been foreign women or slaves and, with few exceptions, had no standing in respectable society.

War was a looming concern for every Greek male, who could expect at some time to face the enemy in hand-to-hand combat and throughout his life prepared for that moment. Half would die by the pike or the sword. In the Bronze and Dark Ages, warfare seems to have been conducted between relatively unorganized gangs from which some hero might emerge, an Achilles eager for glory and reputation, to challenge the best fighter from the other side; so do men fight in Homer's *Iliad*. In the Classical Period, by contrast, a citizen fought for the glory of his *polis*. War was conducted on open plains between opposing lines, many ranks deep, of heavily armed men called hoplites (*hoplon* = "shield," "armor"). Each man had to pay for his own equipment. The principal weapon was the thrusting spear, but a fighter also carried a one-edged sword for slashing in close encounter. Advancing in tight ranks, each pushing on the one in front, one phalanx (a unit of massed infantry) attempted to break the other and win the battle. Afterwards, a truce was called, the dead buried, and a trophy (*tropaion* = "place of turning") set up by the winning side. In Homer the heroes go into battle in chariots, then jump down and fight on foot. Cavalry—warriors mounted on individual horses—was not important in Greek warfare until the Hellenistic Period, and even then the lack of saddle and stirrup (introduced to Europe from China in the Middle Ages) and the small size of the horses limited the cavalry's effectiveness against a phalanx clad in bronze. Most hoplites were small-farmers, the backbone of the *polis,* and not wealthy enough to own horses.

Social institutions encouraged the cultivation and refinement of the warrior's spirit. In the *gymnasium* (from Greek *gymnos,* "naked"), the Greek male practiced nonlethal forms of war. Our tradition of athletics (from Greek *athlos,* "contest") began in Greece. As sport to the Greek was practice for war, war was a kind of sport, and strict rules governed the behavior of the citizen armies; by contrast, war is not a sport in modern warfare and few rules govern an army's behavior. Competitive rules similar to those regulating Greek warfare extended off the battlefield into every realm of social life. In the Archaic and Classical Periods, a man divided his social relations into clear camps of friends and enemies; a man was measured by the richness of gifts to his friends and the thorough punishment he gave to his enemies. In Athenian tragedy, poets recast ancient myths to reflect contemporary concerns as they competed vigorously for first prize under the critical gaze of their fellow citizens. In Athenian law courts, one sought not justice, but victory. The notion of "natural rights" to life or property or happiness, so prominent in our own thinking, simply did not exist.

## Greek Women

While our lack of sources hinders the study of all aspects of ancient Greek society, we find it particularly difficult to form an accurate picture of the lives of women. Almost all literary sources were composed by male authors, who often present a biased, unsympathetic, and contradictory picture of the opposite sex. On the one hand, these sources suggest, the ideal Greek woman was tall, beautiful, submissive, fertile, chaste, and silent, and virtually invisible to those outside the home. As the statesman Pericles told the widows of soldiers killed in battle, "Your reputation is great when you do not prove inferior to your own nature and when there is the least possible talk about you among men, whether in praise or in blame" (Thucydides 1.45.2). But the sources also imply that real women were likely to behave in ways that contrasted sharply with this ideal. Fired by an insatiable sexual appetite, the women depicted in literature are often ready to lie and scheme to achieve their aims. In myth Hesiod's description of Pandora, Zeus' punishment for mankind, encapsulates this attitude:

> With a nasty smile, the father of men and gods
> told famous Hephaestus to hurry, to knead the water and clay,
> to add human speech and strength, to give it a goddess's form
> and the lovely face of a maiden. Next he ordered Athena
> to teach her womanly skill, to weave on a well-built loom.
> Aphrodite the golden he told to crown her head with desire,
> but with heartbreak as well, and all the aching sorrow of love.
> Last of all he had Hermes the herald, the killer of Argus,
> to give her thievish morals, and to add the soul of a bitch.
>
> HESIOD, *Works and Days*, 60–66

It is difficult to distill the truth about women's lives from the sources that are available to us, but we can make at least some observations with a reasonable level of confidence.

A little girl learned the values of modesty, obedience, and restraint in the care of a nurse as she grew up in the *gynaikeion*, "women's quarters," located in the back of the house or on an upper floor. In the *gynaikeion* she also learned the female arts of spinning wool and making cloth, a woman's principal occupation throughout life, except for childbearing and care of the dead. Only rarely did women learn to read and write. In the inner rooms of the *gynaikeion*, women met with other women friends and entertained one another with gossip and music. Although women may have told stories, myths, to one another and to their children, we have no direct evidence that they did; as far as we know, Greek myth, like Greek literary education, was an invention of the male, a fact of paramount importance in our attempts to understand it.

A Greek proverb noted how a woman knew two great moments in her life: her marriage and her death. Unlike other ancient peoples (except possibly the Etruscans), the Greeks were monogamous; that is, offspring from one wife at a time were the man's legitimate heirs. The origins of Greek monogamy are unknown, but no other social practice affected more deeply the way Greek men and women behaved toward one another. Marriage was not based on mutual affection, but arranged between families on political and economic grounds. Even the Athenian *polis*, despite the institutions of democracy, was governed by its leading families. The family provided the woman with a dowry, a way that the bride's family retained some control even after marriage: In case of divorce the husband was compelled to return the dowry intact. The bride may never have set eyes upon her husband until the wedding day. The groom was a mature adult, usually in his thirties, with wide experience of life and war; the bride was a girl in her teens, around fourteen years old, who offered her dolls in a temple as her last act before marriage. The husband had wide sexual experience, sometimes orgiastic, with women and other males; the bride was a *parthenos,* "virgin." No respectable man would knowingly marry a woman who had prior sexual experience, and a father could sell into slavery a daughter guilty of it, even if she were the victim of rape. For these reasons Greek girls were married off as soon as possible after first menstruation.

The period between first menstruation and marriage was one of great danger to the girl, her family, and to society itself. As *parthenos,* the female was thought to be wild and dangerous, like the goddess Artemis, to whom the *parthenos* was often compared and whose cult young girls served. Most heroines of Greek myth are *parthenoi,* in a momentary position of freedom to do immense harm or bring great advantage to her people. Fortunately, in marriage a woman could gain *sophrosynê,* "self-control." Tamed by the authority of her husband, in willing submission to the weighty demands of pleasing her husband sexually and bearing him children, a woman could overcome her natural weakness and live a modest and silent life away from the scrutiny of others.

The wedding, the highpoint of a girl's life, was ordinarily held at night, when the new bride moved out of her mother's *gynaikeion* into that of her mother-in-law, where she first experienced intercourse, bore children, and lived until she died, often in childbirth at a young age. The myth of Hades' abduction of Persephonê must reflect the young Greek girl's psychological experience on the wedding night. Terrified when snatched up by Lord Death as she played with her virgin friends, she soon accepted her changed condition in life.

The groom traveled to the bride's house in a cart, where he took her wrist in a special gesture implying a staged abduction. At this moment she left behind the authority of her father and entered within the authority of her husband and of her husband's mother. To the accompaniment of music, dance, song, and crackling torches, the cart made its way to the house of the groom, where the couple had intercourse. In the morning, the girl's friends visited her in the bridal chamber and brought gifts.

As a virgin, or *parthenos,* the Greek female was called *korê* (an alternate name for Persephonê). After marriage and intercourse she was a *nymphê,* "bride" (whence our word "nymph"). Not until she bore her first child did she become a *gynê,* "woman" (as in *gyne*cology), when she assumed full authority over the *oikos,* "family,"[1] which included not only the female and

---

[1]From which come our words *economy,* "the management of the family," and *ecology,* "study of the habitat." The Latin *familia* had approximately the same meaning.

young unmarried male members of the household, but also the slaves, domestic animals, the physical house itself, and its inner storeroom filled with storage vessels (in myth, women are closely associated with vessels, as they are with textiles). By her late teens a Greek woman was a mother, and by age thirty a grandmother. By age forty-five she was a great-grandmother, if she lived that long.

A Greek wife did not even eat with her husband, but monogamy placed enormous power in her hands (about which we hear endless complaints in Greek myth). Monogamy also isolated her in a way unknown within the polygamous societies of the rest of the ancient world, where women of the harem had constant companionship. Increased prosperity heightened still more the isolation of Athenian women of the Classical Period, for whom abundant slaves now performed such menial but social work as gathering water or nursing children. Ordinarily, a respectable woman went outdoors only during certain religious festivals, when she averted her eyes from the gaze of men and covered her head.

Several festivals were restricted to women alone, and close study of their symbols and rituals shows how in these festivals the fertility of the earth, and by extension the well-being of the community, were connected closely to the female's ability to bring forth from her body new life. Childbirth was a moment of personal crisis, because many women died from it, but also of enormous pollution, called *miasma,* "stench," because of the blood and other fluids that attend childbirth. No man would come close to a woman in labor. Woman's ability to purify the chamber and the child after birth extended to their care of the dead. Only women could touch a dead body to clean it for burial. After burial they tended the family graves, pouring offerings and tying ribbons around gravestones. Myths are filled with events surrounding birth and death and the special power of woman to withstand and control the two crises through which every human being must pass.

Our evidence concerning family size from the Classical Period is poor, but in the Hellenistic Period an average Greek family consisted of three children, preferably two boys and one girl: One boy to die in the endless wars, another to carry on the family line, and one girl to assist in the formation of interfamilial alliances. Girls were disadvantageous because they required a dowry and did not carry on the family lineage, transmitted by the sons. Additional children were often exposed, abandoned in the wilds. Most died, but some were found and raised as slaves or prostitutes. There are famous foundlings in Greek myth, including Oedipus of Thebes.

Athenian women probably fared somewhat better in the Archaic Period, when great families were in power, than in the Classical Period under the democracy, when citizenship became all-important. To be a citizen meant not to be a woman or a slave or a resident foreigner. In affirmation of the solidarity of the group, Athenian males met together every year in a gigantic civic symposium, the festival of Dionysus, god of wine, where they witnessed the tragedies and lighthearted satyr plays for which the chorus dressed as sexually excited males.[2] Although powerful women often appear in Greek plays, their fascination emerges directly from the shocking reversal of ordinary roles. Clytemnestra, in Aeschylus' tragedy *Agamemnon,* ruled the city of Mycenae while her husband Agamemnon fought at Troy, then murdered him in a bathtub. In Aristophanes' comedy *Lysistrata,* the women of the Greek cities band together, go on a sex strike, and take over Athens. To the male audience, this amusing reversal seemed as absurd as if the birds in the sky were to conquer the world, as they actually do in Aristophanes' play the *Birds.*

Although social tensions between Greek men and women were high and never resolved (nor are they today), the sexes were capable of genuine affection toward each other. Helen's infidelity, so the story went, caused the Trojan War, but Odysseus' longing for home and family led him to abandon an offer of immortal life with a nymph far more beautiful than his wife. Among the most touching works of Greek art are the sculptured gravestones showing the deceased in loving company with husbands, wives, or children. In rare cases, women even participated in public life: Aspasia, the non-Athenian mistress of Pericles, from the city of Miletus, was highly cultivated, could read and write, knew Socrates and other powerful people, and was said to have advised Pericles on his foreign policy.

## THE MEANING OF THE AMAZONS

A good Athenian woman of the fifth century BC was expected to be submissive, sexually chaste, productive of male heirs, and zealous to preserve the stability of the family. The Amazons, by contrast, were brazen, licentious, and murderous to males and did not live in families. Amazons defied their destiny as women and lived like males, fighting, hunting on horseback, ruling themselves, and having sexual intercourse out of doors and when they pleased. They lived in a perennial confusion between childhood and maturity, neither girls nor women, neither male nor female, at the edge of the world in a twilight zone between civilization and barbarism. In myth they are a perversion of all that is proper and correct, a threat to the family, the basis of Greek society. Although the myth of the Amazons is a refinement of the traditional motif of female hostility to the hero, the threat is magnified by being directed against all society; thus are the Amazons always an army. They do not tempt the hero with their sexuality (although this motif is submerged in Heracles' labor to acquire the belt of the Amazon queen). Their incursion

---

[2]Although no clear evidence shows whether women were present at tragedies, their presence would nullify the all-male esprit that the citizen festival was intended to affirm, and of course violate the sense of conventional feminine modesty, at least for well-born women.

into the civilized world is the encroachment of darkness into light, and Greek heroes always overcome them just as they defeat other denizens of the nightmare realm, ruthlessly and without mercy.

The Athenian myth of the Amazonomachy became especially vigorous after the astounding victory of Athenian hoplites over the Persian invaders in 490 BC at the battle of Marathon. After this time the Amazons were represented in Greek art as Persians, wearing long leather trousers and with Persian leather caps. Theseus' victory over the Amazons symbolized and justified Athens' superiority—moral and political—not only over the Persians, but over all peoples who would oppose its imperial democracy. The Amazonomachy was represented on a metope frieze of the Parthenon, begun in 447 BC, on the shield of Phidias' celebrated gold and ivory statue of Athena that stood in the Parthenon, and on the frieze in a temple to Hephaestus that still stands just off the Athenian agora.

## FURTHER READING

Blundell, S., *Women in Classical Athens* (London, 1998). A concise summary of what is known about women and their status in Athens in the fifth and fourth centuries BC.

Bothmer, D. von, *Amazons in Greek Art* (Oxford, 1957). The best review of the artistic evidence.

Dover, K. J., *Greek Homosexuality* (Cambridge, MA, 1978). Scientific treatment of a difficult topic.

Fantham, E., H. P. Foley, N. B. Kampen, and S. B. Pomeroy, *Women in the Classical World* (Oxford, 1994). Superb review of artistic and literary evidence, clear and jargon-free.

Hawley, R., and B. Levick, eds., *Women in Antiquity: New Assessments* (New York, 1995). Wide-ranging topics, both Greek and Roman, in essays by different scholars.

Lefkowitz, M. R., *Women in Greek Myth* (Baltimore, 1990). The types of women in Greek tragedy and their relationship to real Greek women, by a leading scholar; good on the Amazons.

Neils, J., ed., *Goddess and Polis: The Panathenaic Festival in Ancient Athens* (Princeton, 1992). Beautifully produced book, with evidence for the cult of Athena in Athens.

Peradotto, J., and J. P. Sullivan, eds., *Women in the Ancient World* (Albany, 1984). Excellent collection of essays from a feminist perspective, by leading scholars.

Pomeroy, S., *Goddesses, Whores, Wives and Slaves* (New York, 1975). A pioneering survey of the roles assigned to women in ancient Greece.

Pomeroy, S., *Families in Classical and Hellenistic Greece: Representations and Realities* (Oxford, 1997).

Reeder, E. D., ed., *Pandora: Women in Classical Greece* (Princeton, 1995). Lavishly illustrated, with illuminating, sometimes penetrating essays.

Rowlandson, J., ed., *Women and Society in Greek and Roman Egypt: A Sourcebook* (Cambridge, England, 1998). Excellent collection of original sources for the lives of women in Greco-Roman Egypt.

Sergent, B., *Homosexuality in Greek Myth,* with a preface by G. Dumézil (Boston, 1986). Explores the social practice as reflected in traditional story.

Tyrrell, W. B., *Amazons. A Study in Athenian Mythmaking* (Baltimore, 1984). Argues that Amazons take their character from an inversion of traditional Greek values.

# CHAPTER 12

# MYTH AND LAW: THE LEGEND OF ORESTES

THE ONLY SURVIVING TRILOGY (sequence of three plays) in the body of Greek tragedy, and according to many the greatest triumph of the Athenian theater, is Aeschylus' *Oresteia,* so called after Orestes, the son of Agamemnon. Aeschylus has taken an old story, important in the *Odyssey* and in other earlier poems and remade it to serve the self-vision of the mid-fifth century Athenian *polis* and its struggles with emerging theories of justice, of right action and right punishment in an ever more complex world.

The first play is the *Agamemnon,* which tells of Agamemnon's murder by his wife Clytemnestra after he returned victorious from Troy. The second play of the trilogy is the *Libation Bearers* (or *Choëphoroe,* kō-**ef**-o-rē), so called after its chorus of Trojan female captives who carry a libation to the grave of Agamemnon; in this play, which takes place several years after the *Agamemnon,* Orestes returns from exile, where he has grown up, and in conspiracy with his sister Electra kills his own mother Clytemnestra and his cousin Aegisthus, Clytemnestra's lover. In the third play, the *Eumenides* (yu-**men**-i-dez), a euphemism for the Erinyes (e-**rin**-i-ez, or Furies), also named after its chorus, Orestes' murder of his mother is adjudged in an Athenian court of law. He is acquitted and the Furies are tamed and receive their new name, *Eumenides,* "Beneficent Ones." A lost satyr play was performed in fourth place, called the *Proteus* after the sea-god who could change shape at will.

## A HOUSE OF HORRORS: THE MYTHICAL
## BACKGROUND TO THE *ORESTEIA*

The woes of the House of Atreus (see Figure 12.1) went back many generations, when hideous crimes of treachery, adultery, cannibalism, incest, rape,
and murder were committed. The story begins with Tantalus of Lydia, in Asia
Minor, a mortal so blessed that he dined with the gods. In his arrogance he
stole from them nectar and ambrosia, the divine food; then to crown his insane
folly, he invited the gods to a banquet and, to test their omniscience, chopped
up his son Pelops and served the pieces in a stew. All the gods recognized the
dish as human flesh and rejected it, except for Demeter, too preoccupied with
the disappearance of her daughter Persephonê to notice. At this time Oenomaüs (ē-nō-**mā**-us) ruled as king over Pisa, a village beside the Alpheus river in
the district of Elis in the northwest Peloponnesus, in classical times the site of
the Olympic Games. Oenomaüs was in love with his own beautiful daughter
Hippodamia (hip-po-da-**mē**-a). She refused to sleep with him, but he pre-
vented her from marrying anyone else by offering her as a prize in an un-
winnable contest. The suitor had to carry her away in a chariot, was given a
head start, and sent racing toward Corinth. Oenomaüs, who had a team of
horses sired by the wind, always caught up with the suitor, speared him from behind, cut off his head, and nailed it to the door of his palace. Hippodamia was
so beautiful that these gruesome conditions were no deterrent; soon the door
was covered with twelve decaying heads of unsuccessful suitors.

Pelops heard of Hippodamia's beauty and was determined to win the
contest. He crossed the sea from Lydia, bringing a golden-winged chariot

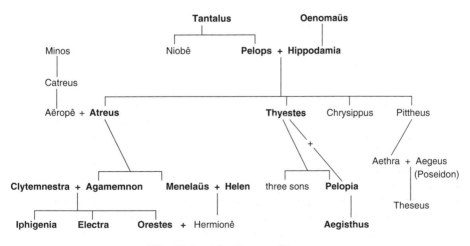

FIG. 12.1.   The House of Atreus.

drawn by horses that never tired, gifts from his divine lover Poseidon. Just to be sure, Pelops also bribed Myrtilus (**mir**-ti-lus), the king's charioteer, promising him the first night in bed with Hippodamia. Myrtilus removed the bronze linchpins[1] from Oenomaüs' chariot and replaced them with wax, so that when Oenomaüs raced toward the Isthmus after Pelops, the heated axle melted the wax and the wheels flew off. Oenomaüs was tangled in the reins and dragged to death.

Myrtilus, Hippodamia, and Pelops traveled on together. They stopped on a headland so that Pelops could get some water for his new and thirsty wife. When Pelops returned, he found Myrtilus clawing at Hippodamia, eager for his reward. In a rage, Pelops threw him from the towering crag into the sea. As Myrtilus fell, he screamed out a curse on Pelops and all his line. Curses on the lips of dying men are particularly effective, and many attributed the later horrors of the House of Atreus to Myrtilus' curse.

Pelops, ritually purified of his murders of Oenomaüs and Myrtilus, returned to Pisa and became its king. He named the land Peloponnesus, "island of Pelops," and produced many sons, including Thyestes (thī-**es**-tēz), father of Aegisthus (ē-**jis**-thus), and Atreus, father of Menelaüs (men-e-**lā**-us) and Agamemnon.

When Eurystheus, persecutor of Heracles and last descendant of Perseus to sit on the throne of Mycenae, was killed by the Heraclids ("descendants of Heracles"), an oracle ordered the Mycenaeans to choose a child of Pelops as the new king. The Mycenaeans sent across the mountains to Pisa and asked for Atreus and Thyestes. Which was to be king? Atreus, as the older, was the obvious choice, but Thyestes declared that a token was needed, a sign, and suggested that whoever could produce the fleece from a golden lamb should be king.

Years before, Atreus had vowed to Artemis to sacrifice his finest lamb to her, but when a lamb with golden fleece appeared in his flocks, he killed it and hid the skin in a trunk instead of burning the fleece on the altar. The only other person who knew about this was his wife, Aëropê (a-**er**-o-pe), a granddaughter of Minos. Unknown to Atreus, she was carrying on a love affair with her brother-in-law Thyestes and had secretly given him the fleece. When Thyestes proposed that whoever could produce the skin from a golden lamb should be king, Atreus hastily agreed, only to see Thyestes produce the very fleece he thought safe in his trunk.

But Atreus was sure that Zeus, god of kings, wanted him to be king, and to prove it, Atreus declared, Zeus would on the next day make the sun rise in the west. Thyestes thought this was impossible, but when the sun did rise in the west, crossed the sky backward, and set in the east, Thyestes withdrew his claim on the throne. Atreus banished him from the land.

---

[1]The linchpin was a sort of cotter-pin at the end of an axle to keep the wheel from falling off.

Atreus began to wonder how Thyestes had acquired the fleece and discovered his wife's infidelity. Burning for revenge, he invited Thyestes, now living abroad, to return to Mycenae; bygones would be bygones. While Thyestes was entertained in an outer room, Atreus murdered his three little boys, cut off their extremities, and roasted their trunks in the kitchen, then served the parts to Thyestes. After a tasty meal, Atreus asked Thyestes whether he knew what he had eaten. He showed him the heads and limbs of his children.

Thyestes fled, his mouth filled with cursing, and traveled to the Delphic Oracle, to inquire how he could even the score with his brother; some attribute the suffering of the House of Atreus to Thyestes' curse, an example of overdetermination, common in myth. Thyestes learned that he must beget a child by his own daughter, Pelopia (pe-**lō**-pi-a). Ignorant of his daughter's whereabouts, Thyestes left Delphi by night and came to a stream near Sicyon. In the flickering light of a sacrificial fire, he saw a girl go to the water. He saw his chance, jumped from the bushes, and raped her, but in the confusion left his sword behind. He did not know that the girl was in fact Pelopia, nor did she know her attacker.

In the meanwhile, Atreus was searching for Thyestes, sorry that he had let him off so lightly. He came to Sicyon and saw the pretty Pelopia, whom he thought was a daughter of the king. Atreus took her as his new wife. When Pelopia bore a son, Atreus naturally thought it was his own and named him Aegisthus.

Years passed, but Atreus continued to search for Thyestes. At last he sent his two older sons, Agamemnon and Menelaüs, to Delphi to ask Apollo where his brother was. Amazingly, Thyestes was at Delphi too; unable to find his daughter (he thought), he sought new advice from Apollo on how to take revenge on Atreus. Agamemnon and Menelaüs seized Thyestes and dragged him back to Mycenae.

Atreus, delighted that he could finally settle scores with the brother who had seduced his wife, summoned his other "son," Aegisthus, and ordered him to finish off Thyestes. Aegisthus entered the prison house, drew his sword, and prepared to behead Thyestes. Suddenly Thyestes called out, "Where did you get that sword?" "From my mother," Aegisthus replied. "But that's my sword!" cried Thyestes.

Pelopia was summoned in secret. She revealed how she had taken the weapon from a nocturnal rapist, Aegisthus' real father. As she spoke, she realized what had happened—that she had had intercourse with her own father. In horror at the deed, Pelopia seized the sword and plunged it into her heart. Aegisthus, realizing his true paternity, drew out the bloody weapon and carried it to Atreus, seeming proof that his murderous command had been performed. Relieved, Atreus offered sacrifice to the gods, then went to the river to wash his hands. Aegisthus came up from behind and knifed him in the back.[2]

---

[2]This complex, detailed, and extravagant myth is a distillation of typical plots of lost plays by Euripides, who must be responsible for the myth's general shape.

With Atreus dead, Thyestes mounted the throne of Mycenae. Agamemnon and Menelaüs fled and took refuge with Tyndareüs (tin-**dar**-e-us), king of Sparta. He was sympathetic to their cause and raised an army. Together they returned to Mycenae to drive Thyestes from the land and place Agamemnon on the throne. Eventually, Thyestes died in exile.

In the meanwhile, the king of Sparta Tyndareüs had married Leda (**lē**-da), whose beauty was so great that even Zeus took notice. Zeus appeared to her in the form of a swan, seized her by the nape of the neck (as swans do to one another), and had his way with her. Tyndareüs also had intercourse with her on the same night. She gave birth to four children: Polydeuces (= Roman Pollux) and Helen, fathered by Zeus, were semidivine; Castor and Clytemnestra, fathered by Tyndareüs, were mortal. According to one version, Leda actually laid a pair of eggs—from one egg hatched Zeus's children, from the other those of Tyndareüs!

Tyndareüs married Clytemnestra to Agamemnon, but was worried about Helen, who had grown up to be the most beautiful woman in the world. The richest and best-born young men from all Greece gathered in Tyndareüs' halls to seek her hand. Among them were Odysseus, son of Laërtes; Diomedes, son of Tydeus who fought against Thebes; Ajax,[3] son of Telamon; Philoctetes (fi-lok-**tē**-tez), son of Poeas, who had dared to light the funeral pyre of Heracles; Patroclus (pa-**trō**-klus), son of Menoetius, who became Achilles' best friend; Menelaüs, son of Atreus; and many others. Being young, headstrong, and dangerous, the rejected suitors were likely to turn on Tyndareüs once he had made a choice.

Odysseus understood Tyndareüs' position and realized that he was too poor to be chosen Helen's husband, coming as he did from Ithaca, an obscure rocky island in the western seas. He therefore went to Tyndareüs and offered a solution to his dilemma, if only Tyndareüs would arrange Odysseus' marriage with Tyndareüs' niece, Penelopê (pen-**el**-o-pē). Odysseus' solution is called the Oath of Tyndareüs, described by Hesiod in a fragment from a poem that cataloged the famous women of olden time:

> Of all the suitors her father° demanded unbreakable pledges,
> making them swear an oath, with libations poured in the fire:
> "The victor, be he who he may, can rely on my giving support
> in defense of his marriage with Helen, maiden of beautiful arms."
> He ordered the suitors, moreover, to assent to another condition:
> if anyone carried her off, forgetting his own reputation,
> and with it the vengeance to come, then all the suitors together

*her father:* Helen's, that is, Tyndareüs.

---

[3]The common Latin form for the Greek *Aias.*

must join in pursuit and exact due punishment from the offender.
Most of the suitors assented, in empty hopes of the marriage,
but the son of Atreus was victor, Menelaüs, delighting in battle,
who offered a price for the bride greater by far than the others.
  Now off in Pelion's forests Chiron was training Achilles,
nimble of foot, the bravest of men, though only a stripling.
Had nimble Achilles come home from the wooded valleys of Pelion
while Helen still was a maiden, not Menelaüs the warlike,
nor any man of the suitors would have met success in his wooing.
But long before then Menelaüs had won and had wedded fair Helen.

HESIOD, *Catalogue of Women*, fragment 204.78
(Merkelbach-West), 78–93

When Paris eloped with Helen, Agamemnon and Menelaüs invoked the
oath of Tyndareüs, and so the heroes assembled at the port of Aulis in order
to sail against Troy. But the winds blew constantly in the wrong direction.
They waited while the troops grew restless, food ran short, and disease
threatened. At last the prophet Calchas revealed how Artemis was behind it
all: Agamemnon once had boasted, while hurling his spear at a deer, that
"even Artemis could not do so well." To save the expedition, Agamemnon
would have to sacrifice his own daughter Iphigenia (if-i-jen-ī-a). Agamemnon
sent a herald to bring Iphigenia to Aulis, pretending that he wanted to marry
her to Achilles. Decked out in saffron wedding clothes, Iphigenia was led to a
wood, where Agamemnon slashed her throat on an altar.

According to another tradition, perhaps the invention of Euripides, at
the last second Artemis sent down a doe as a substitute for Iphigenia. The
doe was killed while the goddess carried Iphigenia to the land of the Tauri-
ans in the remote northern regions of the Black Sea, the modern Crimea.
There she became priestess to a foreign and even more savage Artemis, who
demanded the human sacrifice of all strangers.

## AESCHYLUS' *AGAMEMNON*

The general outlines of the background to the action, as sketched above,
would have been familiar to many of Aeschylus' audience. This is why he is
able to refer so obliquely, and in such abstruse language, to details of the
story and expect to be understood. A genre of ancient epic called *nostos*
("homecoming") told of the returns of the heroes from Troy and all that
happened to them—the *Odyssey* is our best example—and the *Agamemnon* is
an example in drama of this genre. Whereas Homer in his *Odyssey* concen-
trates on the tribulations Odysseus suffered while coming home and the dif-
ficulties he faced when he arrived, Aeschylus is concerned with the bitter
conflict within the family of Agamemnon and its resolution.

Homer refers to the story nineteen times in the first twelve books of the *Odyssey*. Telemachus, the son of Odysseus, is compared repeatedly to Orestes. In either case, an unprotected wife has received the sexual solicitations of other men. Clytemnestra gave in, Penelopê did not. Orestes avenged his father's death; and so should Telemachus be prepared to fight for the family's honor. But in Homer's version of the story, Aegisthus is the principal agent in Agamemnon's murder and the object of Orestes' wrath. Orestes is therefore a model of heroic behavior, because he defended the honor of the *oikos*, the household. Aeschylus, by contrast, attributes principal responsibility to Clytemnestra, making his drama a powerful study of gender in conflict.

In the opening scene a watchman perches on the roof of the palace, waiting for the beacon fire that will signal from across the sea, by a sort of primitive telegraph, that Troy has fallen. The watchman's opening words reflect the gloom enveloping the palace, where Clytemnestra has been having an affair with Agamemnon's cousin Aegisthus, apparently begotten after the cannibal feast. Suddenly the fire blazes up, the signal that Troy has fallen.

Clytemnestra comes onto the stage and explains in detail the meaning of the fire's beacon. She speaks "as a man," taking the man's role of a master of words and persuasion. A war-weary herald arrives, reporting the imminent appearance of the great and triumphant king, Agamemnon.[4] The herald presents a gloomy picture of this famous conquest of wide-wayed Troy, the burning of its temples to the ground, an outrage against the gods.

Troubles for the Greek victors had already begun with a great storm that beset the fleet when it set out from Troy, a storm usually attributed to Athena's anger because in the sack of the city, amidst every other outrage, a Greek warrior had raped Cassandra, prophetess and the daughter of Priam, as she clung to an image of Athena. Where Menelaüs was driven, no one knew, but Agamemnon's ship, at least, has survived.

Agamemnon arrives in a chariot, accompanied by his mistress and "prize," the raped Cassandra. He greets the city and is himself greeted by Clytemnestra, who comes out from the palace. She publicly and deceptively complains of the awful suffering during her husband's absence that nearly drove her to suicide. She then invites her husband to enter the palace over a purple cloth, a central symbol in the play. The cloth is a metaphor of the net by which Clytemnestra will trap and kill him, a symbol of the blood-red destructive woven arts of woman. At first Agamemnon refuses, saying to walk on the scarlet cloth would be presumptuous, not befitting a mortal's place, but Clytemnestra, arguing cleverly and like a man, urges him to put such thoughts from his mind. His triumphant return merits special display. Persuaded, and ignorant of her real prayer, Agamemnon removes his sandals,

---

[4]Aeschylus has little interest in presenting the sequence of events in real time.

steps from the chariot and enters the palace across the purple cloth, doomed and in the woman's power.

The old men of the chorus are wise and have speculated on the meaning of the mysterious omen that greeted the fleet when it set out, two eagles tearing at a pregnant hare, appearing on the right hand, the side of good omen. The eagle is the bird of Zeus, so their victory is Zeus' will, and the two eagles are Agamemnon and Menelaüs, but Artemis, the chorus explains, is outraged by the death of the unborn young, sure foretelling of further misfortune. Cassandra, whom Apollo loved, sees the truth directly and, although a woman, she declares publicly Agamemnon's doom and her own. No one understands her prophetic babble, because although Apollo gave her prophecy, he declared that no one would believe her. She has a vision of Thyestes' curse hanging heavy on the house and over the lintel of the palace sees a vision of the cannibal feast.

Cassandra turns and goes into the palace. From within a cry is heard as Clytemnestra strikes the death blow. Clytemnestra comes forth, drenched in blood, looming over the murdered bodies of her husband and his mistress. Exulting, like a male warrior triumphant, she declares how delicious was the murderous deed, which she prepared with her lover, Aegisthus. She killed him like an ox led to sacrifice, and she killed his whore too. In an obscene parody of agricultural metaphor, she compares the drops of blood to the spring rain that nourishes young crops. Clytemnestra defends her treachery and murder, claiming as her motive Agamemnon's sacrifice of her daughter Iphigenia. The spineless Aegisthus, compared to a woman, joins her on the stage, and the play ends.

## AESCHYLUS' *LIBATION BEARERS*

The second play of the trilogy takes place years later. Agamemnon's son Orestes, spirited from the house as a child and raised in Phocis (the territory around Delphi), has come to manhood. Ordered by Apollo through the Delphic Oracle to avenge his father's murder, he returns to Argos in the company of his friend Pylades. He goes to his father's grave and leaves a footprint, a lock of hair, and a piece of cloth upon it.

The night before, Clytemnestra had a horrible dream: She gave birth to a viper that sucked at her breasts and bit them. Thinking the dream sent by the angry ghost of Agamemnon, she sends her daughter Electra to his grave to make drink-offerings, in company with a band of Trojan slaves—the "libation bearers" who make up the chorus. Electra recognizes Orestes from the tokens she finds on the grave. Bitter and filled with hatred toward the mother who killed her father, and the perversion of sexual roles and sexual behavior that she represents, she allies with Orestes and together they plot the murder of Clytemnestra.

Orestes pretends that he is a messenger from Phocis, come to Argos to report his own death. Thus he gains admission to the palace. Aegisthus is summoned to hear the good news; Orestes kills him on the spot. Clytemnestra discovers the corpse—and the truth. Orestes draws his sword to fulfill his mission, but Clytemnestra, desperate for life, bares her breasts and pleads:

> No, no, my child! have pity on these breasts,
> from which, still half asleep, your baby gums
> so often sucked the milk that gave you strength.

AESCHYLUS, Choëphoroe, 896–898

Orestes hesitates, but his friend Pylades, in the only words he speaks in the play, urges him to remember Apollo's command. Orestes buries the sword in his mother's belly, then exults over the two bodies lying at his feet, as Clytemnestra had exulted over the bodies of Agamemnon and Cassandra. Already the Furies, the persecuting spirits of murdered kin, surround Orestes and work their vengeance by disturbing the mind of their victim. Orestes has gone insane.

## AESCHYLUS' *EUMENIDES*

The last play of the trilogy, in which the Furies make up the chorus, opens in Delphi. Orestes has gone there for Apollo's protection from the Furies, for it was Apollo who advised him to kill his mother. Apollo orders Orestes to go to Athens to seek justice from the Athenian law court presided over by Athena. The scene shifts (rare in Greek drama) to Athens, where Orestes falls down, a suppliant, at the statue of Athena. The Furies arrive and insist that the spilled blood of blood relatives must be atoned by more spilled blood, but Orestes claims that Apollo has purified him of pollution and appeals to Athena for help. The Furies claim that it is their divine and eternal right to persecute those who murder their own blood kin and that the upstart Olympians have no right to interfere with ancient privilege. Athena, seeing justice on either side, turns the case over to a jury of twelve Athenians, who hear the case on the Areopagus ("hill of Ares") below the Acropolis, the first trial scene in Western literature.

The Furies present their case: Without the ancient restraints there will be no check on crime. Orestes asks why they did not persecute Clytemnestra for killing Agamemnon—because, they reply, Clytemnestra and Agamemnon did not share the same blood. Apollo now takes up Orestes' case and claims the authority of Zeus, the protector of kings: Agamemnon's death is not to be compared with that of an adulterous woman. As for the primacy of blood-ties, the child's blood comes from the father who plants the seed, not from the mother who is but the soil in which the seed is sown. Athena herself is proof that the child is of the father—she had no mother, but was born from Zeus' head. Therefore, Orestes' murder of Clytemnestra was, strictly speaking, not the shedding of kindred blood. Orestes was obliged to avenge the murder of his father, a scepter-bearing king.

Even after Apollo's ingenious application of traditional tale, the story of Athena's birth, to prove a point in a court of law, the jury's vote is evenly divided. Athena, who always sides with the male, casts the deciding vote: Opinions differ whether before Athena's vote the jury was evenly divided, or whether her vote created an even division. In either event, Orestes is acquitted. Still the Furies are vengeful, but Athena appeases their anger by assigning them a permanent place in a grotto beneath the Acropolis. As beneficent spirits, no longer malignant, they will further the prosperity of the *polis;* hence their new name Eumenides, "the kindly ones."

Apollo's argument, that the son is closer to the father than to the mother, is based on the ancient agricultural metaphor applied to human biology. The seed is planted in the earth, but is not of the earth; the rain from heaven, like semen, makes the seed grow, which otherwise would die. So the human female provides a soil in which the child may grow, but the child comes from the father. The reasoning is typical of arguments offered in real Athenian courts of the fifth century, when conclusions based on the plausibility of evidence were first being refined. A century and a quarter after the production of the *Oresteia,* Aristotle speculated on the roles of father and mother in producing children. Although he recognizes that both sexes contribute, he assigns the generative force (which includes the form the fetus is to assume) to the male contribution; the female contributes only its formless matter. In fact, the female's genetic contribution to human reproduction was not clarified until about two hundred years ago.

## THE *ORESTEIA:* A PARABLE OF PROGRESS

Aeschylus, born in 525 BC, grew up when the tyranny of Pisistratus and his sons was breaking down. He lived through the radical democratic reforms of Cleisthenes around 510 BC and fought in the battles of Marathon, 490 BC, and Salamis, 480 BC. Alone of the major Athenian tragedians, he brought to his poetic vision the boundless optimism of the young democracy. In the *Oresteia* we see him refashion the myth so important to Homer's *Odyssey* to proclaim this vision.

A leading theme in the trilogy is the question, "What is justice?" In the Greek text, the Greek word for justice, *dikê,* which can also mean "vengeance," "right," "judgment," and "trial," recurs dozens of times in the speculations of the chorus and the actors. According to the ancient unwritten law of the clan, justice is revenge. Thyestes slept with Atreus' wife; Atreus gave Thyestes his own children to eat. Agamemnon killed Iphigenia;

Clytemnestra killed Agamemnon; Orestes killed Clytemnestra. This is blood-vendetta, rooted in the ancient fear of ghosts who demand blood for blood, an eye for an eye, the old law that the Furies embody and execute.[5]

But the constant killing for revenge has no logical limit. Clytemnestra claims justice for her murder of Agamemnon, then herself becomes the murderer, the object of revenge. The old justice has placed Orestes in a "double bind": Either course of action before him is disastrous. Either he must not avenge his father's death, or he must kill his mother. Agamemnon had been in a similar position at Aulis. Either he must allow the expedition to perish, or he must kill his own daughter. It is a theme in the trilogy that the males place social responsibility above obligation to family. Hence Orestes restores the legitimate male succession at Argos by killing his own mother; Agamemnon allows the expedition to advance by killing his own daughter.

Earlier in Greek religion, at Delphi, an advance over the primitive blood-vendetta had appeared. In a rite of purification performed there, a pig's blood was dripped over a murderer to release him and those who had contact with him from persecution by a ghost. The progressive Athenian system of civic law to settle homicide, which Aeschylus proudly celebrates, was a momentous improvement over the Delphic system of magical purification (but note that Aeschylus gives Apollo credit for inspiring this advance). We use a similar system of civic law in the West today.

In Athenian civic law the juridical power of the family is curtailed and overridden by the authority of the state, whose will is communicated through laws recorded in writing. Most upper-class Athenian males could read this script, and from 621 BC onward Athenian laws were engraved on wood or stone and displayed in the agora, where anyone could examine them and argue over their meaning. Some written law had existed before in Mesopotamia (never in pharaonic Egypt), but such laws were presented as handed down by gods, immutable, divine, and inexorable; the Hebrews, too, viewed law as divinely willed. In Athens, by contrast, laws were drafted and approved by the people, constantly revised, and interpreted in open courts by a jury of one's fellow citizens. There was nothing divine about these laws, and there were no lawyers in Athens to present a definitive interpretation: A defendant had to represent *himself* in court.[6] The system of Athenian popular democratic laws recorded in alphabetic writing contributed greatly to the dvelopment of the arts of persuasion and led directly to the invention of logic and the elaborate philosophical speculations of Plato and Aristotle.

---

[5] Cf. the biblical "If any harm follows, then you shall give life for life, eye for eye, tooth for tooth, hand for hand, foot for foot, burn for burn, wound for wound, stripe for stripe" (Exodus 21.23–25).

[6] Athenian females, who were never citizens, were excluded from this system of public governance and were ordinarily not allowed into court; when a woman was charged with a crime, a male would speak on her behalf.

The Furies, on the other hand, stand for traditional, familial, and tribal ways. The avenging spirits of spilled blood take no interest in why familial blood was shed, but only that it was shed. These ancient powers of ghost-vengeance, the children of Night (Nyx), are by nature opposed to the younger Olympians, Athena and Apollo. They are also female, as the man-like murderous Clytemnestra is female, as Helen is female, whose adultery began the Trojan War. Although they cannot be cast out completely or destroyed, anymore than the female can be gotten rid of, they can be tamed and transformed into propitious powers that will support the new order—the Eumenides. Thus Athens, the ideal *polis,* replaces the violent, archaic, and heroic world with one that looks to a brighter future in which human intelligence can resolve primitive, self-destructive fear.

Aeschylus also incorporates numerous etiological details in the *Eumenides.* The institution of the Areopagus, a court with jurisdiction over homicide during Aeschylus' day, is traced back to the trial of Orestes; the rule, still true, that a tie vote stands for acquittal may begin with Athena's ruling (if that is what happened); the cult of the Eumenides (which actually existed in caves beneath the rock of the Areopagus) is hereby explained; and the traditional political alliance between Argos and Athens in Classical times is traced to Orestes' gratitude for being freed of the Furies' persecution at Athens. Aeschylus' *Oresteia* is a good example of how the Greeks modified and transformed ancient, traditional tales to reflect contemporary issues and to justify contemporary practice.

## FURTHER READING

Arthur, M., "Early Greece: Origins of Western Attitudes Towards Women," in J. Peradotto and J. P. Sullivan, eds., *Women in the Ancient World* (Albany, 1984). Explores the myth of matriarchy overthrown in the *Oresteia.*

Fagles, R. *Aeschylus: the Oresteia* (New York, 1966). Good modern translation.

Goldhill, S., *Reading Greek Tragedy* (Cambridge, England, 1986). Has two chapters on the *Oresteia.*

Goldhill, S., *Aeschylus: The Oresteia* (Cambridge, England, 1992). The best short book on the trilogy.

Zeitlin, F., "The Motif of the Corrupted Sacrifice in Aeschylus' *Oresteia,*" *Transactions and Proceedings of the American Philological Association* 96 (1965). Seminal essay on the trilogy.

# CHAPTER 13

# ROMAN MYTH AND ROMAN RELIGION: THE *METAMORPHOSES* OF OVID

**M**YTHS HAVE HIDDEN STRUCTURES that are communicable across racial and linguistic lines. They spring alive anew in new ground and take on new meanings. The Greeks took their myths from the East, and the Romans took theirs from the Greeks. In so doing, the Romans more than the Greeks fashioned our popular notion of a myth.

The Romans themselves seem scarcely to have had any myths. In the native tradition there is no creation story and almost no divine myth. Roman myth is really legend, stories about great men and great deeds in the Roman past. Well-known examples include the story of the founding of Rome by Romulus and Remus, the one-man stand of Horatius at the bridge crossing the Tiber, and Brutus' overthrow of the Etruscan tyrants after the king's son raped the noble Lucretia. Roman legend is intimately bound up with Roman history and equated with it by the Romans themselves. Nonetheless, there is little that is truly historical in these legends. Mostly they are myths in our modern sense, propaganda designed to elicit support for social patterns.

Such Roman stories did in fact prove remarkably effective in maintaining Roman power. The Romans knew that their legends worked as propaganda, but accepted their validity, just as Americans still teach children that George Washington cut down a cherry tree and, because he could not tell a lie, confessed to his father. Even if Washington never did this, he might have done so; the moral of the story is more important than its historical truth. Roman "myth," then, looks like traditional story and in its story patterns is modeled after Greek myth, but ethical and political purposes (as to some extent in Athenian myth) have become preeminent.

The stories of early Rome have exercised a profound influence on Western civilization and continue to do so today. Whenever one is asked to suppress one's personal interests for the common good, as Brutus[1] did when he executed his own sons for disloyalty to the state, the wonderful deeds of early Rome come to mind and take on fresh meaning. Such has always been an important function of myth: to define a culture to itself, to inform a people what is real in the world and important in one's personal and social life, and to offer bases for the difficult decisions everyone must face.

## ROMAN RELIGION AND ROMAN MYTH-MAKERS

Careful students of Greek culture from an early date, the Romans eventually took over the whole body of Greek myths, with minor modifications, substituting similar Roman divinities for the Greek gods and goddesses (see chart at back of book). Catullus (c. 84–54 BC), a contemporary of Julius Caesar, is best known for his love poems, but also wrote on mythical themes. Vergil (70–19 BC), the greatest Roman poet, told the story of Aeneas in his epic, the *Aeneid*. This poem has one of our fullest descriptions of the underworld and our most vivid account of the sack of Troy. The poem also preserves the legends of Dido, queen of Carthage, and of Hercules' (= Greek Heracles) battle against the monster Cacus (see Chapter 14). The poetry of the Roman Ovid (43 BC–c. AD 18), a generation younger than Vergil, is our most important source from any period, and we will examine his influential poem *Metamorphoses* (met-a-mor-**fō**-sēz), "Transformations," later in this chapter.

We have noted how myths are stories, whereas religion is belief and the course of action that follows from belief. Religion is a system of assumptions about how external powers affect our behavior and the things we do to maintain good relationships with these external powers. Greek myth was inextricably mixed with religion, as we have seen. Roman myth was too, but the profoundly different nature of the Roman divinities created special conditions for the development of Roman myth. Greek religion as reflected in Greek poetry regarded its deities as endowed with superhuman powers and, in general, with immortality, but the Greek poetic anthropomorphic gods also possess a human psychology: They lust, lie, cheat, fight, love, forgive, hate, and avenge, and many help the humans they favor. Native Roman deities, by contrast, seem to have been mostly personifications of various

---

[1]Not the Brutus who killed Caesar, but the legendary Brutus who lived at the founding of the Roman Republic (claimed as an ancestor by Brutus the assassin).

abstract qualities and were strictly limited in their function, having only the right to refuse or assent to requests. The Latin verb *nuo* means "nod" and hence "assent," and from this word such deities are called *numina* (singular *numen*), "nodders." The *numina* are spirits that can inhabit almost any object or serve almost any function, petty or grand.

A good example is the *numen* called by some authors Robigus, grammatically masculine, and by others Robigo, grammatically feminine—that is, a spirit whose gender was unimportant. Robigus/o had one power, either to bring or hold back fungus disease in the grain crop. At a sacrifice called the Robigalia, held annually on April 25, the priest of Quirinus (kwi-**rī**-nus), a *numen* representing the Roman people, would ask Robigus/o to hold back the blight. In return, the priest offered him/her a sort of bribe of wine, incense, the gut of a sheep, and the entrails of a filthy red dog. The ceremony was called *sacrificium*, a "making sacred," the origin of our word *sacrifice*.

*Sacrificium* was a legal transfer of something into the ownership of the *numen*, who was then expected to fulfill his or her side of the bargain. Both parties to a contract gave something in order to receive something in return—*do ut des*, "I grant you this, so that you will give me that in exchange." Such a notion, applied to the gods, removed them from moral responsibility. The priest acted as a lawyer for the Roman people in fulfilling their side of the contract, and the *numen* was expected to fulfill his or her obligations as well.

The functions of *numina* were sometimes subdivided by anxious souls eager to do everything exactly right. We have several lists of such subdeities, who had no temples or cult, but were invoked separately on appropriate occasions. For example, at the Cerealia, a ceremony on April 19 in honor of Ceres (**sē**-rēz), *numen* of the grain harvest, and *Tellus Mater* ("Mother Earth"), a priest invoked the favor of First-Plower, Second-Plower, Maker-of-Ridges-between-Furrows, Implanter, Over-Plower, Harrower, Hoer, Weeder, Harvester, Bringer-in, Storer, and Bringer-out. Such beings later excited the scornful mirth of the fathers of the Christian church.

Although the Roman *numina* were remote and colorless, some of them took on roles of service to the state and the family and enjoyed a central place in Roman civic and home life—roles that grew as Greek influence helped them assume more personality. One of the best-known Roman *numina* was Janus (**jā**-nus), "gate-god," in origin a *numen* of bridges, hence of going forth and returning. He was represented with two faces, one looking forward, the other back. He came to be viewed as presiding over beginnings of all kinds, and the first month of our year was named after him. In the Forum stood a gate without a building: Janus himself. His doors were opened when Rome went to war, and closed when it was at peace. Until the final victory of Augustus in 31 BC in the terrible civil wars that had long afflicted the Roman world, they had stood open for more than two hundred years; the first emperor proudly proclaimed, "I closed Janus." From this *numen* seems to come the Roman triumphal arch.

When the Roman poets fell under the influence of the Greeks living in southern Italy, they began to think of these bloodless abstractions, the *numina*, as being like the anthropomorphic gods of the Greeks. The Roman equivalents to Greek gods, as named in Vergil, Ovid, and other poets, were largely a poetic invention, then, with little basis in native Roman religion, although there were also important political motivations, especially during the reign of the first emperor, Augustus (ruled 27 BC–AD 14).

The first syllable of the name of Jupiter[2] (also called Jove), originally *numen* of the sky, is etymologically identical to Zeus; he must descend from the common cultural, linguistic, and racial heritage shared by all speakers of Indo-European languages. Jupiter was worshiped in many manifestations (for example, as *Juppiter pluvius,* "Jupiter as the rain"). As *Juppiter lapis,* a sacred stone supposed to be a thunderbolt, he received pigs sacrificed with a stone knife, a rite descended from neolithic times. Jupiter became the incarnation of the striking power of the Roman state, and his emblem, the eagle, appeared on the standards of the Roman legions.

Juno was the *numen* who presided over women as members of the family, hence her equation with Hera; she had close ties with the moon. Ceres, *numen* of wheat, was from an early time equated with Demeter. Diana, the Roman Artemis, shares the same Indo-European root *di-*, "shining," with Zeus, Jupiter, the Indian sky-god Dyaus, and the Norse war god Tiu. Perhaps in origin a spirit of the wood, Diana, like Juno, was associated with women and childbirth.

Mercury has no ancient Italian heritage, but is Hermes introduced to the Latins under a title suggestive of his commercial activities (*merx* is Latin for "merchandise"). Vulcan's name is not Latin. Identified with Hephaestus, he may have come from the eastern Mediterranean through Etruria north of Rome; he was a god of volcanic and other forms of destructive fire. Neptune (equated with the Greek Poseidon) was the *numen* of water, although not specifically the sea until identified with Poseidon. Apollo was never successfully identified with a Latin *numen,* but came early to Latium through Etruria and the Greek colonies of southern Italy.

The origins of Mars, assimilated to the Greek Ares, are obscure. Closely associated with the wolf, he may once have protected flocks, or have been a primordial god of war (a spear kept in the forum had the name Mars). He gave his name to the month of March, a good time for beginning military operations. Minerva, an Etruscan import, was *numen* of handicrafts, hence asso-

---

[2]His name is spelled with two p's in Latin, one in English.

ciated with the Greek Athena. Liber (lē-ber, "free"), *numen* of wine, was equated with Dionysus; according to the etymologizing of the Romans, always suspect, his name was taken to be a translation of the Greek epithet for Dionysus, *luaios,* "looser" from care. Liber had a female counterpart, Libera. Faunus (**faw**-nus, "kindly one") is named euphemistically: He was *numen* of the unreasoning terror of the lonely forest and was identified with Pan.

Venus seems once to have been a *numen* of fresh water, especially springs; an early inscription from the volcanic country in southern Italy is a dedication "to the Stinking Venus," presumably the *numen* of a sulphurous spring. Water is, of course, essential for the cultivation of plants, especially in gardens, and the name of the *numen* may derive from the Latin word for "pleasant," *venustus* (unless the name of the *numen* came first). From being a *numen* of vegetable fertility, Venus, under Greek influence, also took animal and human fertility under her protection.

A literary passage reflecting the transformation of Venus appears in the opening of the *De rerum natura,* "On the Nature of Things," a philosophical poem by one of Rome's finest poets, Lucretius. Venus, Lucretius writes, is a being "who stings every heart on land and sea and air, the leaf-laden trees and the birds, the green and flourishing land, with insistent desire that lures them on to propagate their kind." In these lines she functions still as *numen,* a natural force with a name. A few lines further, however, she becomes the Greek Aphrodite, in whose arms "reclines fierce Mars,[3] stabbed with love's undying wound. His head droops back; he feeds desire with gazing in your [Venus'] eyes, and his breath is locked to your responsive lips." The humanization of Venus presented by Lucretius around 60 BC has much advanced forty years later in Vergil's *Aeneid,* where she functions as does any Greek god, protecting her son Aeneas in his trials.

To Hercules belongs the earliest foreign cult received at Rome. The form of his name reflects Western Greek pronunciation, as does Aesculapius, the Latin form of Asclepius, and Proserpina (pro-**ser**-pi-na), the Latin form of Persephonê (as Ulysses is the Latin form of Odysseus). Dis (dis), the Roman Hades, is an abbreviation of Latin *dives,* "a rich person," a translation of the Greek Pluto (which in Greek means "enricher"), a euphemism for Hades.

## OVID'S METAMORPHOSES

Such identifications between native spirits and abstractions and the Greek gods was long since complete by the time that Ovid wrote his *Metamorphoses* around the time of the birth of Christ. Transformation is not only the central

---

[3]That is, Ares.

theme to the *Metamorphoses,* but the poem is itself ever-changing in style, jumping from the solemn to the hilarious to the burlesque. The poem begins with the transformation of chaos into cosmos and ends with the transformation of Julius Caesar, Augustus' great-uncle, into a star. But in Ovid's literate and urbane retelling, the old Greek tales have lost the religious overtones of the Greek versions; a large percentage of his stories are love stories, appealing to the refined, good-humored taste of the powerful but often idle Roman elite. Clever, engaging, irreverent, sometimes salacious, his *Metamorphoses,* more than any other single work, defines what the world thinks of as classical myth. Ovid wrote much love poetry besides the *Metamorphoses* that also alludes to myth. For centuries, from the Roman Period through the Middle Ages and the Renaissance, Ovid was the most important source of classical myth for artists, writers, and others. Every art museum has pictures inspired by his accounts.

## Structure and Genre

Scholars have long argued, and continue to disagree, about the genre of Ovid's poem. Some view it as a kind of epic because it is written in dactylic hexameter verse, like Homer and Vergil's *Aeneid,* and is very long. Also, it contains epic catalogues and high-flown epic similes, considerably more than in the *Iliad* or the *Odyssey.* Yet Ovid's poem lacks utterly the focus on heroic achievement and the struggle with the meaning of human and moral action that we expect in epic. In fact the poem's endless variety and shifts of mood and tone make it impossible to place the poem into any specific genre. In this respect, Ovid owes a great debt to Greek literary predecessors who lived predominantly in Alexandria in Egypt, who composed poetry in which myth had lost its deep meanings to become the subject of play and a way of showing off learning. The Alexandrians even had a genre of poetry devoted to metamorphosis, although no Alexandrian poet attempted anything remotely so ambitious as Ovid's effort.

Apparently Ovid himself, however, invented the device of organizing his tales in a chronological framework, beginning with the creation of the universe, proceeding to the universal flood and the repopulation of the earth. He places the myths of Hercules and of Jason and the Argonauts before the stories about Troy, according to a conventional scheme of mythical chronology. Then come adventures of Greek leaders, then the early heroes of Rome, ending with the ascendance of Augustus Caesar, the first emperor. The chronological arrangement gives to Ovid's mythical handbook the dimensions and the look of a universal history. Yet very few of the actual connections between the individual stories are chronological. Rather, connections between stories depend on fancy, free-association, or even preposterous relationships. For example, he makes a transition from the story of Callisto, a virgin follower of Diana turned to a bear, to the story of Coronis, struck dead for sleeping with another man while pregnant with Apollo's child, in this way. Juno, bitter that Jupiter has raised the transformed Callisto and her son to the stars, asks that they at least never bathe in the pure waters of Ocean:

> The sea gods nodded assent and Juno, mounting her swift car
> Came to the clear heaven, borne by her colored peacocks,
> Peacocks just recently decorated with the eyes of Argus,
> At the same time that your plumage, loquacious crow,
> Was changed from white to black.

OVID, Metamorphoses 2.531.5

Juno's car is pulled by peacocks; peacocks got their eyes at the same time that the crow was turned from white to black: Both peacocks and crows are birds, and there we would expect Ovid to make his connection, but the actual connection is temporal. Argus was the many-eyed monster that watched over Io, beloved of Jupiter and changed to a cow by Juno, until he was killed by Mercury. In the story of Coronis, Apollo changes the crow from white to black because the crow brings to him the news of Coronis' infidelity.

## Ovid's Style: Erysichthon

In spite of the poem's title and of the important theme of transformation, only rarely do stories focus on a change of form, a detail commonly added perfunctorily to a tale whose real interest lies in the brilliant or unusual way in which it is told. A good example of Ovid's method is found in the tale of Erysichthon (8.738–878), an obscure subject treated in the *Hymn to Demeter* by the Alexandrian scholar and poet Callimachus (c. 305–240 BC), but otherwise almost never mentioned (Hesiod refers to it). As Callimachus tells it, the basic story is simple. The young Erysichthon wants to build a banqueting hall, so he goes to the forest and comes to a grove sacred to Demeter (= Roman Ceres). His men begin to cut it down, when a tree screams aloud at the blows of the ax. Demeter, disguised as a priestess, appears and asks Erysichthon to desist. When he replies that he needs the timber to build a banquet hall, she afflicts him with an insatiable and eternal hunger, a condition that brings disaster on Erysichthon's family and on himself. After eating everything in sight—including the family cat!—Erysichthon goes out on the road to beg and eat the filth left behind by others.

Ovid's telling of the story, by contrast, is anything but simple. Constantly and without apology, Ovid shifts his tone from the serious to the grotesque to the comic and playful, showing little interest in metamorphosis as such, but rather in the tones and postures that his theme will allow. He begins with a solemn description in epic style of the mysterious wood, realistically described. He declares Erysichthon's wickedness and criminal personality, leading us to expect a moral tale of crime and punishment. But the serious and realistic tone he has carefully constructed evaporates when, to fulfill her curse, Ceres sends a nymph to the land of Hunger, a fantastic and wondrous realm. Ovid abandons his earlier solemn style of description and never returns to it. Hunger is described with the kind of elaborate and grotesque detail that so delighted European artists of the European Renaissance:

> The nymph sought Hunger, and she found her in a stony field,
> Digging with her nails and teeth in the scanty grass.
> Her hair hung down in matted locks, her eyes were sunken,
> her face pale white, her lips had lost all color, and her throat
> was rough and scaly, the skin so tight you could see the guts right through,
> her skinny hips bulged out from the loins. Her belly was a hole,
> You'd say her breasts dangled, held up, barely, by a spine
> So thin that her joints seemed huge, knees swollen and her ankles
> big overgrown lumps.
>
> OVID, *Metamorphoses* 8.799–808

Ovid loves to exaggerate, to go on and on, and in this way he now describes how Erysichthon's appetite explodes, consuming everything that the sea, the earth, and the sky can produce. What would feed a city is a tidbit to him. The more he eats, the more he wants. In exorbitant, even ridiculous, descriptions, Ovid has abandoned entirely any plan to tell an effective story about retribution for a sinful nature and impious behavior.

Here, in accordance with his theme, Ovid at last introduces a transformation. Reduced to dire poverty, Erysichthon sells his daughter as a slave. She prays to Neptune, who loves her, for help, and Neptune grants her the power to change shape. Her new-found power only enables Erysichthon to sell his daughter over and over again, as she adopts ever different forms! The metamorphosis of Erysichthon's daughter underlines the horrendous effects of his hunger, but the effect of the device is to divert attention from a true moral solution to the plot, whereby evil is suitably punished. Erysichthon's fate is too exaggerated to provoke a moral response in the audience. Finally, tired of his story, Ovid reports that Erysichthon ate himself up, a comical image. The ancient deep meanings of myth, their meditations on cosmic origins and moral behavior and the meaning of human experience, are gone. What remains is a delight in the narrative itself, in the brilliant telling of the story.

## Other Themes

Such is the rule, that metamorphosis robs the story of a tragic and moral dimension, usually by preventing a crushing finale. Daphnê, for example, is turned to a laurel to escape Apollo's amorous pursuit; Syrinx, turned to a reed, never submits to Pan; and Niobê, all of whose children lie dead around her, is turned to a rock as she grieves. By being transformed, these figures never feel the weight of tragic suffering, but escape their dilemmas through a literary device. Often Ovid adds editorial comments that cast doubt on the accuracy of his description and further lessen the story's potential gravity. For example, when the bestial Thracian king Tereus rapes his wife's sister Philomela, Ovid remarks

And then—the story goes on, *scarcely deserving of credit*—
the sadist returned in his lust again, and again, to his victim.

OVID, Metamorphoses 6.561–562

When Ovid does describe the psychology of metamorphosis, his focus is on the anguish of the human being trapped inside the beast, where its human mind continues to think and feel as it did before the transformation, as when the angry Diana transforms Actaeon into a stag:

From his forehead antlers erupted,
the horns of a terrified stag, just where the water had spattered.
She forced his neck to grow long and crowned it with pointed ears;
she turned his hands into hooves and traded his forearms for forelegs;
his body she veiled to the view with a spotted velvety deerskin.
To crown it, she gave him the heart of a deer. Actaeon
was astonished to find how nimble he was, how speedy of foot,
But O! what a horror to see his antlers reflected in water.
"Can that be your face, Actaeon?" was what he attempted to utter.
Not a word would come out. He groaned; that was all he could manage.
Tears dropped down from a pair of eyes no longer his own.
Yet still the mind of a human was left. "What can I do?" he debated,
"Shall I flee to my father's house and the apparatus of power,
or hide in the forest?" but shame blocked one and terror the other.

OVID, Metamorphoses 3.185–199

Often the transformation embodies the inner qualities of the human suffering it, as in the first transformation in the *Metamorphoses,* when the wicked king Lycaon (lī-**kā**-on) is turned into a wolf:

His mouth gathers foam and with its accustomed lust for slaughter
He attacks the sheep and even now rejoices in blood.
His clothing changes to hair, his arms to legs.
He is a wolf, yet preserves traces of his former shape.
The gray hair is the same, the same violent face,
The same glowing eyes, the same image of the wild.

OVID, Metamorphoses 1.234–9

Lycaon's character remains unchanged; his new outer form of a wolf only expresses his inner lasting nature.

Because Ovid does not focus on the metamorphosis, he is free to concentrate on events leading up to it and to punctuate his narrative by elaborate descriptions of states of feeling. As the narrative undergoes constant metamorphosis, a shifting of tone, mood, and posture, Ovid concocts melodramatic situations and sometimes bizarre overdrawn images. For example, after Tereus rapes Philomela

> as she vainly struggled to call the name of her father,
> he seized her tongue with pincers and sliced it off at the root.
> The stump convulsively twitched, as the rest lay writhing about,
> trying to add its protest to the dark and blood-stained ground;
> like half of an injured snake, it jerked in its mistress's track.
>
> OVID, *Metamorphoses* 6.555–560

Another example of Ovid's taste for the grotesque is the skinning alive of Marsyas, who competed with Apollo in a musical contest:

> The skin is torn off the screaming Marsyas from the top of his limbs,
> He is nothing but one great wound, gore everywhere,
> the nerves exposed, his veins throb and quiver
> without skin to cover them, you could count his innards
> as they palpitate in the gleaming fibers of the tissue in his chest.
>
> OVID, *Metamorphoses* 6.387–91

When Ovid's stories do have morals, they are of the homespun variety—so the story of Tereus, Procnê, and Philomela proves that one should not give in to irrational desire, as if we needed to be told that. We are never sure how far Ovid is mocking the reader's expectations and using such simplistic morals simply to justify his touching or lurid descriptions.

Although Ovid's humans pay for their mistakes, we also sense that the god or goddess who punishes them metes out an excessive punishment, that humans are the innocent victims of petty but divine emotion. Did Actaeon really deserve to be torn apart by his own dogs? His fate seems far out of proportion to his crime of accidentally seeing Diana as she bathed. In fact Ovid introduces the story by saying that it is a good example of how unjust the gods can be.

## Love Stories

One type of Ovidian love story tells of a deity having intercourse with a mortal woman, who is then turned into an animal (so Io became a cow). Procris and Cephalus is an example of another type of love story, where the conflict is not between men and gods, but within a human family. Cephalus, a king of Athens, tests the love of his beloved wife by disguising himself and offering a rich bribe to sleep with her; when at last she gives in, she must go into exile. Later they are reconciled, but continued suspicion leads to her accidental death. It is a tale of lovers who love too much until suspicion destroys them; lovers should trust one another, another homespun moral. The story of Procnê and Philomela is about perverted love, where uncontrolled sexual desire leads to bestial acts of impiety—Tereus brutally rapes his sister-in-law, then cuts out her tongue—and to a punishment equally savage, where the avengers are as twisted as their attacker. The metamorphosis into birds of Tereus, Procnê, and Philomela is nearly an afterthought, a device allowing Ovid to attach the tale to his general scheme.

Another kind of love story is when an impossible love is made possible. Pygmalion, for example, falls in love with a statue he has made. He can never consummate his love, but then Venus brings the statue to life. Or the love is forbidden, as when Byblis incestuously loves her brother Caunus, or Myrrha has an incestuous passion for her own father. When the great weaver Arachnê weaves a tapestry in a weaving contest with Minerva, she presents a catalogue of the types of love stories we can expect from Ovid, who ranges from the self-love of Narcissus, the animal passion of Tereus, to the pure love of Pygmalion and the idealized conjugal love of Ceux and Alcyonê, with every variation in between.

## Ovid's Gods

Unlike the human actors, no god or goddess is ever given a compelling psychological portrait in Ovid's poem. Like humans, the gods are amorous to a fault, but they never have an interior life where they doubt or ponder or find conflict in their efforts to make decisions. When they punish humans for their foibles, they do so from wholly human motives. The gods behave as petty and ill-tempered humans, features also found in Homer, but Ovid greatly exaggerates these features in accordance with his rejection of the searching and speculative quality of Greek myth.

The gods are so humanized as to be divided according to social class into "nobles" (*nobiles*) and "commoners" (*plebs*). They rarely inspire action: Humans of their own will commit crimes against each other, making their lives a misery, allowing passions to run unchecked so that innocent and guilty are destroyed alike. Often the gods are the subject of humor, as for example when Jupiter changes into a darling and lovable bull in order to seduce Europa:

> Majesty and love do not go together, nor remain in the selfsame place.
> That father and ruler of the gods, whose right hand holds

The three-forked lightning, whose nod shakes the world,
Put down his heavy scepter and his majesty,
and took up the shape of a bull and in this form
went lowing with the cattle, wandering over the tender grass,
beautiful to see, the color of snow on which no foot has set,
or a raindrop stained. The great muscles bulged on his neck,
and the dewlaps hung to his chest; his horns were small,
but of perfect shape as if a sculptor made them,
cleaner and more shining than any jewel. His eyes and brow
were not threatening, and the mighty stare was filled with peace.

OVID, *Metamorphoses* 2.847–858

To underline the bull's absurdity, he jumps about playfully on the grass, then lies down on his side to encourage the attention of the pretty Europa, as if real bulls behaved in this fashion.

A deeply human instinct is to feel kinship with the natural world, to think of animals and plants and even stones as inhabited by intelligence somehow like our own. The mutability of nature, and of ourselves who are destined to die, suggests that the same being can take on more than one form, human or inhuman. Much religious cult is based on efforts to communicate and negotiate with the humanlike powers in nature. In theory, we reject this interpretation of the natural world, but many who own pets treat them as equals (or superiors!), and the popularity of Bugs Bunny, Mickey Mouse, the Lion King, and other cartoon characters shows how easy it is for us to accept that animals can behave and think like ourselves.

Ovid does not, however, tell stories about metamorphosis in order to appeal to an instinct within us to explain nature by humanizing it. Ovid is a sophisticate who created his poems in writing to be read aloud to upper-class Romans, women as well as men, who could themselves read and write and who were intimately familiar with the monuments of Greek literature. He is utterly unlike the *aoidoi* Homer and Hesiod. He gave contemporary relevance to old stories, which contained primitive elements, by embellishing them with the rhetorical display familiar to the Romans from their education (as in the highly wrought speeches of Philomela and Procnê). In the elegant high society of Ovid's Rome, unparalleled even in modern times, where freeborn men and women freely mixed, where love affairs and sexual passion were a principal preoccupation of the great and the amorous, such stories no doubt had a special appeal and poignancy, as they did in similar later epochs.

## FURTHER READING

Dumézil, G., trans. P. Krapp, *Archaic Roman Religion* (Chicago, 1970). Learned study from the point of view of Indo-European comparative mythology.

Feeney, D. *Literature and Religion at Rome: Cultures, Contexts, and Beliefs* (Cambridge, England, 1998). Argues for a creative model of cultural interaction in relations between Greek and Roman religion and literature.

Forbes-Irving, P. M. C., *Metamorphosis in Greek Myths* (Oxford, 1992). Thorough review of this feature, based on early religious belief, in Greek myth.

Galinsky, G. K., *Ovid's Metamorphoses, An Introduction to the Basic Aspects* (Oxford, 1975). The best general book on Ovid's poem, with excellent analysis of the differences between Greek and Roman myth.

Hinds, S., *The Metamorphosis of Persephonê: Ovid and the Self-Conscious Muse* (Cambridge, England 1987). Discusses Ovid's important treatment of the myth of the rape of Persephonê.

Myers, K. S., *Ovid's Causes: Cosmogony and Aetiology in the* Metamorphoses (Ann Arbor, 1994). Modern study of these pervasive themes.

Otis, B., *Ovid as an Epic Poet*, 2nd ed. (Cambridge, England, 1970). Excellent general studies of the poet, with emphasis on the *Metamorphoses* taken to be a kind of epic.

Tissol, G. *The Face of Nature: Wit, Narrative, and Cosmic Origins in Ovid's* Metamorphoses (Princeton, 1997).

Wheeler, S. M., *A Discourse of Wonders: Audience and Performance in Ovid's* Metamorphoses (Philadelphia, 1999).

Wilkinson, L. P., *Ovid Recalled* (Cambridge, England, 1990). Excellent survey (a shorter paperback version published as *Ovid Surveyed*).

# CHAPTER 14

# MYTH AND POLITICS: THE MYTH OF THESEUS AND THE *AENEID* OF VERGIL

OVID'S *METAMORPHOSES* REPRESENTS one kind of Roman poetry, deeply indebted to literary models from Alexandria in Egypt and designed to delight and entertain. In the generation before Ovid, however, several Roman poets, and above all Vergil (70–19 BC), told stories to explain the origins of Roman power and its obligations to the Roman ruling class. Myth, for such poets, was a kind of propaganda, reinforcing the high ideals of Roman government.

The Romans did not, however, invent myth as political propaganda. This honor, as so many others, goes to the Athenians. By the fifth century BC, the golden age of Greece, the days of Aeschylus, Sophocles, Euripides, Pericles, and the Parthenon, Theseus had become the official hero of Athens and its empire, celebrated in sculpture and in song, as was Aeneas in Rome, and in our efforts to understand Vergil's poem, it will be useful first to examine briefly this earlier Greek model of myth as political propaganda.

## THESEUS OF ATHENS

In the sixth century BC, Theseus was scarcely known, except for the adventure of his flight from Crete with Ariadnê, his descent to the underworld, and his participation in the battle between the Lapiths and the Centaurs; these are his oldest myths, mentioned in passing in the *Iliad* and the *Odyssey*.

No important family claimed him as its ancestor, no town or village was named in his honor, and an obscure Menestheus commanded the Athenians at Troy. Only in the sixth century BC did Theseus rise to prominence, when a festival was named after him and he began to appear more often in Athenian art. Before the end of the sixth century, an epic called the *Theseïs,* now lost, was composed, which must have given form to what became the standard cycle of legends about Theseus.

The popularization of the legends of Theseus, including the composition of the *Theseïs,* took place under the sponsorship of Pisistratus (pi-**sis**-tra-tus), the famous leader of Athens who first came to power in 561 BC and governed Athens off and on until his death in 527 BC, when his sons, Hippias and Hipparchus, succeeded him. The dynasty began to come apart in 514 BC after the assassination of Hipparchus in a homosexual intrigue. Like Theseus, Pisistratus unified Attica under the political and cultural rule of Athens and fought for Athens' interests overseas, in Ionia and on many islands. Parallels were constantly drawn between the accomplishments of Theseus and Pisistratus. Theseus was often given credit for Pisistratus' important deeds, such as the unification of Athens. Such parallels served to increase Pisistratus' reputation as a benevolent and powerful leader.

By the fifth century BC, Theseus was claimed as the founder of Athenian democracy, but it was Pisistratus who, in the sixth century BC, encouraged the individualism and cultural enlightenment that made the democracy of the fifth century possible. In myth, Theseus founded the Panathenaic games, which celebrated the unity and glory of Attica; in reality, Pisistratus gave to this old festival its special character, including a festival of special magnificence every fourth year, when the entire *Iliad* and *Odyssey* were recited. Theseus defeated a wild bull on the plain of Marathon; Pisistratus returned from temporary exile in 546 BC on this same plain, from which he drew much of his support, and shortly afterward Athenian vase painters began to portray the Bull of Marathon. Coinage, one of the most important economic innovations of the sixth century BC, was attributed in myth to Theseus, but Pisistratus was probably the first Athenian to strike coins in Athens, and his coins bore a bull's head. In myth Theseus stopped at the island of Delos after escaping from the Labyrinth; in history it was Pisistratus who exerted powerful influence over this strategic island, site of the ancient cult of Apollo and Artemis. Theseus destroyed the bandits living on the edge of the gulf from Troezen to Athens; Hippias, Pisistratus' son, rid the Saronic gulf of pirates. Scenes showing the opponents of Theseus—Sinis, the Crommyonian sow, Sciron, and Procrustes—appear in sculpture and painting soon after Hippias' achievements.

After the murder of Hipparchus, Hippias' rule became oppressive, and he was soon driven out. One might have expected the myths of Theseus, which glorified the Pisistratids, to decline in popularity, but the opposite occurred. Old cults were remade in Theseus' honor, and he was ever more commonly represented in art. From the model for benevolent autocratic rule by the Pisistratids, Theseus became the hero of the Athenian democracy, founded in 510 BC by Cleisthenes (**klīs**-then-ēz). Attic drama celebrated Theseus' kindness to such suppliants as Oedipus, Adrastus, the sons of Heracles, and Orestes, all refugees from cities hostile to Athens in the fifth century BC. Theseus was said to have renounced autocracy in favor of democracy (although there was no democracy in Greece before the reforms of Cleisthenes). The new style of government, a drastic departure from traditional forms, was legitimized by modifying the traditional tales.

In 490 BC a badly outnumbered Athenian citizen army under the leadership of Miltiades (mil-**tī**-a-dēz) turned back the Persian host on the plain of Marathon. Once again, the act of a mortal was given prominence by being linked to an act of Theseus. Eyewitnesses reported that the ghost of Theseus rushed up before the Athenian lines: On the plain of Marathon Theseus had captured the bull. Earlier myths telling of Theseus' rape of the Amazon queen (Heracles had performed a similar deed) were altered to emphasize the Amazons' invasion of Attica and Theseus' destruction of their army. Theseus was transformed from the swashbuckling adventurer and loverboy to the magnanimous and stalwart defender of homeland and freedom, and Miltiades was his successor.

Cimon (**sī**-mon), the son of Miltiades, further politicized the myths of Theseus. An aggressive general and politician like his father, Cimon led an alliance of Greek states formed after the Persian invasions to victory after victory, sponsored trade, captured slaves, and took booty that enormously enriched the city of Athens. He, too, made use of Theseus' story when, after an outbreak of piracy in the northern Aegean, he occupied the pirates' hideout on the island of Scyros, where Theseus had died. An oracle directed Cimon to find the bones of Theseus, a task proper for the son of one who, aided by the ghost of Theseus, had led the Athenians to victory at Marathon. On Scyros, Cimon saw an eagle clawing at a mound of earth. He dug down and found an enormous skeleton, bronze spear and sword at its side (did Cimon find a Bronze Age tomb?). These were obviously Theseus' bones, and Cimon proudly brought them home to Athens. A new Festival of Theseus was added to the calendar and a shrine constructed in the agora to house the relics. The shrine was decorated with scenes from the Amazonomachy, the Centauromachy, and the story of Theseus' dive into the sea to retrieve the ring of Minos. Such activity redounded to the credit of Cimon, the new Theseus who brought fresh glory to a new Athens.

When the threat of Persia receded, and Athens and its often unwilling allies began to square off against Sparta, the myths underwent further transformation. Theseus now stood for the Ionians under Athens' leadership, while the Dorian states under Sparta claimed Heracles as their hero. Parallels between the two cycles of myth were carefully drawn; the Labors of Theseus were surely designed on the model of older stories about Heracles.

Such developments furnish a good example of the use of myth as propaganda. The legends of Theseus encapsulated, symbolized, and justified Athenian policies—ascendancy at sea, suppression of marauders, and determined resistance to the barbarian. It took only about a century for Theseus to become the official hero of Athens, because Pisistratus, Miltiades, and Cimon all consciously, for political gain, made Theseus their model. To accomplish this goal successfully, they often had to remake or reform the traditional legends. The Athenians pioneered use of myth for political ends, but the Romans brought it to perfection.

## ROMAN GODS OF THE FAMILY AND STATE

We saw in Chapter 13 how the Romans incorporated Greek anthropomorphic deities into their native traditions by identifying them with abstract spirits, the *numina*. The divinities associated with the Roman family, by contrast, always retained their own identities, despite Greek influence. This may have been because the Greeks had no deities to correspond to these particular gods, or because they were so embedded in Roman life that nothing could replace them. Such deities played an important role in Roman patriotic legend. One such deity was the Lar (plural Lares, **lar-**ēz), protector of the people in a household; the name is apparently derived from the Etruscan word for a spirit of the dead. The Lares were worshiped in small shrines at crossroads where the boundaries of four farms came together; there every year a doll was suspended for each member of the family and a ball of wool for each slave, perhaps a substitute for human sacrifice. The Penates (pe-**nā**-tēz), often confused with the Lares, protected a household's things and especially its food. In origin the *numina* of the storehouse (*penus* means "cupboard"), the Penates became identified with the welfare of the state. The Trojan gods whom Hector's ghost entrusted to Aeneas as he fled the burning city of Troy were identified with the state Penates.

The Romans felt that the state was a family writ large. This notion becomes clear in the cult of the *numen* Vesta, whose name corresponds etymologically to the Greek Hestia. Like her, Vesta is protectress of hearth and home. In Rome she was served by six Vestal Virgins, each chosen at the age of seven from the great families. The Vestals served for thirty years, after which they could marry, although few did. In their round temple in the Forum near the ancient house of the Roman kings, they performed services for the state analogous to the work of unmarried girls in a private home: ritual baking, spring cleaning, and tending the sacred flame on the hearth, said to have been brought from Troy by Aeneas and never allowed to go out. If a Vestal was caught having sexual relations, she was buried alive in a tomb containing a loaf of bread, a jug of water, and a lighted lamp (some did meet their end in this way). Although Vesta was among the most sacred and revered deities of Roman religion, she has few myths (like the Greek Hestia), but remained a *numen* throughout Roman history.

Perhaps the Romans' vision of the state as an enlarged family is most clear from the exaltation in myth and other propaganda of a set of duties called *pietas* (**pē**-e-tas). The term has little in common with its derivatives piety and pity but refers, rather, to the extraordinary devotion that one shows first to the *paterfamilias,* then, by extension, to the abstraction of the state itself and its gods. The Roman exaltation of *pietas* as the highest virtue was prominent from an early time and was claimed in titles used by Roman emperors and the poets who wrote for them, especially Vergil, who constantly calls his hero *pius Aeneas.* The virtue of *pietas* could legitimize the suppression of political opposition because the ruler embodies the country and opposition to him shows a lack of *pietas.* No doubt it was the native Roman predisposition to regard abstractions as divine that enabled them to transfer pious devotion to the head of a family to an invisible entity, the state. Greek religious anthropomorphism, by contrast, stood in the way of granting obedience to a divine abstraction. Although the Greeks (in Athens, especially) made tentative efforts to replace family moral authority with that of the city (in Athens, embodied in the figure of Theseus), their political divisions continued, and they never—until the Roman conquest—united as a single nation.

## THE *AENEID:* AN EPIC OF NATIONAL REBIRTH

The most important Roman myth is told in Vergil's poem, the *Aeneid.* Vergil, in his immensely complicated and influential poem, used the legend of Aeneas, the founder of Rome, to create a document to rival those of the Greeks, even Homer. Vergil was born in 70 BC near Mantua, in the north of Italy. In 41 BC, if we can believe suggestions in his own verses, he lost his farm. Helped by Maecenas, a friend and minister of Augustus, he became a trusted member of Augustus' art council. He wrote the *Eclogues,* graceful pastoral poetry celebrating the uncorrupted emotions and clever wit of imaginary shepherds, and the *Georgics,* a long poem, ostensibly on farming, in four books that praises the physical beauty of Italy and the old-fashioned virtues of its people. The last ten years of his life, Vergil spent on the *Aeneid,* which he left not quite finished when he died in 19 BC. Although the poet had ordered his literary executors to burn the incomplete poem, Augustus intervened.

In Homer's *Iliad,* Aeneas was the son of Anchises and a cousin of Hector; he hoped to succeed Priam as king, although they were on bad terms. His mother was the goddess Aphrodite. It is unusual for a hero to have a mortal father and a divine mother, although the same was true of Achilles. Aeneas was destined to survive the Trojan War:

> The son of Peleus in close combat would have taken Aeneas' life
> with his sword, had not Earthshaker Poseidon seen what was happening.
> And so he spoke among the immortal gods: "Now look, I am sad about
>     great-hearted Aeneas,
> who soon shall go to the house of Hades, killed by the son of Peleus . . .
> But why should he, a man without guilt, suffer pain because of sorrows
>     not his own?
> Especially since he has always given fine gifts to the gods in heaven.
> Let us head him forth from death, or the son of Cronus will be angry
> if Achilles kills him; for it is destined that he will escape and that the race
>     of Troy
> will not perish and be seen no more. . . . Truly will the mighty Aeneas be
>     king
> among the Trojans, and his sons' sons born in days to come."
>
> HOMER, *Iliad* 11.290–308, trans. A. T. Murray, modified

Because the Romans had no ancient explanation for their origins, this passage from the *Iliad* suggested a possible illustrious ancestor for them, complete with a divine parent. By the time of Augustus, the story had been elaborated: Aeneas had fought valiantly for Troy, but when the city burned, he escaped to the far west and founded Lavinium in Latium, where he ruled for three years before his death. His son Iulus (ī-ū-lus), who allegedly gave his name to the Julian clan to which Julius Caesar and Augustus belonged, ruled Lavinium for thirty years, then founded the town of Alba Longa. Three hundred years later his descendants, Romulus (**rom**-yu-lus) and Remus (**rē**-mus), born in Alba Longa, founded Rome. But Aeneas was *pater*, "father," of the whole race of victorious Romans and the direct ancestor of Augustus, who united the Roman world about the time of Christ.

At first glance, the *Aeneid* and the *Iliad* or *Odyssey* look much the same: Both authors use an apparatus of gods to manipulate the action, both set their poems in the days of the Trojan War, treat issues of honor and destiny, and present gory descriptions of death and physical violence. Vergil constantly invokes Homer's *Iliad* and *Odyssey*. So the first line of the *Aeneid* is *arma virumque cano*, "I sing of arms and the man." The reference to *arma*, "arms," invokes the martial *Iliad*, whereas *virum*, "man," invokes the first word of the *Odyssey* in Greek, *andra*, "man." The first half of the *Aeneid*, Books 1–6, is a sort of *Odyssey*, a tale of a hero's wandering as he tries to reach a new home in Italy. In these books Vergil develops the Odyssean themes of a father's relation with his son, a dangerous woman who would deflect the hero from his purpose, and the search for a bride when the hero reaches his goal; Aeneas even finds one of Odysseus' men, left behind on the island of Cyclops. The second part of the *Aeneid*, Books 7–12, begins with a second invocation and resembles the *Iliad*, a chronicle of warfare between Aeneas and local peoples in Italy, over whom, at the poem's end, Aeneas triumphs. Familiar Iliadic themes are the gathering of the troops, the hero's special relationship with his mother, the death of the hero's best friend, councils of the gods, and the intervention by gods who quarrel among themselves. The meter is the same dactylic hexameter of Homer, introduced to Latin about two hundred years before Vergil and by his time fairly well naturalized (although Vergil was the first Roman to use it with true facility). All three poems use many of the same technical devices—for example, the use of such fixed descriptive epithets as "swift-footed Achilles" in the *Iliad* and "pious Aeneas" in the *Aeneid*.

But the differences are profound. Homer was an oral entertainer in a boisterous, unlettered age that lacked political unity or great wealth. Vergil, like Ovid, was highly literate, steeped in written Greek poetry and philosophy, and in personal contact with the most powerful men who had ever lived. Homer composed on the fly to entertain. Vergil's poem was painstakingly learned, self-conscious, and created in writing with deliberate compression and elegant expression. Greek oral epic, usually complete in a single sitting, differed with every performance; our Homeric poems are snapshots of a single artificially extended performance. The *Aeneid*, composed in writing, was not finished even after ten years. An early commentator reports how Vergil wrote ten or twelve lines in the morning, then spent the rest of the day compressing them down to three or four.

In Homer's stories people act—they become angry, do clever things, kill cruelly, or die nobly. The meaning of the story is in the action, and the characters are who they pretend to be. But Vergil's myths, like the Athenian myths of Theseus, are purposeful propaganda, to prove that Augustus deserved his place in the world and that Rome's destiny in history was willed by divine intelligence. Homer did not sing to prove that his audience deserved power in society. Vergil, in vigorous contrast, ties his myths to real history. On the shield that Vulcan makes for Aeneas, parallel to the shield that Hephaestus makes for Achilles in the *Iliad*, Vulcan shows historical events that occurred within Vergil's lifetime, including the epoch-making battle of Actium (31 BC) in which Augustus, Vergil's sponsor, was victorious over Marc Antony and Cleopatra. When Aeneas visits his father Anchises in the underworld, Anchises speaks of the spirits there who will become great men in Rome's distant and very recent past, including the spirit of a beloved nephew of Augustus, whose early death shocked and saddened the ruling household.

Characters and events in Vergil's myths have various levels of meaning; they stand for more than meets the eye. All events and characters are subordinated to the patriotic purpose of satisfying Rome's need for a tradition of national origin, a tale telling in the language of legend how this great empire was made. Its story of far away and long ago, when cows munched grass on the Palatine hill, satisfied contemporary literary taste for an escapist setting, yet made it possible for Vergil to proclaim, in symbolic form, the divine necessity of Rome's conquest of the world and Augustus' ascendancy in it.

In order to provide justification for Augustus' new regime, Vergil needed a philosophy that could explain the whole sweep of Roman history, culminating in the purposes and achievement of Augustus. The old Roman *numina* lacked the authority to satisfy this requirement. Vergil needed a theory of destiny, an unchanging and inescapable plan laid down by immortal power, operating through all the ages. He found this theory in the philosophy of Stoicism, widely studied by the Roman ruling class, which taught that the world is ruled by a divine *logos,* meaning something like "purpose," "structure," and "order" (the origin of our word logic). The Stoic *logos,* although it lacked personality, was close enough to the Judeo-Christian God to appear in the opening of the gospel of John (1.1): "In the beginning was the *logos,* and the *logos* was with God, and the *logos* was God, and without the *logos* was nothing made that was made" (the usual translation, *word,* is inadequate here). Stoicism was founded by Zeno, a Semite from Citium in Cyprus, about 300 BC; it is named after a colonnade (= *stoa*) in Athens where Zeno taught. A central moral theme of this complicated philosophy was that one should live in harmony with nature, whose transformations reflect the underlying logos. The force of the logos permeates all history. Rome's triumph is the working out among mortals of divine will.

To Vergil, his hero must be shown as obedient to his country, above all other obligations. Aeneas is *pius,* placing duty above all, and he is not an independent agent; he is *fato profugus,* "driven by Fate." Homer's Achilles must make a choice between a short glorious life or a long inglorious one. Homer's Odysseus too must choose repeatedly: to take his revenge now or wait until victory is sure. Aeneas has no such choices, because he must obey what Fate has established. The Roman Fate is comparable to the Greek *logos;* Latin *fatum* means "something spoken" or "decreed," and the Greek *logos* is derived from *legô,* "to say."

The world of the *Aeneid,* and hence by implication the world of Rome under Augustus, is not really controlled by a self-indulgent sky-god who squabbles with his wife and lusts after young women. As Anchises reveals to his son in the underworld, where Aeneas visits him in *Aeneid* Book 6, even Jupiter serves the impersonal *logos/fatum,* the divine order. Juno in her hatred of the Trojans opposes the fulfillment of Fate's decree, but all the obstructions she interposes can only delay the inevitable. Aeneas may appear to be heartless for placing his duty to found Rome above his love for Dido, but the *pius* man must do his duty to the divine command, regardless of consequences to his personal life. He does what he must do, the only behavior that admits the possibility of human happiness, according to Stoic philosophical teaching. For the founding of empire, one must place personal interests behind those of the state.

In Book 2 Vergil tells us how Aeneas left behind in Sicily the Trojan women who had tired of wandering: They were not worthy of empire, of destiny. The weak must be purged before the great task, Fate's will, can begin.

Palinurus, the helmsman who fell from the ship and drowned off the Bay of Naples, is not just a member of the crew, but stands for every noble Roman who gave his life, at divine behest, that Rome might be great. The individual will perish, yes, but empire and its benefits to civilization will grow.

Vergil's complex myth therefore places empire in the context of a divine plan for human history while glorifying the moral qualities necessary for the foundation of empire. The quality of *pietas,* devotion to duty, is the most important positive quality in a ruler, and he certainly means to imply that Augustus possessed such qualities. Vergil also shows what features rulers should not have, and many modern scholars have detected undercurrents of criticism of Augustus and life under a monarch; again and again the reader is reminded of the telling price exacted by an empire without end or limit. Aeneas during his seven years of wandering must purge himself of material and sexual excess, which the exotic eastern city of Troy symbolized in ancient literature, where gold-drenched Priam produced fifty sons, each with his own bedchamber. Aeneas spurns the glorious new city that Dido is building in Carthage and he rejects his passion for her, so similar to that between Paris and Helen, who in placing personal desire above communal good started the catastrophic Trojan War. Now a new city will rise in the Western Land, purged of the burden and the mistakes of the past, sheltering peoples with its impartial laws and its toleration of difference in race and religion.

In Dido, Vergil embodies many mythical and historical associations. We may feel sorry for Dido and be impatient with Aeneas for spurning her, but Dido stands against history and must succumb. Dido is not only like Helen of Troy, who gave in to passion, but also like Homer's Circê and Calypso, enchantresses who would sway the hero from his purpose, and like Euripides' savage Medea, who represents all that is Eastern and barbaric. In Dido the contemporary Roman reader would also recognize Cleopatra, who seduced that great Roman Marc Antony and turned him against Augustus and his own city, Rome. In short, Dido represents the moral failings of broken faith and Eastern passion. Although she had sworn to her murdered husband Sychaeus that she would have no other, she was happy to sleep with Aeneas when a storm led them to take shelter in a cave. Then, when Aeneas abandoned her, instead of transcending her heartbreak and pain as a Roman woman would, she took her life in an act of vindictive self-destruction. Even so did Cleopatra kill herself after being defeated in the battle of Actium in 31 BC. Dido also is an incarnation of Semitic Carthage, Rome's greatest enemy, who under the extraordinary general Hannibal (247–183 BC) nearly destroyed the Roman state. Such was the working out of Dido's curse that she shouts against Aeneas and his descendants, before taking her life. But ultimately Rome destroyed its ancient enemy and razed Carthage to the ground in 146 BC.

The Romans were an amalgam of many clans and tribes, whose primitive tribal identity was submerged in the greater being of the state and the peace and good government that the state offered. In Vergil's poem, Latinus the

Latin, Tarchon the Etruscan, and Evander the Greek, military allies of Aeneas, stand for the diverse peoples fused into Rome. All work together toward the common enterprise. Brazen and hotheaded, Aeneas' greatest enemy, the "mad" and "fanatical" Turnus, is too like Achilles—or Marc Antony!—to survive. He is bent on personal glory. He indulges in hurt feelings, and he cannot understand the greater good. Morally, he is not wrong; he may be right. After all, he was engaged to the local woman Lavinia before Aeneas appeared and carried off Turnus' promised bride. Lavinia's own mother favored Turnus and opposed Aeneas. In killing Turnus, Aeneas forgets his father's advice in the underworld that he should "spare the downtrodden" and gives in to the *furor*, "war madness," of which Turnus is guilty. Still, Turnus must lose because he opposes the pattern of destiny. The personal and local pride that Turnus represents must succumb if empire will bestow its many benefits on all of humankind. Just so, the enemies of Augustus' order must yield so that a new Golden Age might return, a human universe under one government where war is obsolete.

In our own day, stories of the exemplary lives of George Washington and Abraham Lincoln inculcate values useful to a modern democracy, but bear small resemblance to the actual deeds and thoughts of these men. History and myth are a perennial tangle. Humans are myth-making animals, retelling ancient stories to fulfill present needs.

## FURTHER READING

Bloom, H., *Virgil: Modern Critical Views* (New York, 1986). Collection of essays by scholars.

Bremmer, J. N., and N. M. Horsfall, *Roman Myth and Mythography* (London, University of London, Institute of Classical Studies, No. 52, 1987). A scholarly but readable and original study of several Roman myths, including Aeneas and Romulus and Remus.

Cairns, F., *Virgil's Augustan Epic* (Cambridge, England, 1989). The interrelationship between poetry and politics in Vergil's Rome.

Galinsky, G. K., *Aeneas, Sicily, and Rome* (Princeton, 1969). The origins of the legend of Aeneas, with much interesting evidence from art and archaeological finds.

Gardner, J. F., *Roman Myths* (Austin, 1993). Succinct review with good illustrations.

Grant, M., *Roman Myths* (New York, 1971). A complete review, accessible to the general reader and attractive to the specialist.

Hurwit, J. M., *The Athenian Acropolis: History, Mythology, and Archaeology from the Neolithic Era to the Present* (Cambridge, England, 1999). Superb review of Athenian traditions, including myth, focused on Athens' most prominent landmark.

Livy, *The Early History of Rome,* trans. Aubrey de Sélincourt (Baltimore, 1960). A principal source for Roman myth. Contains Books 1–5 of Livy's great *The History of Rome from Its Foundations.*

Rose, H. J., *Religion in Greece and Rome* (New York, 1959). Contains succinct, scholarly, although somewhat old-fashioned synopses.

Ward, A., ed., *The Quest for Theseus* (New York, 1970). Abundantly illustrated, has chapters on the development of the myth of Theseus, archaeological background, and survival of the myth into medieval and modern times; the essay by Robert Connor is excellent on the political uses of the myth of Theseus.

Wiseman, T. P., *Remus, A Roman Myth* (Cambridge, England, 1996). Ingenious and learned attempt to explain the origin of the myth of Romulus and Remus.

# CHAPTER 15

# MYTH AND ART

WE MIGHT ASSUME that the relationship between myth and the related artistic image was a relatively straightforward matter, with images created to illustrate preexisting stories. But the relationship between myth and art turns out to be much more complex, and in some cases a mythical story seems to have been invented or adjusted to fit a preexisting image.

Myth may be a traditional tale, with or without serious content, but as we have seen, myths are not historical truth. Myths are stories and stories are narratives, the report of a sequence of events with beginning, middle, and end. Narrative is prominent in the monumental art of the ancient Near East, but the representation of myth in art seems to have been a Greek discovery, made at a certain time and under certain influences. In this chapter we will explore the outlines of how this remarkable invention took place, the ultimate origin of the feature film and one of our most important inheritances from the ancient world.

## GREEK MYTHS FROM EASTERN ART

Although delightful scenes of everyday life survive from Bronze Age Greece, not a single scene can be confidently associated with a surviving myth. Nor did the Egyptians portray myths: The art of their astonishing tombs recreated everyday life for the benefit of the dead, or portrayed scenes of magical resurrective power, while scenes of pharaonic prowess decorate Egyptian temples. Much Mesopotamian art, too, is historical in the same way as the Egyptian, portraying military conquest, sometimes vividly. In Mesopotamia, however, we find another class of objects that *do* have designs that sometimes appear mythical, especially engraved on the tiny hard-stone cylinder seals that survive in the tens of thousands, produced over a span of 4,000 years. When we try to identify what myths are meant exactly, however, we encounter serious difficulty.

Figure 15.1, for example, from a cylinder seal from the age of the conqueror Sargon the Great, c. 2500 BC, shows in the center a god emerging from a mountain, holding the saw of the sun-god. Rays spring from his shoulders. The tree sprouting from the hill shows that the rising of the sun promises the renewal of nature. Beside the tree stands Ishtar, who will become Aphrodite among the Greeks. On the right, the clever water-god Ea (ē-a) steps over a goat onto the mountain. A bird, perhaps the dangerous Anzu bird mentioned in Mesopotamian poetry, alights on the streams of water that flow from his shoulders. On the far right is the two-faced messenger god Isimud, about whom little is known. On the left stands a hero with bow and spear. Could he be Gilgamesh? A lion stands at his feet.

It is not hard to understand this scene in terms of religious symbols, in which the powers of sexuality (Ishtar), the sun, and water (Ea) make plants grow, nourishing the beasts of the field, but we can never confidently tie such illustrations to Mesopotamian stories.

One of the most common type of scenes in Mesopotamian art is the "Presentation Scene," where a seated king, or god, receives a series of figures

FIG. 15.1  Seal of the scribe Adda, 2500–2000 BC.
(British Museum WA 89115. ©The British Museum.)

who stand before him. In Figure 15.2, a typical example, two goddesses, distinguished by their peaked crowns, introduce Hashhamer to Ur-Nammu, "strong man, king of Ur." Countless variations of such scenes are found on seals and other objects.

Figure 15.3, a Greek representation with similar iconography has, however, taken on a very different meaning, one of our earliest representations of the myth of the Judgment of Paris. On the left, Paris (not a king) sits in a chair, extending his hand to what appear to be the three goddesses Athena, Aphrodite, and Hera, waiting to hear who is most beautiful. In his right hand he seems to hold the Apple of Discord, tossed into the wedding of Peleus and Thetis, with the proclamation, "For the most beautiful woman!" The scene is identified positively as portraying the myth of the Judgment of Paris by Figure 15.4 on a somewhat later vase from the early sixth century BC, where the goddesses are named. Before the figure on the left, here standing, is written "Alexandros," another name for Paris. The figure to the far right is labeled "Aphrodite" and the one in the middle, "Athena." The presentation of a man before a god or king, a religious emblem from the East, imported

FIG. 15.2 A greenstone seal of Hashhamer, governor of Ishkun-Sin, servant of Ur-Nammu, "strong man, king of Ur," 2112–2095 BC; the very first Sumerian text published, in 1820. (British Museum WA 89126. ©The British Museum.)

FIG. 15.3  Ivory comb from sanctuary of Artemis Orthia at Sparta. Late seventh century BC. (National Archaeological Museum, Athens)

FIG. 15.4  Judgment of Paris, from the "Chigi Vase," c. 575 BC.
(Villa Giulia 22679)

into Greece, has been reinterpreted to represent a scene in one of the most famous Greek myths. Someone has seen an Eastern picture, failed to understand its meaning—no Greek could read cuneiform writing—and generated a story, a *muthos,* to explain the picture. Presumably, the picture has come first and inspired the myth. If true, the myth of the Judgment of Paris does not precede the early classical period (800–600 BC), when such Eastern images began to flood into Greece.

Another striking example of the shift in meaning when iconography passed from East to West is found in early representations of the Trojan Horse. Figure 15.5, from c. 725 BC, nearly within the lifetime of Homer, seems to be our earliest illustration of this myth. On the right-hand scene, partially destroyed, surrounded by birds, is engraved a horse with small wheels. We can be sure this is the Trojan Horse, because Figure 15.6, on a vase from Mykonos of about 675 BC, which certainly represents the Trojan Horse, shows the same small wheels. In this case, the men inside peek out, drop armor to their companions, and walk beside and on top of the contraption. Such illustrations appear, however, to depend on roughly contemporary portrayals of Assyrian siege engines, as in Figure 15.7, from a palace wall in Assyria.

The wheeled engine, covered in a leather coating and concealing fighters within, advances up a siege mound to attack a city with powerful rams that protrude from the front. Such engines were the terror of Levantine

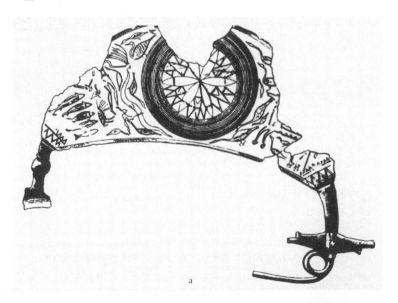

FIG. 15.5 Boeotian fibula. (London British Museum B 3205; after Walters, *Catalogue of Bronzes in the British Museum* [London, 1899], pl. 87)

FIG. 15.6  Trojan Horse, on a relief pithos from Myconus, c. 675 BC.
(Myconus Museum, 2240)

cities in the ninth century BC, the real destroyer of the great citadel of
Lachish in southern Palestine, shown here, and the destroyer of the city of
Troy in a myth, recorded in the *Odyssey* from about the same time. The Assyrian advance against the coastal Semitic seafarers, the Phoenicians, strongly
encouraged Semitic migration to Africa, Sicily, and Spain and set in motion
the massive transference of culture from East to West.

We glimpse real historical fact, then, behind the myth of the Trojan
Horse, but the myth distorts what the device really was, as pictures that illustrate the myth of the Trojan Horse are distortions of Assyrian artistic illustrations of siege engines. Again, the picture must come first, and the story
explaining it second. If so, again, the myth of the Trojan Horse cannot pre-
date the late Iron Age, c. 900 BC, when siege engines were first used. We can
only wonder what was the original explanation for Troy's fall, and how this

FIG. 15.7 Assyrian siege engine from the palace of Tiglath-pileser III at Nimrud, 744–727 BC. (British Museum 115364. ©The British Museum.)

odd story has so thoroughly displaced it. The harder we look at Greek myth, the more recent and the less traditional it appears.

Illustrations of the myths of Heracles probably offer our best examples of the precedence of artistic representation over story. Although Heracles is said to be the most popular of Greek mythical heroes, the surviving literary works hardly support this claim. He figures importantly only in Sophocles' *Trachiniae* and Euripides' *Heracles Insane* and *Alcestis,* all performed in the second half of the fifth century BC. Not until that century is there clear evidence, from the metopes on the temple of Zeus at Olympia, of Heracles' canonical twelve deeds. As we have noted, the last-known poet who may have been an *aoidos,* Panyassis of Halicarnassus, composed a lost poem on Heracles, which may have given shape to the legends reported in the handbook of Apollodorus (second century AD) and later handbooks. But in art, he figures prominently much earlier, from the sixth century BC.

Figure 15.8, an Akkadian seal from c. 2500 BC, found in a temple dedicated to the "Lord of Vegetation," represents an attacker, presumably the Lord of Vegetation himself, who attacks a four-legged, seven-headed dragon. Four of the heads droop as if dead. Two worshipers, a man and perhaps a child, stand behind the hero, beneath a star. A second attacker stabs the dragon in the rear. Six waves protrude from the monster's back, perhaps

FIG. 15.8 Two heroes attack a seven-headed dragon, Akkadian cylinder seal, c. 2500 BC. (Oriental Institute 7237; after Frankfort, H., *Cylinder Seals. A Documentary Essay on the Art and Religion of the Ancient Near East* [London, 1939], no. 478)

waves of fire. A story seems to lurk behind the picture, a dragon-combat, but we have no idea what it was exactly. In the much later Babylonian poem *Enuma elish,* Marduk fights the monstrous Tiamat, but she is never said to have seven heads. But a seven-headed dragon is mentioned in texts from the north Syrian Bronze Age port town of Ugarit, written in a script antecedent to the Greek alphabet, so such stories must have circulated in the ancient Near East, although we still cannot make a close association between literary account and artistic illustration.

When we examine a Greek example of the same motif, however, we are very clear about the myth. Figure 15.9 shows a scene first found on the same fibula with the earliest Trojan Horse (Figure 15.5, left) and later often represented on Greek pots and referred to in Greek literature. In Figure 15.9 Heracles, on the right, attacks a seven-headed serpent, while his nephew Iolaüs cuts at one neck with a scimitar of Eastern type (like that used by Perseus). He leaps over a fire because, according to the Greek story, Iolaüs cauterized the stumps of the necks that Heracles severed, to prevent their growing back. As in the Eastern story, two men attack the serpent, and the fire on the dragon's back has become the bonfire beneath the feet of Iolaüs. Evidently, some Greek has seen an Eastern illustration of the slaying of a seven-headed serpent and elaborated a myth from it, explaining such small details as the attack by two men, not one, and the presence of flames. It is scarcely plausible that an extraneous image illustrated accidentally and perfectly a preexisting unrelated tale.

Another example is the myth most commonly represented on Greek pots, Heracles and the Nemean lion, of which about 500 examples survive. Men struggling against lions are common in Eastern art, as for example

FIG. 15.9 Heracles and Iolaüs kill the Hydra. Black-figured vase from Caere, c. 530 BC. (J. Paul Getty Museum, Malibu, 83.AE.346)

Figure 15.10, from a Babylonian seal of about 800 BC. Some see this man as Gilgamesh, but there is no certainty. Similar scenes appear in very early Greek representational art. Figure 15.11 shows the leg of a tripod found in the cemetery at Athens, in which the iconography is clearly indebted to Eastern models. But who is he? Many commentators have identified him with Heracles. The scene on another leg, however, showing a man holding an ani-

FIG. 15.10 Neobabylonian cylinder seal, eighth century BC.
(British Museum, WA 134767 ©The British Museum.)

FIG. 15.11 Man killing lion,
c. 850–750 BC (Ceramicus Museum 407,
Athens)

mal while it is attacked by a lion (?), cannot be explained in this way. Yet Figure 15.12, on an Attic black-figured pot from around 530 BC, certainly *is* Heracles and the Nemean lion.

Curiously we cannot say what is the *first* representation of Heracles and the Nemean lion. Evidently, many of the best-known stories about the greatest Greek mythical hero are not traditional tales at all, reaching back to the Bronze Age or earlier and passed down by *aoidoi*, but are fresh inventions from the Archaic Period, when Eastern influence became strong in Greece and inspired artistic representations.

Who is responsible for this reinterpreting of Eastern images, the making of new stories from old pictures, this myth-making? It can only be the *aoidoi*, who improvised song at symposia, where imported Eastern metal vessels, or Greek vessels imitating them, adorned the tables and Eastern textiles covered the couches, whose images cried out for explanation. Intimacy between Eastern art, *aoidic* composition, and alphabetic writing used to record *aoidic*

FIG. 15.12 Heracles and the Nemean lion, Attic black-figured jar by the Euphiletos Painter, c. 530 BC. Athena stands to the right, while Heracles' nephew Iolaüs (probably) stands to the left. (Elvehjem Museum of Art, Madison, WI, 68.14.2)

compositions in the late eighth century BC had led to a momentous discovery: how to present a mythical narrative in pictures. We cannot approach classical myth as something confined to literary expression.

## THE GREEK INVENTION OF MYTHIC ILLUSTRATION

To invent a myth to explain an Eastern representation is one thing—and the myths of Heracles are deeply indebted to this process—but to learn how to illustrate a preexisting story is quite another. We seem actually to witness the Greek discovery of the representation of mythic narrative in art in an illustration of the blinding of Cyclops made around 670 BC. Here in Figure 15.13, we are confident that in this case the story, *not* the picture, has come first. The details of the imagery tie the illustration explicitly to Homer's version: For example, the wine cup Cyclops holds in his hand refers to Homer's statement that Odysseus made him drunk before blinding him. The artist has taken a preexisting Greek story—how Odysseus blinded Polyphemus—and modified an Eastern iconographic type of great antiquity to illustrate it. Near Eastern im-

FIG. 15.13 The blinding of Cyclops, on a large vase from Eleusis, c. 675 BC. (Eleusis Museum 546)

FIG. 15.14 Terracotta plaque of man killing female Cyclops, c. 2000 BC. (Oriental Institute 3195, University of Chicago)

agery even includes, in its artistic stable of monster-killers, a man stabbing a one-eyed monster, as in Figure 15.14, but we do not know the name of either monster or killer, whereas clear details tie the Eleusis vase to the story in Homer's *Odyssey* (Book 9). By 670 BC Homer was long dead, but texts preserving his poems, or portions of his poems, were circulated in Greece.

Some have supposed that the myth of Odysseus and Polyphemus as preserved in Homer was everywhere abroad in the land independent of Homer, told and retold in oral tradition, so that we can dissociate the Eleusis vase from the written text of Homer's *Odyssey*. However, our only knowledge of this story is from Homer's *Odyssey*, which the Eleusis vase aptly illustrates and in a way that no pre-Hellenic representation ever illustrated a myth. My own view is that we cannot dissociate the text and its vase. The picture makes use of Eastern iconography, yet transforms it to suit a literary exemplar, to portray a sequence of events described in a text, the mythic narrative of how Odysseus got Cyclops drunk, then blinded him.

In the Eleusis vase, we have the earliest certain illustration of a Greek myth, but the principle was quickly extended and bore rich fruit in the famous pictured vases of the sixth and fifth centuries BC that illustrate Greek tragedies and other Greek poems. For example, Figure 15.5 must illustrate the famous play of Euripides, the *Medea*, about an Eastern princess who murdered her children to take revenge on her unfaithful husband Jason.

On the right Jason, with raised sword, curses his wife Medea, who flies away in a chariot drawn by dragons, as described in Euripides. In the play the children are in the chariot, while in the picture they are on the ground: The artist, inspired by the literary exemplar, is not a slave to it, but allows his own imagination to assist in telling the tale, here the sorrow of Jason.

Such illustrations depend on a written text, even if the artist's actual experience of the story was through "oral" public presentation of that text in a theater and even if the artist prefers to take liberties of all kinds with his pre-

FIG. 15.15    Jason and Medea. Lucanian water jar, c. 400 BC, Policoro painter. (Museo Nazionale della Siritide, Policoro)

sentation of characters and events. By the sixth and fifth centuries BC, the creative roles of the ancient *aoidoi* diminished rapidly against the new poetry created in alphabetic writing, also for memorization and reperformance. Attic tragedy was the finest flowering of this development.

For the Greeks of the Archaic Period, myth, made universal through alphabetic writing, was the natural medium for understanding the world. In the East, where only a handful could read or write, military victory inspired historical narrative in art. In Greece, where many could read or write, military victory was commemorated in art through mythic narrative. Except for a painting of the battle of Marathon on the Painted Stoa in Athens, the great battles of the Persian wars were never displayed directly in art, as they surely would have been in Assyria. Rather, they were represented through such mythic exempla as Heracles' victory over the Amazons or the Lapiths' victory over the Centaurs. Such is part of the meaning, at least, of the celebrated sculptures of the battles of the Lapiths and the Centaurs, Figure 15.16, on the pediment of the temple of Zeus and Olympia, built about 460 BC. We might understand such representations as a rough allegory wherein Apollo = Hellenic spirit, Lapiths = Greeks, Centaurs = Persians, and the whole relief reminds the viewer of the victory of Hellenes over Persians at the sea-battle of Salamis (480 BC) and the land-battle at Plataea (479 BC).

Yet the mythical frieze expresses much more than that: broad cultural ideals of the transcendence of *eunomia* ("rule by good law" under the protec-

FIG. 15.16 Apollo extends his hand toward a Lapith who assaults a Lapith woman, c. 460 BC. (Olympia Museum, University of Wisconsin Photo Archive)

tion of Zeus) over *hybris* (violence), wherever *hybris* might be found. Paradoxically, the Greeks, the inventors of history, have in their art put myth back into history, seeing historical events in mythical terms, whereas their Eastern forebears, who had not discovered history, kept historical and mythical realms separate. Alexander the Great was so infected by the myth of the Trojan War that in his conquest of Persia he saw himself as a new Achilles attacking a new Troy, living out in battle after battle the story of the fearless Hellenic fighter against strange and savage Eastern kings.

Such is the power of myth.

## FURTHER READING

Carpenter, T. H., *Art and Myth in Ancient Greece* (London, 1991). The representation of Greek myths in Greek art, arranged by subject, with many illustrations.

*Lexicon iconographicum mythologiae classicae (LIMC)* (Zurich, 1981–1999). Massive multi-volume compilation of every representation of every myth, with scholarly commentary, in many languages (but mostly English). The single leading resource for the study of myth and art in the ancient world.

Powell, B. B., "From Picture to Myth, from Myth to Picture: Prolegomena to the Invention of Mythic Representation in Greek Art," in S. Langdon, ed., *New Light on a Dark Age: Exploring the Culture of Geometric Greece* (Columbia, MO, 1997), 154–193. Earliest publication of the analysis presented in this chapter.

Shapiro, H. A., *Myth into Art. Poet and Painter in Classical Greece* (New York, 1994). A study of Greek iconography, focusing on the depiction of myth on Greek painted pottery.

# INDEX

*Note:* Names are indexed by their Latin forms, as given in the text, but the Greek transliterated spellings, often seen in modern translations, are given in parentheses after the pronunciation.

## A

# The Greek and Roman Pantheon

| Greek Name (Roman Name) | Parentage | Origin | Concern | Attributes |
|---|---|---|---|---|
| Zeus (Jupiter, Jove) | Cronus + Rhea | Indo-European sky-god | Kingship, law; weather | Thunderbolt, scepter |
| Hera (Juno) | Cronus + Rhea | Mother-goddess | Marriage, family | Middle-aged, round hat |
| Demeter (Ceres) | Cronus + Rhea | Mother-goddess | Harvest | Grain; with Persephonē |
| Poseidon (Neptune) | Cronus + Rhea | Consort of earth? | Water, sea; earthquakes | Trident, team of dolphins |
| Hestia (Vesta) | Cronus + Rhea | The hearth | Household | Rarely shown |
| Artemis (Diana) | Zeus + Leto | Mother-goddess | Hunting, wild things | Bow, short dress, often with animals |
| Aphrodite (Venus) | Zeus + Dionê (or born from the foam) | Asian - fertility goddess | Human sexuality | Nudes, doves, with Eros |
| Hermes (Mercury) | Zeus + Maia | Personified road marker | Travel, trade, lies, thieves | Winged shoes, caduceus |
| Hephaestus (Vulcan) | Hera (alone) | Fire spirit | Crafts | Lame, bald, hammer |
| Apollo | Zeus + Leto | Lycia, Thrace; shaman | Music, healing, plague, prophecy | Beardless; lyre, bow |
| Ares (Mars) | Zeus + Hera | Thrace | War, violence | Spear, shield |
| Athena (Minerva) | Zeus + Metis | City-goddess | Civilization; crafts | Helmet, aegis |
| [Dionysus][a] (Liber) | Zeus + Semelē | Thrace, Phrygia | Ecstasy; the vine, wine | Ivy, panthers, Maenads |
| [Pan] (Faunus) | Hermes + nymph | Woodland spirit | Cattle; terror | Horns, hoofs, pipes |
| [Heracles] (Hercules) | Zeus + Alcmenē | Deified hero | — | Club, lion-skin, bow |
| [Asclepius] (Aesculapius) | Apollo + Coronis | Deified hero or Eastern healing god | Medicine | Staff with snake entwined |
| [Hades] (Dis) | Cronus + Rhea | Underworld | The dead | Rarely shown |
| [Persephonê] (Proserpina) | Zeus + Demeter | New crop; doublet of Demeter | The dead | Young woman, with Demeter |

[a]Deities in brackets are not Olympians.